ALSO BY PETER MAY

THE BIG THREE

THE
LAST
BANNER

The Story of the 1985–86 Celtics,
the NBA's Greatest Team
of All Time

PETER MAY

SIMON & SCHUSTER

Simon & Schuster
Rockefeller Center
1230 Avenue of the Americas
New York, NY 10020

SIMON & SCHUSTER and colophon are registered trademarks
of Simon & Schuster Inc.

Designed by Kathryn Parise

Manufactured in the United States of America

1 3 5 7 9 10 8 6 4 2

LIBRARY OF CONGRESS CATALOGING-IN-PUBLICATION DATA
May, Peter, date.
The last banner : the story of the 1985–86 Celtics, the NBA's
greatest team of all time / Peter May.
p.   cm.
Includes index.
1. Boston Celtics (Basketball team)—History.   I. Title.
GV885.52.B67M39   1996
796.323'64'0974461—dc20   96-35854
                                                                    CIP

ISBN 0-684-80085-3

All photos not credited below appear courtesy of the Boston Celtics:
1 Courtesy of the Portland Trail Blazers; 2 © Steve Carter;
6 © Lipofsky; 8 © Fred Mirliani; 13 © Byron Testa Photo;
17 © Mike Montes

ACKNOWLEDGMENTS

Stop! Don't skip this page! These are the people who made this book possible and they deserve to be thanked. Needless to say, the cooperation of all those connected to the 1985–86 Celtics team is gratefully appreciated. The coaches, family members, and players themselves gave up time to revisit that season. Obviously, without their support, this book never would have been written. Bill Walton gets a special thank-you. He was never too busy to find time to reminisce about that season. Another big thank-you also goes to Scott Wedman, who, thanks to my own ineptitude, had to do twice what he should have had to do only once. The Boston Celtics were immensely helpful. General manager Jan Volk gave freely of his time and also proofread the manuscript. Dave Zuccaro and Jeff Twiss of the public relations office were also quite helpful. At the *Boston Globe,* thanks to sports editor Don Skwar for allowing me to pursue the project and to the several colleagues, notably Bob Ryan, who helped me along the way. Sean Mullin again helped solve my many computer problems. Thanks also to Barbara Colangelo of the NBA's international public relations office, who helped me track down

David Thirdkill in Israel. My editor at Simon & Schuster, Jeff Neuman, got the ball rolling in his own, inimitable style, and his assistant, Frank Scatoni, remained focused and unfazed in shaping the many revisions. Thanks also to my agent, Faith Hamlin, for keeping me on course throughout this project.

To my family.
Thanks for being there.

CONTENTS

CONTENTS

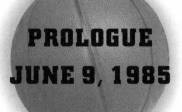

PROLOGUE
JUNE 9, 1985

He remembers the drive home as being unlike all others that year. Normally, after a game, Dennis Johnson would hop into his Jeep Cherokee with his wife, Donna, and head to the Back Bay for something to eat. After a leisurely meal, the two would chat on the way home to Lexington, a thirty-minute drive.

On this particular Sunday, however, there was no stop for food and no time for conversation. Dennis Johnson felt incapable of even the most innocent chitchat. After the game, Donna Johnson had given her husband a hug, but that was the extent of their interaction.

It hadn't been until the final minute of the game that Johnson knew, for sure, that the Celtics would lose, and, with the loss, that the season was over. The Los Angeles Lakers were replacing them as the champions of the National Basketball Association, and they were doing it in Boston Garden.

Had he bothered to leave the Boston locker room right after the game, Johnson would not have had to wander far to hear the cheers and the champagne bottles popping down the corridor. He could not have missed Lakers owner Jerry Buss exulting in doing something no opposing owner had ever done before or since: celebrate an NBA championship in Boston. The Lakers' victory was especially rewarding, for the franchise had been humbled and defeated by the Celtics in eight NBA Finals dating back to 1959 when the team was located in Minneapolis, and including the previous year, when the Celtics had prevailed in seven exhausting games.

The 1984–85 Celtics had tried to do what no NBA team had done since 1969: win back-to-back championships. They won the most regular season games that year, and they opened the 1985 Finals with a 148–114 rout of the Lakers on Memorial Day. Los Angeles had quickly regrouped, however, and won four of the next five, including two games in Boston Garden.

The clinching victory exorcised so many ghosts from the Lakers' past. They had lost Game 7 in Boston, in overtime in 1962, when Frank Selvy's 10-foot shot at the end of regulation spun out; they had led that series 3–2 and lost Game 6 at home. In 1966, they had watched Red Auerbach retire in triumph as the Celtics won the series in seven games. Three years later, in 1969, they had blown leads of 2–0 and 3–2 before losing Game 7 at the Forum; then-owner Jack Kent Cooke had balloons tied to the ceiling, ready to be released when his Lakers, starring Wilt Chamberlain, Elgin Baylor, and Jerry West, won the title. Instead of the planned celebration, Bill Russell, in what was to be his final game, led Boston to a 108–106 victory. The balloons came down without fanfare the next day. Then in 1984, the Lakers dominated the first four games of the series but blew two of them with late-game mistakes, finally succumbing to the Celtics in seven games. That is why the 1985 win was so sweet for the long-suffering Lakers' fans: yes, the team had won championships in 1972, 1980, and 1982, but never against the hated Celtics.

Johnson saw it all and was stunned to see how happy the Lakers were—and how devastated he felt. That was when it hit him, the disappointment crashing down and enveloping him.

"That one really hurt," he recalled. "We were so close to re-peating and we just didn't. It was a day I felt about the worst I can feel. We had given everything that year to win. And we got so close."

In the Boston locker room, there were the predictable muf-fled sounds of a team in defeat. A year before, they had been celebrating as the Lakers were now. The 1984–85 Celtics didn't win the championship, so by the standards of presumptive greatness that ruled the team in those years, the season was a disappointment. They had won 63 games. They had the two-time MVP Larry Bird, an imposing front line, and a talented backcourt. They had the best starting five in basketball with Bird, Kevin McHale, Robert Parish, Dennis Johnson, and Danny Ainge, but, as the season progressed, it became apparent that the bench—along with the inability of forward Cedric Maxwell, the MVP of the 1981 Finals, to recover from knee surgery—would be the team's undoing.

Beyond the starting five, there was not a whole lot of support. Maxwell hadn't, in the opinion of management, worked hard enough to come back from his injury and was therefore deemed to be excess baggage. His future would have to be elsewhere. The top reserve, former All-Star forward Scott Wedman, aver-aged just a shade more than 14 minutes a game. M.L. Carr, once a valuable sixth man, was now almost a full-time cheerleader. Guards Quinn Buckner and Carlos Clark were all but forgotten, losing time to the erratic and eventually doomed Ray Williams.

The defending champions had been pushed hard in the postseason. A Cleveland team that had won only 36 games took the Celtics to four games in the first round, equaling Boston's point total over the series. Detroit took the Celtics to six games in the second round, and the 76ers, two years removed from their title and rapidly disintegrating, were vanquished in five.

The Celtics had fallen behind 2–1 in the Finals and then tied the series in Los Angeles when Johnson hit an 18-foot jump shot at the buzzer to win Game 4. The Lakers then took advantage of a new Finals format, 2-3-2, and won Game 5 at home, 120–111.

By then, the Celtics' personnel disadvantage was becoming more and more critical. The Lakers had more of everything, or so it seemed, and after that humiliating loss in Game 1, they controlled the series. Worse, they seemed undaunted by the task of wrapping it up in Boston.

The Celtics flew home after the Friday night loss in Los Angeles and then had to turn around and play Game 6 on a Sunday afternoon. There was nothing that could be done on Saturday, other than to go over what they already knew. The starting five accounted for all but 26 of the 240 minutes in Game 6. The Celtics were worn down and beat up and they fell quietly in the second half. Finals MVP Kareem Abdul-Jabbar had 29 points. Magic Johnson had a triple-double. Larry Bird, worn down by the relentless Michael Cooper, missed 17 of 29 shots. A jubilant Pat Riley, the Lakers' coach, shouted, "They can no longer mock us." It was the highlight of his coaching career.

On that particular Sunday, Celtics coach K.C. Jones never used Carr, Buckner, Maxwell, Clark, or Williams. It was a sign of things to come, as all five would be somewhere else in the fall of 1985. Even then, the players who watched had an inkling that major changes were on the way.

"We were all sitting in the training room talking about who was going to be back and who was not going to be back," Carr recalled. "And Max had his roster all ready. He said, 'You know, Froggy [Carr's nickname], you and I won't be back. And Quinn, you too.' We all knew there was going to be a change and change was needed. But the reality was that it hadn't begun to sink in because we had been together for a long time and we'd accomplished so much. But in a real sense it was a sad time. You knew that you couldn't go on and battle the Lakers with what we had at that point."

Johnson knew that, too, but he could not shake the emptiness he felt after the 111–110 loss. When he and Donna arrived home, he paid the baby-sitter and went off and sat by himself for the rest of the evening. Finally, at four A.M., he went to bed, but sleep didn't come easily that night. He was far too preoccupied with the immediacy of the defeat, and the pain that he felt, to even contemplate what lay ahead.

"Next year? No, I wasn't thinking about that," he said. "There was no way I could do that on that day."

But others were doing just that. When you are on top of the mountain and someone displaces you, it's time to find another way back. The Celtics were not that far away, but as presently constructed, they were not good enough to win an NBA championship. Certain adjustments needed to be made.

Alan Cohen, one of the team's three owners and the driving force in management, was already thinking ahead. He was a shrewd judge of talent, knew the inner workings of the league as few of his peers did, and had an insatiable desire to win. As he sat in his loge seat on that day, he recalled dual feelings of helplessness and determination.

"It was clear we had to make changes," he said. "It didn't bother me at the time that we lost to the Lakers, maybe because I didn't have enough Celtics heritage in me. I had only been involved for two years. Personally, I felt that if we had lost to anyone else *but* the Lakers, I would have committed suicide; the Lakers were a great, competitive team, and if you're going to lose to anybody, it might as well be them. If we had lost to anyone else with the team we had, *that* would have been unthinkable."

After the loss, Cohen and Jan Volk, the Celtics' general manager, quietly walked over to the team officers located on the ninth floor of a building adjacent to Boston Garden. They sat down, dissected the roster, and unemotionally began the rebuilding process. "It's not like we were weeping in our beer," Cohen said. "We just talked about what we had to do."

The first order of business was Cedric Maxwell. Cohen was convinced Maxwell had to go. Maxwell had been a far cry from his usual self for most of the season, and then had undergone arthroscopic knee surgery in February. It was thought he would make a full recovery and be back in time to be a factor in the playoffs. He never was. In his few appearances in the post-

season, he was inconsistent or ineffective and ended up playing
sparingly against the Lakers. This was the same player who, the
year before in Game 7 against the Lakers, told his teammates to
jump on his back and he would carry them to the title. They did,
and he delivered, dishing off eight assists and scoring a team-
high 24 points.

Now, however, there was bad blood between Maxwell and the
front office. Red Auerbach, the longtime Celtics master builder
and still team president, was furious with him; Red felt that
Maxwell had lay down on the job after signing a lucrative contract extension the previous fall. The players liked Maxwell too
much ever to say a bad word about him, although some were
privately concerned about his ability to come back.

Cohen told Volk that they no longer could count on Maxwell
to be an integral part of the team. And that meant only one
thing: getting rid of him and getting another big man in return.
No one's name popped up as a suitable replacement, but the
message was clear: Maxwell was history and someone had to
take his place if the Celtics were going to be able to compete
with the Lakers.

"We identified some areas where we were deficient," Volk remembered. "We felt we needed to upgrade our outside shooting and our rebounding. We wouldn't have needed to if Max
was playing, but he wasn't. He had not come back from a knee
injury and there was a lot of disappointment that he didn't put
his heart into the rehab. By normal standards, he should have
been ready to play and he wasn't."

The second problem they had to address was the backcourt.
Dennis Johnson and Danny Ainge were solid as starters but, beyond them, there was no relief. Quinn Buckner couldn't shoot
and had never been the player the Celtics hoped he would be.
Ray Williams was a human Dow Jones chart. Carlos Clark was a
step out of the Continental Basketball Association. And M.L.
Carr was on his way to retirement.

For a team that had finished the season 63-19, and had advanced to the NBA Finals for the second straight year and al-

most repeated as champions, the Celtics were surprisingly active and intent on making changes—even though the nucleus of the team was, with the exception perhaps of Parish (then 31 years old), entering or already in the prime of their careers. When a championship is your only yardstick for success, change becomes a game of one-upmanship with your rival. The Lakers, beaten up in 1984, got physical in 1985 and won. The Lakers also got great contributions from their bench in 1985, far surpassing their efforts in 1984. Given that the landscape in the Western Conference was unlikely to change as long as the Lakers still had Magic Johnson, Kareem Abdul-Jabbar, James Worthy, Michael Cooper, and Byron Scott, the Celtics measured their moves with one eye on the Lakers.

That 1984–85 Celtics team would be strong enough to win 80 percent of their games. It would be strong enough to win title after title in today's talent-diluted NBA. But back in 1985, there were only twenty-three teams and a team needed at least three Hall of Famers, not one, simply to compete for an NBA title. As the Celtics learned that year, the champion also needed depth. If the Celtics couldn't improve their bench, the likelihood of winning another title in 1986 would be even slimmer. No one wanted to reflect on the possibility that the 1984 team might have been the last of the Bird-era champions. There had to be at least one more out there. One more banner.

That was the theme that drove the Celtics through the summer of 1985. And by the time the 1985–86 season started, they had assembled what may well have been the greatest team in NBA history. It wasn't a simple, fill-in-the-blanks process. Along the way they endured countless setbacks. They made creative financing deals that would have made fugitive banker Robert Vesco envious, deals that prompted the NBA to change the way it handles player contracts. And, they worried about Bird's back, a lingering injury that threatened to deep-six the season before it ever got going.

Almost a year to the day after losing to the Lakers in the NBA Finals, the Celtics reclaimed the NBA championship, emphatically, by defeating the Houston Rockets 114–97 in Game 6. They had steamrolled through the season, through the conference playoffs, and through the Rockets, surprise conquerors of the Lakers out west. The two priorities from the previous summer, rebounding and shooting, had been addressed with the additions of Bill Walton and Jerry Sichting. Walton made a huge difference and managed to stay healthy enough to play in 80 games, 13 more than his previous best. Unbeknownst to management, he even played the final three months with a broken wrist. Sichting, a sharpshooting guard, played in all 82 games and, by the end of the year, was a valuable third guard, just what they had been missing the year before.

Amid the jubilation in the Boston locker room that Sunday afternoon, someone asked Bird how many years he had left on his contract and Bird raised four fingers. That person then concluded that celebrations like these might be a familiar sight for the next four years, something Bird thought to be quite probable.

What no one could have imagined at that moment was that the Celtics would not be in this position for another decade, possibly into the millennium. And what no one could have imagined at that juncture was that this was the last time this team would be healthy and together, a one-year phenomenon the likes of which the NBA had never seen and was unlikely ever to see again.

CHAPTER ONE

Along Came Bill

Prior to the summer of 1985, the very last thing Bill Walton had hoped or figured to be doing was developing a plan to leave the equable climate and, in his biased view, the unsurpassed charm of San Diego, California. Other than a few years in Portland, most of them personally and professionally unrewarding, he had never lived anywhere else in his life. Walton was a veritable human billboard for the area, relishing in the recreational opportunities the area had to offer: bike riding, mountain climbing, or year-round basketball in the driveway of his sprawling home near the San Diego Zoo.

But the beautiful city lacked one essential: a place where he could play in the National Basketball Association. Only two years earlier, there had been a team in San Diego and he had been a part of it, though not as big a part as he or the team had anticipated. Injuries had left Walton unable to compete on a nightly basis, and the team's incessant losing sapped his will and his seemingly boundless reserve. Had he been healthy and playing, he believed, the Clippers would still be in San Diego.

Instead, the Clippers were now in Los Angeles, the home of

their fabulously wealthy owner, Donald T. Sterling, who envisioned them as the soon-to-be "in" team in a city that exists on trends and fads. But in 1985, the Clippers were having no luck chipping away at the Los Angeles Lakers' flighty fan base and impressive winning percentage. Walton was supposed to revive them when he signed as a free agent in 1979, but injuries limited him to only 14 games in his first three seasons, during which the team averaged fewer than 30 wins a year. The ensuing three years were marginally better both for the team and for Walton, who was able to play each season, but never more than 67 games. By 1985, six years had come and gone, the Clippers had moved north and were still losing, and Walton was tired of it all.

"The whole thing went south," he says today. "It finally dawned on me that I wasn't going to be able to compete for a championship. That was the only point in playing as far as I was concerned. I have to play to win. I just couldn't continue to play knowing that we were going to win 30 games. I was just a very slow learner, that's all."

But Walton knew winning. He had experienced it in college and in the NBA, and he wanted that feeling again. He had hoped to find it in San Diego, but he now understood that was not going to happen. During his early years with the Clippers, when injuries made him a basketball nonentity, he took classes at Stanford Law School with the full blessing of the organization.

Returning to law school was a distinct possibility, but as long as he felt he could play well, he had to play. There was no other solution. Abandoning basketball would be a decision of gut-wrenching proportions, one he could not and would not make. Ever since he had started playing the sport at the Blessed Sacrament Elementary School under the watchful eye of coach Rocky Graciano, the game was the dominant fixture in his life. It dictated where he went to college and where he worked as a professional. It paid him handsomely and gave him satisfaction he could not get elsewhere. It was his raison d'être.

"Basketball was always a celebration for me and I had gone

almost ten years without celebrating," he says. "I live for basketball. To never again know and experience the fun, the joy, the
satisfaction . . . I wasn't ready to give that up. I couldn't give it up."

He was thirty-two years old. He had, if he was lucky, a year or
two left, although one could make a convincing case he had
nothing remaining. Walton looked at his age, his waning career,
his dwindling opportunities, and the NBA landscape. He
wanted one more chance to compete for an NBA championship, and in 1985 that meant only two teams were on his list:
the Lakers and the Celtics. They had played for the league title
in each of the last two years and there was every reason to believe that would be the case again in 1985–86 because they had
the two best players in the game in Larry Bird and Magic Johnson, and future Hall of Famers surrounding them.

The more Walton thought about returning to play for the
Clippers, the more unappealing it became. He had to find a way
out. He had a termination clause in his contract that enabled
him to become a free agent and solicit offers from other teams.
The Clippers, however, would have the right to match any offer.

"I had," he said, "pretty much come to the conclusion that I
was at the end of the line with the Clippers. It was all so frustrating."

The Clippers were coming off a 31-51 season. They had fired
head coach Jim Lynam and replaced him with Don Chaney.
There were some "names" on the team—Marques Johnson, Junior Bridgeman, Michael Cage, Norman Nixon—but the players were, with the exception of Cage and a soon-to-be-injured
Derek Smith, all past their prime and soon to be ex-players.

Walton first tried the Lakers. He always admired Kareem
Abdul-Jabbar to the point of obsession, and he thought the Lakers
would need help for the aging center. Jerry West, the astute Los
Angeles general manager who had known Walton well for years
(they frequently ate breakfast together when Walton was at
UCLA), said he didn't think it would work. West, like most
everyone, feared Walton's injured feet were too beat up for him
to make much of a contribution. When Walton called West to

inquire about a job with the Lakers, West's response was: "Thanks for the interest, Bill, but I've seen the X-rays of your foot."

Having watched the Lakers defeat Boston in six games in the NBA Finals, Walton knew that the Celtics also needed help at center. He picked up the phone in his San Diego home and made a call: "This is Bill Walton of the Los Angeles Clippers," he said to the voice on the other end. "I would like to come play for your team. I think I can help."

The voice at the other end told Walton to hold on and turned to talk to another individual in the room.

"It's Bill Walton. He wants to come here," Red Auerbach said.

"Go get him" was Larry Bird's reply.

•

The Bill Walton of 1985 was a very different Bill Walton from the one who once had basketball purists salivating every time he touched the ball. He had been, in one brief, scintillating season, perhaps the greatest center who ever played the game—better than Bill Russell or Wilt Chamberlain or Kareem Abdul-Jabbar. He could score, defend, pass, and run. If you had to pick a 12-man team to defend the planet, and could have any center, the one who played in Bill Walton's body in the 1976–77 season would be an excellent and irrefutable choice.

"I thought he could develop into the greatest center who ever played," Pat Riley said. "He had the level of intensity and the super quickness. There's Russell, Chamberlain, and Kareem, but he may have been the most complete player of all."

That year, his third with the Trail Blazers after a glorious career at UCLA, ended with the Blazers winning their only NBA championship. Walton, despite missing 17 games, averaged 18.6 points a game and led the team in both rebounds (14.4) and blocked shots (3.25). He also averaged almost four assists a game, extraordinary for a center. He was named the Most Valuable Player in the playoffs, and the Blazers, despite having only the fourth best record in the league, won the championship in six games over a talented Philadelphia team featuring former ABA stars Julius Erving and George McGinnis.

The Trail Blazers were huge underdogs in that series and they lost the first two games in Philadelphia. They came back to win four straight with the unselfish, team-oriented game that Walton loved to champion.

"We knew we were going to win," Walton said. "We were young, we didn't know any better, and we thought the world was ours. [Maurice] Lucas and I had been so dominant. We oozed confidence. We just thought it was part of the natural order of life. We were not surprised or shocked that we won. It was supposed to happen. Then came the injuries, the operations, and I was never without pain again.

"It was awful. I was getting shown up by terrible players. And there's nothing more embarrassing than that, especially when you can't do anything about it. All the defeats. All the injuries. It wasn't pretty and I had to leave."

That was his unfortunate history. In some respects, he was a basketball version of Mickey Mantle, a terrific but injury-prone player, a player who made everyone wonder how good he could have been had he been blessed with good health. Mantle, however, was generally able to find a way to play despite his ailments. Walton had no such luck. That's why the Celtics in 1985 were so important to him. It was, he knew, his last chance. In contacting Boston, he was in no way looking for personal glory, he merely wanted to fill a subordinate role on a good team that would have a shot at winning the championship. The year before, he had led the league in rebounds per minute and had played in 67 games, his personal best. He knew he still had something left and could make a contribution if only given the chance.

In retrospect, Bill Walton and the Celtics were a natural fit. Growing up, he had embraced the Celtics' traditional style of play, a game predicated on rebounding, running, and defense. His college, the University of California at Los Angeles, played a

similar style under the watchful eyes of John Wooden. His favorite NBA team had always been the Celtics because they
played the way he played and, in Walton's mind, that made
them the superior team. He had been a great admirer of Bill
Russell, arguably the greatest team player in sports history, a
player whose impact on the game came in the areas Walton believed to be critical.

His views were formulated at an early age, starting in the
fourth grade. His coach, Rocky Graciano, remembers a fragile,
nervous, but incredibly committed youngster who was eager to
play, eager to learn, and had a limitless capacity to absorb all he
was taught.

Walton's basketball days at Blessed Sacrament began with an
auspicious start: in his first game, he threw a court-length pass
to a teammate that went through the basket instead.

"What really got me," Graciano said, "was that here was this
tall, gangly, fourth-grade kid who could dribble the ball. [Wal-
ton modeled his game after Pete Maravich.] When we got in
trouble with the press, he brought the ball down. He knew how
to rebound and could make what I called the uncoachable release, but I could never understand how he did that. It was just
amazing."

All three Walton boys played basketball, but Bill's brothers,
Andy and Bruce, eventually gravitated to football. Bruce, who
was a year older than Bill, played football at UCLA and then
joined the Dallas Cowboys as a reserve offensive lineman. Bill
stayed with hoops. As he made his way through Blessed Sacrament, Bill went by the nickname "Spider," partly because of his
physique and partly because he would try to frighten the nuns
by hanging spiders from the classroom ceilings. He was also incredibly shy and introverted, a character trait exacerbated by a
brutal stuttering problem.

Those who knew Bill Walton growing up find it much more
amazing that he has conquered his diffidence and speech im-
pediment and made it in television than that he played basketball well enough to make it to the Hall of Fame. His high school

coach, Gordon Nash, said he felt Walton's shyness made him a better all-around player, because he could see to it that others got involved and, therefore, got some attention and acclaim after the game.

"People always wanted to interview him and it was such a trying process," Nash said. "Bill would be reticent to talk and if he did, it was in very short, clipped sentences. He was very conscious of it and he would go out of his way to avoid a confrontation. But he was so bright and perceptive that you hoped one day he would get over it. And when I retired from teaching at Helix High [in 1992], he gave a speech, off-the-cuff, for thirty-five minutes. Everyone was flabbergasted. It couldn't have been the same person who went to Helix."

At UCLA, Walton took a speech class and stuttered so horribly during a presentation on New Orleans attorney Jim Garrison that he was laughed out of the classroom. He still occasionally stutters to this day, but has learned to control the problem sufficiently to make a career in television.

Walton's mother, Gloria, a former librarian, stands 5-11. His father, Ted, who is 6-4, was once a county welfare department supervisor whose interests—music and literature—were decidedly unathletic. The Waltons were a strong, middle-class, Roman Catholic family in which the children were encouraged to be independent and resourceful. Music training was important and the kids all played instruments. Ted Walton had a wonderful singing voice and would often break into song at the dinner table. Education was also a priority and attending college was a given.

When high school beckoned, Walton had two choices: the Catholic high school, St. Augustin, or Helix, the public school in La Mesa, a suburb of San Diego. He had gone to Catholic school growing up and he wanted no more of it. "St. Augustin's wanted me, but I had no intention of going there. I mean, it was all boys. I had had it with Catholic school at that point. I was going to Helix."

Walton was only 6-1 then, with the body of a swizzle stick. But he could play. Nash, who had been out of the school system when Walton was in eighth grade, returned as a biology teacher and basketball coach and caught his first glimpse of Bill Walton on the blacktop one afternoon. He never forgot what he saw that day.

"It was obvious he was going to be a player," Nash said. "He was skinny, but he had all the coordination skills that you dream about. Then he stepped on a sprinkler head screwing around playing football and broke his foot."

By the time he was ready to play high school basketball, however, the injury had healed and Walton soon developed into one of the best players in the country. With Walton manning the middle, Helix won 49 straight games over his last two years and back-to-back state championships. He was on just about every college's wish list.

Nash recalled meeting one college scout midway through Walton's senior year after his star player had scored more than 50 points and collected more than 30 rebounds in a Christmas tournament game.

"This scout comes up to me and says, 'I've been all over the country and I've seen all the guys,'" Nash says. "'If I could get a letter of intent from him and a copy of this game film, I could recruit the next four best players in the country.'"

Walton always had a special fondness for UCLA, dating back to his first meeting with coach John Wooden at a clinic when Walton was in the sixth grade. The first recruiting letter he received was from Denny Crum, then a UCLA assistant. But other recruiters were pursuing Walton as well. Frank Arnold, who a decade later would be coaching Danny Ainge and Greg Kite at Brigham Young, was at that time a recruiter for the University of Oregon. Arnold's turf was Southern California, and he first noticed Walton in the summer between Walton's sophomore and junior years, when the still-growing redhead was in a cast due to a knee injury.

With letters and calls coming in almost nonstop, the Walton family made a rule: they would have the coach over to their house for dinner and he would make his pitch in their house, not in some quiet restaurant. Few coaches even got that far, but Wooden was one of them.

Arnold also made the select list, although he privately knew he had no chance of getting Walton to come to Oregon. He had been watching Walton for three years and had gotten to know Ted and Gloria Walton well enough to be invited to the house for roast beef dinner. Bill Walton, however, wasn't home when Arnold came; he was up at UCLA, visiting his brother. He hitch-hiked home and arrived forty-five minutes late.

"That wasn't a good sign," Arnold said, recalling the evening. "I asked him if he would like to visit Oregon and he said no. Then he left. But Ted and Gloria asked me to stay and help them through the [recruiting] process."

Initially, Arnold told the Waltons he thought their son was headed to UCLA, but after spending time with the parents he came to a different conclusion. Ted Walton had gone to the University of California at Berkeley and was an active alumnus. The activism at Berkeley also seemed to suit Bill as well. Arnold left the Walton home convinced that Berkeley would prevail.

Nash tried his best to shelter his star from the recruiting blitz. Walton even went so far as to tell Nash he would do nothing but rebound and play defense as a senior to deflect attention to his teammates.

"Bill had absolutely no desire to be an all-time scoring leader or a record buster," Nash said. "He was so totally engrossed in how the team concept applied to him. We'd have these long talks and he could not bring himself to be the center of attention, he was beyond all that. He felt bad because he knew how important his teammates were. He was second on the team in assists. If I could think of one word that described Bill, it would be 'unselfish.' He never showed any inclination to be the big shot. He was totally team-oriented."

Officially, Walton kept everyone guessing about his choice of colleges until after the season. He says he never gave any other school a serious thought. According to Graciano, Southern California offered Gloria Walton a job as a librarian if her son came to USC. One afternoon while Stanford had Walton, Greg Lee, and Keith Wilkes up for a visit, the three came to the same conclusion while eating strawberries on a country club veranda: Let's go to UCLA.

Walton and UCLA were a marriage made in hoop heaven. Less than a two-hour drive from San Diego, the college campus, located in Westwood and bordered by a tony section of Sunset Boulevard to the north, is magnificent.

Prior to attending UCLA, Walton played on an Amateur Athletic Union team in San Diego and he was, at seventeen, the best player on the floor. "I never really knew how good Bill was," Nash said. "But at every level, he elevated his game. I just sat in the stands with my wife and watched him play in that [AAU] tournament and he was so incredible even I couldn't believe it."

Walton also had an opportunity to go overseas with an Armed Forces team, but it would mean leaving high school before classes ended. At first, his parents would not let him go, but Walton, who was in honors classes, got support from the teachers, did his work ahead of time, and joined the team for a tournament in Europe. He hated it.

"We had a lunatic coach who believed in three-hour practices," Walton said. "Looking back, I think my knee problems started then. I had tendinitis from that point on."

Walton was the only high-schooler in the group of twenty-five and as the tour began, he found himself in an unfamiliar position: benchwarmer. He became so mad he offered to play for an opponent just to get on the court. He was allowed to do that in one game in Yugoslavia and his team almost beat the Armed Forces team. The next game, he was back on the Armed Forces team and back on the bench. He couldn't wait to get to UCLA.

Freshmen were ineligible for varsity play at that time, but Wooden already had things in mind for the towering center. Much to Walton's chagrin, Wooden played him in a high post offense to help him with his footwork, passing, and screens. Walton wanted to be on the blocks, but he now recognizes how that one year made him a much more complete player. Wooden also prepared Walton for the physical play of the Pac-8 by bringing in former UCLA player Jim Neilson to work him over in practice. Swen Nater also helped out in that area.

In the three years Walton played at UCLA, the Bruins went 86-4, winning NCAA titles in his sophomore and junior years. UCLA won the first 73 games it played with Walton as its center; the actual NCAA record streak was 88, as the 1970–71 UCLA team started the streak by winning its final 15 games. Walton was Player of the Year as a sophomore and junior, and he remains the school's all-time leading rebounder and field goal percentage shooter.

Frank Arnold was around for the Walton years at UCLA, having joined Wooden's staff as an assistant when Denny Crum left to accept the head coaching job at Louisville. He saw a dramatic change in Walton's personality in those years, which were turbulent on most college campuses, UCLA's included. The war in Vietnam was still raging without an end in sight, Richard Nixon (not a Walton favorite) was in the White House, and Wooden, who ran a straitlaced program, was now all of a sudden out of touch with his players.

Walton became politically active during his years at UCLA, participating in an antiwar demonstration and other campus protests. In 1972, he was arrested for occupying the UCLA administration building, protesting the mining of Haiphong harbor. He said incredibly controversial things that made news simply because of who he was. According to Walton then, no one over thirty-five should be president of the United States. According to Walton, it was "all right" for a white man to be gunned down by a black man because of all the evil that whites did to blacks. According to Walton, the mayor of Los Angeles, Sam Yorty, was a communist dupe.

He wrote a letter on UCLA stationery to Nixon asking him to resign. He got his teammates to sign it. (Wooden was asked to do the same but refused.) Walton wanted to grow his hair long, but Wooden wouldn't allow it. Walton persisted. Wooden finally said, "Okay, Bill, you can if you want to. And we'll miss you on the basketball team." Walton cut his hair.

"I remember the first practice in Bill's senior year," Arnold said. "Coach Wooden had the players on the floor and Bill asked if he could speak. He then starts talking about TM [transcendental meditation], and over the next two or three months, there were players saying 'ooommm' all over the place. But on the court, he was still a fierce competitor."

Between his sophomore and junior years, there was also pressure on Walton to play for the United States in the 1972 Olympics. He was open to the idea and now regrets not being on the team. But he had been through the horrible international experience before entering UCLA and had no desire to relive that. He also wanted preferential treatment, including an exemption from the Olympic tryout camp if he was to play. The U.S. Olympic Committee said no, and Walton did not go. The United States lost the gold medal that year to the Soviet Union on a still-controversial buzzer beater.

Walton's final team at UCLA, the 1973–74 Bruins, lost four games. Notre Dame ended the winning streak at 88. There were back-to-back losses at Oregon and Oregon State, known in UCLA circles as "The Lost Weekend." And there was a season-ending loss to North Carolina State in the Final Four. Walton said he thought the 1973–74 team was the best of the three he played on and is still shaken by the way the season ended.

"If I could have one week back in my life, the week we played North Carolina State would be it," he wrote in his autobiography. The team was, he said, in total disarray. Walton had cracked two bones in his back and had missed two weeks, returning for the Notre Dame game. He did not play well there.

Then, in the semifinals of the Western Regionals, UCLA blew a 17-point lead and needed three overtimes to beat Dayton, 111–110. After the game, Walton removed all his clothing and settled in the hotel Jacuzzi to unwind. Hotel management was not amused and Wooden was furious. UCLA then beat San

Francisco, 83–60, to advance to the Final Four for the eighth straight year.

The Final Four that year was in Greensboro, North Carolina. N.C. State, which had the acrobatic David Thompson, already had lost once that year to UCLA by 18 points at a neutral site in St. Louis. Greensboro was anything but neutral. The bracketing had the two powers, ranked No. 1 and No. 2, paired in the semifinals.

UCLA led by 11 points with 11 minutes to play and couldn't hold it. The Bruins led by seven in overtime and couldn't hold it. They lost 80–77 in double overtime. Neither Walton nor any of the seniors had any interest in playing in the consolation game against Kansas. Wooden persuaded them to play and they did, although Walton went only 20 minutes and took three shots. UCLA won 78–61. North Carolina State went on to defeat Marquette in the finals.

After the game, Walton said he would never get another haircut.

Three months later, he was the No. 1 pick in the NBA draft, having been selected by the Portland Trail Blazers. Oregon wasn't exactly Southern California. But it sure beat the other possibility: Philadelphia.

"I didn't want to go east," he said. "The only time I've ever agreed with Ronald Reagan was when he said that if California had been settled first, the rest of the United States would still be a wilderness. I didn't know anything about the industrial Northeast other than that I didn't want to live there. I was a West Coast guy."

While at UCLA, the ABA offered Walton his own team in Southern California. It also said he could choose any players he wanted, with the exception of Julius Erving. He could also select the coach. But he wanted to play in the NBA. That's where the best players were and he wanted to play against the best.

The league at that time used a coin flip to determine which team would be awarded the first pick. Portland had the worst record in the Western Conference and Philadelphia had the worst record in the Eastern Conference.

"The 76ers had tried to get me out of UCLA after my sophomore year, but there was no way I was going to do that," Walton said. "I loved UCLA. But I also made it clear I was not going to play in Philadelphia, and if they won the flip, I was going to go to the ABA. So Portland won the flip."

•

Portland had in many ways seemed a good match for the professional coming-out party of Bill Walton. Oregon was a progressive state and had a backcountry feel to it, perfect for the man who had shown up wearing a flannel shirt and blue jeans to accept the Sullivan Award as the country's top amateur athlete. It was ideal for the radical-chic life that Walton led at the time, ranging from his vegetarianism to his celebrated relationship with activist Jack Scott and, perhaps, even fugitive Patricia Hearst. He had even been questioned by the FBI about possibly hiding Hearst, but when asked about it a decade later in front of the Nieman Fellowship class at Harvard, Walton smiled broadly and said, "If I didn't tell the FBI, do you think I'm going to tell you?" (Walton later said that Scott had been hiding Hearst, but not when he was living at Walton's house.)

Things initially did not work out for Walton in Portland, and there were times when he was so overcome by frustration, pain, and losing that he would call the owner in the middle of the night and threaten to retire. Basketball was not just about winning for Walton, although that was critical. It was like a gourmet meal to an epicure, everything had to be just so, and in Portland, everything was awry. He didn't like his teammates. He didn't like the weather. He didn't like the idea of not playing, to him the greatest penalty, and he was sitting more often than he was playing. Injuries limited him to 35 games as a rookie, and in his four years in Portland he never played in more than 65 games in any 82-game season. His knees, which had been able to withstand a college schedule of two games a week, were now being asked to endure more. But the Portland team doctors and others who examined him afterward zeroed in on the real problem: his feet. Walton was playing on Royal Doulton china. Eleven years later, Dan Dyrek, the Celtics' physical therapist, was amazed at the extent of the damage done by a long series of injuries and operations.

"When I first saw his X-rays, I said to myself, 'This is not a human foot,'" Dyrek recalled. "One day, I was treating him at the office and he was having a setback and he didn't want to hear about it, although I knew that he knew. He hauled off and punched the wall of the treatment room and cracked the plaster. He was doing it out of frustration. It was the foot and ankle. That was always the problem. It was like when you examined his foot, you threw away all your knowledge of anatomy. But in a way, I think he was immune to that foot that year [1985–86]. There was a small margin of safety and he just kept playing. His mental psyche was, 'I'll listen to the foot later. We have a chance.' Nothing was going to get in his way."

Danny Ainge remembered one game when Walton was being guarded by 6-7 Kenny Fields and could not take advantage of it. "We would tease him all the time because he couldn't post up strong," Ainge said. "His feet were so weak. With the bad feet he had then, and the bad knees, it was pretty amazing he could even play."

The foot pain surfaced in the first quarter of his first season with Portland in 1974–75, and the Blazers floundered. Portland won 38 games that season and just 37 the following year. In that second season, Walton also did something he had resolutely refused to do as a rookie: he took painkillers for his feet. It was something he would come to regret. He broke his leg that season and played in just 51 games.

"I knew what might happen, but I let myself get suckered in," Walton said. "At that point in my life, I wasn't strong enough as a person to say no."

Portland then decided to make a coaching change and brought in Jack Ramsay to coach the team. Ramsay, then the

coach at Buffalo, salivated at the prospect of coaching Walton
and unleashing what he felt would be a force on the rest of the
league.

"I never coached a player who was more attentive to the
game, the detail of the game, had more of a desire to win, and
who loved the team game more than Bill Walton," Ramsay said.
"He was just a pleasure. I never had one difficult day with him."

That might have been true at the outset. Walton and Ramsay
were soul brothers in their basketball beliefs, championing the
running game that would be triggered by Walton's defense and
rebounding. They were also both vegetarians. But probably
more important than Ramsay was the arrival in 1976 of two former ABA stars, Maurice Lucas and Dave Twardzik. Walton felt
Lucas was the best teammate he ever had (prior to Boston), and
the one individual who made him a better player. The two had
dined together when Lucas arrived in Portland and agreed to
work for the betterment of the team instead of their own personal agendas. For one glorious season and two-thirds of the
next, it worked.

Although he did miss 17 games in the 1976–77 season, Walton played in all 19 playoff games. He averaged 18.2 points, 15
rebounds, and 3.4 blocks a game in the postseason.

The following year was even better—until the end of January.
The Blazers were the consensus favorites to repeat and were
39-8 when Walton felt soreness in his right foot. He tried everything from a hypnotist to soaking his feet in a river as part of
a religious experience. Nothing worked. Portland eventually
peaked at 50-10 before finishing the season at 58-24. Walton underwent surgery in early March and then tried to come back the
following month when the Blazers opened the playoffs against
Seattle.

In the first game against the Sonics, Walton was visibly limited
but still managed 16 rebounds in 34 minutes. Before Game 2,
Walton reluctantly agreed to painkiller injections and subsequently broke a bone in his left foot. His season was over.
Less than four months later, and becoming increasingly upset

over what he saw as the Blazers' medical mistakes, Walton demanded a trade. Portland tried to accommodate him, but could not. He then missed the entire 1978–79 season with a foot injury and finally left Portland when San Diego signed him as a free agent.

His signing in San Diego came amid much hoopla and fanfare. The Clippers had been in San Diego for only a year, having moved there from Buffalo in 1978. Walton was a natural— homegrown and enthusiastic. He signed a five-year deal for $7 million, but in those days, a free agent signing required compensation, and the price was usually a steep one, in both cash and players. Walton felt a fair deal would be his old backup at UCLA, Swen Nater, and guard Randy Smith. The one player he did not want the Clippers to lose was power forward Kermit Washington, whom he envisioned playing the same enforcer role that Maurice Lucas had played so well next to him in Portland.

When the Clippers and Trail Blazers could not agree on compensation, NBA Commissioner Larry O'Brien made the final decision: for signing Walton, who was one year removed from an MVP season, but who had nevertheless been injured and missed the entire previous year, the Clippers had to give up backup center Kevin Kunnert and Washington, along with two first-round draft picks. Kunnert and Washington had come over from Boston that summer when the Celtics' and Braves' owners swapped franchises. Walton was floored.

"I really believed," he said, "that because of my circumstances leaving Portland that it wouldn't be the rape of the Clippers. But there was nothing I could do about it. We had to give up the players. But I was the reason we had to."

In 1978–79, the Clippers had gone 43-39. Then they signed Walton. They waited and waited and played reasonably well as he tried to get healthy.

Coach Gene Shue, who had pushed hard for signing Walton, was eagerly anticipating the arrival of the franchise center. He finally got him, but on a very limited basis. Walton, who had lost none of his cerebral powers, was still very iffy from a medical standpoint and had to be brought back on a strict timetable.

"It was unbelievable," Shue remembers. "The doctor gave me instructions on what I could and could not do. The first couple of games, Bill comes out and he is just sensational. He's doing all these great things and I have to take him out of the game. It was craziness, trying to break in a great player like that and make the whole thing work."

For 14 games it did work. But then Walton hurt himself again and did not play for the rest of the 1979–80 season as well as all of 1980–81. During these years, he started law school, but he eventually returned to the Clippers in 1982–83 (33 games), 1983–84 (55 games), and 1984–85 (67 games). The Clippers never made the playoffs and moved to Los Angeles in 1984.

Walton puts the blame squarely on himself for the Clippers' inability to survive in San Diego. The reason, he feels, is simple: he could not play.

"I love San Diego and that failing is and always will be an embarrassment to me," he says. "I would love it if basketball made it back there. I'm the reason it didn't stay there."

But now, he was pushing to leave Southern California altogether for what he once thought was the unlivable, industrial Northeast. The Celtics were interested, but they soon discovered that wanting Bill Walton and actually getting Bill Walton would be two very different things.

•

A week after Walton made his phone call, Auerbach and general manager Jan Volk flew to Los Angeles for a face-to-face with Walton and his representative, Ernie Vandeweghe, at the Los Angeles Airport Mariott Hotel. The meeting was mainly to further the dialogue from the telephone conversation; "a temperature check" is the way Volk remembered it. After the meeting, Auerbach told Volk, "This kid is hungry, and it's a good time in his career for this. We ought to pursue it." It was agreed that Walton would fly to San Francisco in the next few days to meet with Auerbach, who would be there for the annual NBA Board of Governors meeting. The Celtics' doctor, Thomas Silva, would also be in San Francisco and he would give Walton a cursory examination.

Everything went according to plan. Walton again conveyed his interest and the Celtics returned theirs. The organization felt that his health, while questionable, was sufficient to withstand a 15- to 20-minute game regimen in the NBA—not a consensus conclusion at the time.

All that remained was to find a way for Walton to get to Boston. In 1985, there was no such thing as an unrestricted free agent. The Celtics discovered early on that the only way to get Walton would be in a trade, because at first the Clippers, intent on keeping Walton in Los Angeles, would simply match any offer the Celtics extended to him.

The Celtics' proposal was simple: trade Cedric Maxwell for Walton. The Celtics had grown tired of Maxwell and the Clippers would soon be convinced that Walton no longer wanted to play for them. The Celtics figured they were going to get nothing out of Maxwell and might get something out of Walton.

It didn't take long for the Celtics to come to the same conclusion as Walton had: the Clippers made things difficult. "They were not to be believed," Alan Cohen said of the negotiations. Volk and L.A. general manager Carl Scheer conducted the negotiations, but with the Clippers there was always the lurking specter of owner Donald Sterling changing his mind, changing his demands, changing everything.

"Donald is the nicest, sweetest guy who will give you two dimes for a quarter and think he's doing you a favor," Cohen said. "I had some lovely conversations with him that managed to advance the cause not at all. But we didn't have another alternative at the time that we felt made sense, so we decided we should keep plodding along, holding hands, making nice and maybe something would happen. As everybody knows, sports is a business and you can't get too emotional conducting the business part. The object is not to get emotional. It was important for us that we strengthen our team. You can't get so emotional that you can't deal with the guy. You can't do that."

Added Volk, "We'd talk regularly, but with quite a bit of frustration on our part because every time we'd make progress, they'd come back with 'Yes, we'll do that, but we need this, too.' They'd keep adding something to the deal and we didn't feel we could get it done unless it was exceptionally lopsided and probably imprudent from our point of view."

Between mid-June and mid-August, there were several times when Volk felt the deal would not get done. He would answer queries about the deal by saying, "It's not going to happen today. This is a recording." In late July, things were going so badly that the Celtics called off the negotiations and prepared for the likelihood that the deal would never happen.

In Los Angeles, Carl Scheer experienced similar feelings. The year before, he had assumed the job and had re-signed a then-enthusiastic Walton, who had bicycled up from San Diego to sign the contract. Even then, Scheer remembers, there was still optimism. Walton was thin, tan, and still upset about the failure of the team in San Diego. He very much wanted to turn things around.

"We were thinking when we signed him [in 1984] that he would resume his position as one of the premier centers in the game," Scheer says now. "Unfortunately, we could not surround him with the players of comparable stature who could supplement his many talents. And he got discouraged very, very quickly. His very positive attitude completely turned around. There was nothing positive to fall back on. No tradition. No pride."

While waiting to placate an increasingly disconsolate Walton, Scheer also had to deal with an increasingly unpredictable Donald Sterling. "Dealing with Sterling was impossible," Scheer said. "If he took the elevator down, he'd ask the operator what he thought and by the time he reached the lobby, he had changed his mind. It was utter frustration. He could not make up his mind and would not allow you to function as a normal basketball operation. It was so painful."

Eventually, Scheer told Walton that Boston was "not a viable possibility" and a "dead issue." He told Walton to prepare for another season in Los Angeles because he, like Volk, sensed that the negotiations were not going to come to fruition.

By then the Celtics, anticipating a nondeal, quietly extended an olive branch to Maxwell, who was summering in North Carolina and quite aware of what was going on in Boston. The pitch was to get Maxwell recommitted and refocused and back in everyone's good graces by attending the team's annual rookie free agent camp in August. It would also be an opportunity for Maxwell to test his knee.

There is nothing glamorous about rookie camp. In 1985, it was held at a place called Camp Milbrook, a former lumber mill with asphalt basketball courts and metal backboards. The games in which Maxwell would be expected to play were held at a high school gym, always crowded and hot. Red Auerbach was there and always mentally took attendance. That was what the Maxwell invitation was all about: it was as much a symbolic surrender or acquiescence as anything significant from a basketball point of view.

Volk floated this idea to Ron Grinker, who represented Maxwell. He was told that Maxwell had no intention of coming to rookie camp.

"It probably was bad on my part not to go," Maxwell said years later, "but after eleven years, what did I have to prove to the team? I was like a stubborn kid, stomping my feet and saying, 'I'm not coming, I'm not coming.' I felt that I was going to come back in good shape and have a good year."

Years and the benefit of hindsight have not changed Maxwell's opinion as to who was to blame. He lays it all at the doorstep of Auerbach. This was a battle of wills with neither side about to budge. The long-term damage for Maxwell, however, was substantial. Red Auerbach never forgets and that year, in a book he co-authored, he removed Maxwell's name from a list of players who he felt embodied the Celtics traditions of unselfishness and loyalty.

"The only problem was Red," Maxwell said. "He was just as stubborn as I was. It was something that probably should not have happened, but it did. We each had leverage. Red had the power. I had the four-year contract. And I had to change the figures to fit into the salary cap. But after a while, I was so mad, so upset, I just told Ron, 'Whatever you have to do, do it.' At that point, I felt betrayed, hurt, all of the above. It was like they had forgotten everything else I had done—and all those things were factual. We won two championships, and I was a leading contributor. And during the resurgence, I was a big part, too. And I was the person who had to make the sacrifices and change my role. Before Larry [Bird] came, I led the team in scoring. A few years later, I was the sixth option on a five-man team. Everyone knew it. I wasn't a troublemaker. I didn't cut my clothes or dye my hair red. The one thing that still bothers me is that, because I was smiling out there and having fun, people thought I didn't care enough or take it seriously enough. Those who knew me, knew differently."

All these sentiments were expressed through Grinker, further infuriating Auerbach. When Auerbach was told that Maxwell was enjoying his new house, the Celtics executive shot back, "Who do you think gave him the money to buy the house?" Fed up, Auerbach decided Maxwell had to go. He told Volk to reopen negotiations with the Clippers, thereby setting in motion the permanent banishment of one of the team's most popular players.

"He ordered me to resume communications with the Clippers at that moment," Volk said. "I remember going to a janitor's office at Marshfield High School and calling Carl [Scheer] at home and trying to get the deal going again."

Out in California, the news invigorated Walton, who was beginning to think things would never work out.

"It was just an incredibly frustrating time because things were on again and off again and it took forever. But that's the Clippers' way of doing things. I had had so much disappointment with the injuries and the losing teams. I wondered if it was ever going to get done," he said.

Two more weeks went by without a solution and then Labor Day weekend arrived with a major breakthrough. Sterling was going to be out of the country and had delegated the Clippers' staff attorney, Arn Tellem, to handle the talks. Tellem, now a player agent, wanted to finalize the deal, if for no other reason than to be rid of a player the Clippers no longer wanted, a player who wanted to be somewhere else. Tellem further indicated he did not need to get back to Sterling for approval. With Sterling out of the picture, the Celtics saw a chance to finally complete the deal.

The trade still took a while to consummate, mainly because of issues between the Clippers and Walton. Walton had to surrender a year and a half's salary that had been deferred. "It was the best money I ever spent," he says today. The two sides also settled a lawsuit relating to his foot problems. "The Clippers wanted their last pound of flesh," Walton said. Meanwhile, the Celtics stood on the sidelines and waited for a resolution. The details and revisions were sent across country by Federal Express, which had a two-hour fax service. (Both sides thought that amazing at the time.)

In addition to parting with Maxwell, the Celtics also agreed to give up their first-round pick in 1986. They could afford that luxury because, a year earlier, they had acquired Seattle's No. 1 pick in a deal for guard Gerald Henderson, a deal that would eventually give them the No. 2 pick overall in the 1986 draft. Their own pick, they figured, was going to be no better than No. 22.

With Walton sitting in Volk's office, the deal was finally closed late on September 8, one day after, coincidentally, the Lakers announced the signing of Maurice Lucas, Walton's old Portland teammate, to shore up their front line. Both teams now had their much-needed big man. And Bill Walton was finally a Celtic.

Shortly after Walton's signing, M.L. Carr drove to the Celtics' office, picked up Walton, and brought him to Robert Parish's comfortable, secluded home in Weston, Massachusetts. The purpose of this true summit meeting—the two men were seven feet tall—was to give Walton a chance to reassure Parish he was only after a championship ring, not any of his playing time. It was Carr's idea, and both men were grateful for the occasion to simply chat.

"I had been really uncomfortable with all the attention be-cause I fully intended to come in and be a second-string player," Walton said. "And I wanted Robert Parish to know that."

A prescient Carr sensed there might be a potential problem, knowing Parish as he did. He was instantly relieved to hear Wal-ton talk about how delighted he was simply to be on the team as the two drove to Parish's house. Once there, Walton laid it on the line as Parish sat, typically stoic, and nodded.

"I told him I wasn't coming here to take anything from him," Walton said. "I told him it was his team, his center position, and I was coming in to be a part of it. That was all I wanted. I wasn't coming to compete against him. I was coming to help."

Parish welcomed Walton with open arms. The Chief never complained about playing time and he had just been through an arduous year without a reliable, consistent, or productive backup. Bill Walton could be all of that.

While the Walton announcement was a jubilant day for the oft-injured, oft-frustrated center, it also marked a bitter end to Cedric Maxwell's career in Boston. He had crossed the wrong man—Auerbach—and crossed him in a way in which redemp-tion was almost impossible.

Once he left the Celtics, Maxwell never had the success he had in Boston. He played in 76 games for the 1985–86 Clippers, averaging a respectable 14.1 points a game. During the 1986–87 season, he was traded to Houston and reunited with former

Celtics coach Bill Fitch. He retired after the 1987–88 season. It took years for him to make it back on the Celtics' guest list for such occasions as Larry Bird Night and Kevin McHale Night, and his No. 31 has not yet been retired.

"Max gave so much to the team," Carr said. "He was the MVP of the playoffs. He led us to the promised land in Game 7 of '84. To see him go out the way he did, it really wasn't that good. But I understand why. Max, to a certain degree, brought a lot of it on himself, because he would say nonchalantly, 'That's it, boys, let's close the books.' I think it got under Larry's skin that he wasn't serious. And Red felt he lay down on him. I just wish that all that could be forgiven and forgotten because there are two banners up there that he was a big part of. He took the best offensive player night in and night out. He was a pretty good 'other' player. I know Red isn't going to go back on that [not retiring Maxwell's number]. But in a real sense, I wish he would. Red has been bitter about a lot of situations a lot of the time. Even though Max did some things wrong at the end, you don't just say, 'He was a bad boy, a bad kid.' We should really respond to the fact that he is a big reason why two banners are up there."

Despite Maxwell's storied history with the Celtics, he was gone from the team in the fall of 1985, replaced with a risky investment in Bill Walton. But Walton was ready for the challenge, he was ready to play. As he prepared for the upcoming season, the Celtics' front office began negotiations that would shore up their backcourt and solidify the team for a realistic championship run.

CHAPTER TWO

Sam, Jerry, and the
Sly One

The Walton saga occupied most of the headlines in the summer of 1985, but that trade was just one of several personnel moves the Celtics made. Walton fulfilled one of their main goals—relief for Robert Parish—but there was still another shortcoming that needed to be addressed: a reliable backup shooting guard.

The Celtics bolstered their backcourt that June by drafting Sam Vincent, an All-American from Michigan State who was regarded as one of the top guards available that year. Vincent was 6-2 and the younger brother of Dallas forward Jay Vincent, a teammate of Magic Johnson's on the 1979 NCAA champion Michigan State Spartans. The *Sporting News* thought so highly of Vincent that it made him a first-team All-American along with Chris Mullin, Wayman Tisdale, Keith Lee, and Patrick Ewing. He was coming off a season in which he averaged 23 points, shooting 54 percent from the field and 85 percent from the line. Only his big brother and Greg Kelser had scored more points for Michigan State, and only four others—Rick Mount, Billy McKinney, Kelvin Ransey, and Cazzie Russell—had scored more in Big Ten conference games, an indication that Vincent played his best against the toughest competition.

The Celtics at the time looked at the statistics and the impressive reputation but overlooked one critical question: why was Vincent still available when it was their turn to pick? The Celtics had traded a second-round draft pick to Dallas before the draft to move up to No. 20—and with Vincent still sitting there a good move looked even better. But why hadn't the Bulls, desperate for guard help, taken him at No. 11, as everyone, including the Celtics, thought they would? "We never thought about Sam," said Bulls GM Jerry Krause. "We were going to go big and I really liked Oak [Charles Oakley]. The only guards we liked were Joe Dumars and Terry Porter."

Dumars had gone to Detroit with the eighteenth pick; and after the Houston Rockets opted for Tulsa guard Steve Harris, the Celtics were left with a choice: should they take the widely known Vincent or the less-known but highly regarded Porter, of Wisconsin-Stevens Point?

The Celtics back then, along with most other teams, did not bother bringing in prospective draft picks for interviews and workouts, so they were relying solely on scouting reports. In the previous year's draft, the Celtics had watched the University of Houston's Michael Young fall to them at No. 24, and he promptly became the first No. 1 pick in twenty years not to make the team. They vowed not to make a similar mistake this year, but here was a strikingly similar scenario.

Out in Michigan, Vincent and his fiancée waited. "I thought I was going to Chicago," he said. "I hadn't visited any places or played in any postseason tournaments and I later found out that that was not such a good idea. I was thinking to myself, 'What's going on here?' The guys who were supposed to go after me were going ahead of me and they had all played in the tournaments. Maybe if I had played, too, there would have been a different outcome."

The Celtics decided to go with Vincent. In hindsight, of course, Porter would have been the better choice, but back then, they simply felt Vincent was too good to pass up. Vincent's first thought was, "Am I going to be able to go in there and play?" He was excited to be chosen in the first round and by such a strong team, but he also wanted playing time, and those conflicting sentiments plagued him throughout his stay in Boston.

"I thought maybe I would be able to make a contribution," he said, "even though it was a solid, veteran team. I was thinking third guard."

The Celtics had hoped to get Vincent at their rookie camp in August, but as camp approached, he had not yet signed. In the two months since he had been drafted, there was no progress in contract negotiations, mainly because the Celtics had no place for him under the constraints of the salary cap.

Because they paid out large salaries to their established veterans, the Celtics were well above the figure the NBA allotted to each team for its payroll. It was all right to do that; the problem was you couldn't sign anyone else unless you paid him the minimum NBA salary, then $70,000, or you had a larger salary slot available because one of your players had been traded or had retired.

The Celtics could not, in good conscience, offer Vincent the NBA minimum and keep a straight face. Nor would he have accepted it. But if they could work a trade or have a player who made more than the NBA minimum retire, they could sign Vincent. So they waited; Vincent, they figured, was worth the wait.

In many ways, Vincent was an anomaly. The Celtics of the 1980s rarely had "name" rookies in camp—or anywhere else—because the team almost always drafted at a low position. Two years earlier, their first-round pick had been Greg Kite of Brigham Young. The year before that it had been the utterly unknown Darren Tillis of Cleveland State.

Vincent was different. People knew who he was. There was the obvious pedigree with his older brother Jay and the big-name college program. And Vincent was not about to be fazed by NBA competition; he had played all through high school and college with his brother, Magic Johnson, and others in the Lansing, Michigan, area.

For about a decade in the 1970s and 1980s, the Lansing area was the epicenter of Michigan prep basketball. Usually, Detroit or Flint enjoyed that distinction, but with the Vincent brothers and Magic Johnson passing through, Lansing was the place to be. Both Magic Johnson and Sam Vincent led their high schools to state championships, Magic at Everett High and Sam at Eastern.

The Vincents could usually find a basketball game at a park about a block from where they lived. There were five brothers, but Jay and Sam were the basketball players. Ella Vincent, a dynamic woman, had been the sole parent in the house since her husband died when Sam was just four years old.

James Samuel Vincent was the youngest of the five and he soon became known as "Sam," thanks to his big brother Jay. Sam's early days were generally happy, although there was always the gnawing problem of not having a father around. "It was a sore issue," he said. "It was just something that was never openly discussed. It was one of those wounds that you put a patch on and kind of leave alone."

Sam was three years younger than Jay and was well known around Lansing basketball circles as he made his way through the school system. His high school coach, Paul Cook, recalls Sam tagging along with his big brother and playing in all the pickup games.

"He and Jay were a lot alike," Cook said. "They were good kids who had a good, gentlemanly manner about them. They were never associated with drugs or violence or criminal activity and there was plenty of that going around. They were role models, on and off the court."

Cook had coached Jay Vincent at Eastern High School, but never won a state championship with him, always losing to Magic Johnson's Everett team. By the time Sam came along, Magic was gone, and Eastern had no problem winning the title

in Vincent's junior year, only his second on the varsity. He was
not eligible as a ninth-grader. "I wish he had been because he
would have started," Cook said. "But freshmen didn't play. Sam
was so much more mature and physically stronger than most
guards at that age. He'd play along the back line on defense for
rebounding and he always had great leadership qualities on the
court. We always figured we'd win in the last four minutes if he
had the ball or went to the line. He had poise and control on
the court."

Eastern did win most of the time, 74 times in 79 games while
Sam Vincent was there. His sophomore year, Vincent led Eastern to the state semis. As a junior, he averaged 20 points a game
as Eastern claimed the championship. In his senior year, Vincent pushed his scoring average to 30, including 61 in one
game, but the Quakers were ousted by Detroit Murray Wright in
the state semis in triple overtime. Vincent fouled out in the last
two minutes of regulation.

"It was disappointing to see a time of life pass on like that," he
said.

Cook said Sam Vincent was the best guard he ever had in
forty-two years of coaching. After finishing high school, Vincent
became the first winner of the Mr. Basketball award in Michigan, barely edging out a guard from Flint named Eric Turner.
Both would go on to have solid college careers—Turner went to
the University of Michigan—but, four years later, Vincent was
the No. 1 pick of the Boston Celtics while Turner, who left
Michigan after his junior year and was a second-round pick by
Detroit in 1984, never played in the NBA.

Up until a week before the Celtics' rookie camp began, Vincent
did not think he would be there since his agent, Fred Slaughter,
had advised him not to go because of the stalemated talks.
The Celtics needed to create a spot, but were having no luck
doing it.

"A few days before camp," Vincent said, "Fred told me we weren't going to be in camp because the negotiations were going nowhere and it was obvious to him that it was going to be one of those long, drawn-out situations. So he told me to relax, hang loose, lay low, and that he'd stay in touch.

"Then he calls back and tells me to get on a plane, that they are expecting me to be there. I wasn't in shape. I told Fred it was totally away from my current frame of mind. I couldn't figure it out."

The Celtics had found a salary slot for their rookie. All through the summer, the team had been nudging M.L. Carr, ever so gingerly, into retirement. Having been reduced to a bench warmer the previous season, Carr himself was leaning in that direction. He did not have a contract. But he also had not officially announced his retirement.

The Celtics could have simply announced they were signing Vincent and replacing Carr on their roster. But that would have been construed as a cold-blooded thing to do to someone who had meant so much and given so much to the team over the previous six years. The Celtics preach loyalty, and simply replacing Carr with a rookie would have been un-Celtic. He was wildly popular and one of the most recognizable and accessible sports personalities in New England. After all he had done for the team, he deserved more from the organization.

Under NBA rules at the time, if Carr retired, the Celtics could use one-half of his $175,000 salary to sign a player. If he intended to play some more, but not in Boston, the Celtics could use the full $175,000 slot. The Celtics didn't know what to do, so they asked the NBA to determine how much they could spend. Using an impartial basketball expert, Billy Cunningham, the former 76ers head coach, the NBA ruled that Carr was, as far as the league was concerned, retired. That meant that Vincent could get a first-year salary of $87,500.

Carr took some time over the first six weeks of the summer to reach the same conclusions as Cunningham. He would rather

have gone out a winner, as would have been the case had he retired in 1984. Now, a year later, he knew his time had come.

"I had waited long enough," he said. "I knew. The motivated
don't need motivating and I was absolutely spent. I was at the
point where I was starting to complain, and I'm not a com-
plainer. But it was summertime and they weren't playing then,
so there was no hurry. I was kind of glad to get it over with when
it finally did happen. And I'm still thankful and grateful to Red
for allowing me to do it. One of the worst things in the world to
me is that Pete Maravich never had a retirement day. And if Pete
Maravich didn't have one, why should I? I just try to keep it all
in perspective."

When M.L. Carr signed with the Celtics as a free agent in
1979, he set off a chain of events that, two trades later, led to the
lopsided deal with the Golden State Warriors that brought in
Robert Parish and the draft pick Boston used to select Kevin
McHale in 1980. The following year, Carr had his first NBA
championship ring; he added a second in 1984.

Carr had played in 604 regular season games over a nine-year
NBA career, the first three with the Detroit Pistons. He was cut
by the Celtics twelve years earlier and was told by Auerbach to
play in Israel so he could hide Carr. He played a year there but
when he returned, there was still no room in Boston, so he
signed on with the St. Louis Spirits of the ABA. When the ABA
folded, he signed with Detroit. Three seasons later, he was in
Boston. His best year in Boston was his first; after that his contributions became increasingly less important, and he left the
game as arguably the best-known towel waver in NBA history.

The official retirement announcement came August 22, at
Marshfield High School. After a Chinese food lunch with Auerbach, Jan Volk, and Celtics owners Alan Cohen and Don Gaston, Carr appeared at a news conference. Fighting back tears,
he said, "There comes a time when the old guys have to move
on." He had helped reverse a bad situation when he arrived that
year in Boston, and outscored a rookie named Larry Bird 15–14
in their first game together as Celtics.

"I had everything planned that day and what I was going to say," he recalled years later. "But it soon became really emotional. I was thankful and felt grateful. I felt I was the most fortunate person in the world. To see all the great players and to know you are a part of such a great tradition, well, it just doesn't get any better. I never, ever took anything for granted. When I sat next to Red at camp and heard him saying things like 'You played with your heart and you gave everything you had,' I'd think, 'Gee, here's a guy who coached [Bill] Russell and [Bob] Cousy and [Bill] Sharman and he'd say that about a little guy from Wallace, North Carolina, who people said couldn't make it. All that time I spent in Israel. All the rejections. All the hard work. It paid off."

With Carr's retirement, the Celtics now had the money to sign Vincent. Just before entering the Celtics' rookie camp, Vincent signed a contract in the passenger seat of Jan Volk's Corvette that called for a starting salary of $87,500 and quickly ballooned to $300,000. (The NBA eventually cracked down on such deals, limiting yearly increases to 30 percent and then to 20 percent to stop this obvious form of salary cap subterfuge.)

The Celtics, however, did not feel that this signing rectified their need for a shooter in the backcourt. They were loath to play rookies in those days and saw Vincent as a pleasant addition with a good upside. But they needed immediate help in the backcourt and that meant getting someone with an NBA résumé. That someone was Jerry Sichting.

In much the same way Bill Walton sold himself to Boston, so did Sichting, a 6-1 stroker for the Indiana Pacers. In late June, two weeks after Walton called the Celtics asking for a job, Sichting delivered the same message to Boston assistant coach Chris Ford.

Sichting only knew Ford casually, but he figured he had nothing to lose. Like Walton, he was tired of losing and playing in unimportant games. Indiana, like the Clippers, was a perennial loser. His call to Ford came when the Celtics' coaching staff was discussing the upcoming NBA draft; Ford relayed Sichting's message to management.

Sichting was not an unknown to the Celtics. The previous February, during the All-Star weekend in Indianapolis, Volk and Wayne Embry, the Pacers' general manager, almost consummated a deal involving Sichting. The Celtics' offer was a second-round draft pick for the soon-to-be-free agent. Embry didn't go for it. After that fell through, the Celtics went out and signed Ray Williams, then a restricted free agent with the Knicks whom New York had decided not to re-sign.

At that point in his career, Sichting had played five NBA seasons, all with the Pacers. He was an Indiana original, born and raised in Martinsville, the hometown of John Wooden, the legendary UCLA coach. The town is thirty miles south of Indianapolis and twenty miles north of Bloomington, the home of Indiana University.

Martinsville has a rich basketball tradition in Indiana hoop history, having taken the state championship in 1924, 1927, and 1933. Like the small town of French Lick, hometown of teammate Larry Bird, Martinsville was famous in the early twentieth century for its mineral water spas and sanitariums. A town history notes that 25,000 people visited Martinsville in 1911, then called the Carlsbad of America, for treatment of any number of ailments, ranging from rheumatism to gout. The Home Lawn Mineral Springs was rumored to have had Franklin D. Roosevelt as a guest. All the sanitariums were closed by the 1930s.

Both sides of Jerry Sichting's family came from Martinsville. His father, Wilbur (Webb) Sichting, worked as an auto mechanic in Indianapolis and, later, as a manager/dispatcher of a trucking company. When Jerry was three, the Sichtings moved into a house near the Martinsville City Park, and it was only a matter of time before young Jerry started playing basketball on the park's courts. They were twenty feet from the Sichtings' property line.

"I had paradise growing up," he said. "That park had a swimming pool, baseball field, basketball court. I played every sport there was."

Sichting's big sports in high school were football and basketball. He was an all-state quarterback his senior year at Martinsville and was recruited by Notre Dame. It was Ara Parseghian's last year in South Bend, and the new coach, Dan Devine, was also interested in him. Sichting, however, stuck with basketball.

"If I had gone to Notre Dame," he said, "I would have been in the same class as Joe Montana. I guess I made the right choice."

Now, ten years later, he was making another career decision. The Celtics liked Sichting for many reasons, but toughness was at the top of the list. This was someone who had seen the bottom of the canyon and lived to tell about it.

Sichting was originally drafted by the Warriors in the fourth round of the 1979 draft, eighty-second overall. He stayed with the team all through veterans camp, only to be cut as a victim of a numbers game. Frustrated and angry—"I think I played four minutes in the entire preseason and I lit up John Lucas in an intrasquad game," he said—he briefly (for forty-eight hours) tried the CBA in Maine and then returned to Indiana to work in a sporting goods store, playing basketball in AAU and industrial leagues around Indianapolis.

The following year, the Pacers conducted a tryout camp in Indianapolis. It was, the team said, a "Walter Mitty Camp." Anyone who harbored any hopes of ever playing in the NBA was urged to attend and fulfill his dream. In the searing heat at Hinkle Field House on the campus of Butler University, Sichting, incredibly out of shape, joined some twenty others for two-a-days. He was good enough to get invited to the Pacers' summer league team in Los Angeles, was invited to veterans camp, and this time was the last player to make the team, beating out Kenny Natt. As the Pacers waited that day for the team picture, neither Sichting nor Natt put on his uniform, each afraid he was going to be the casualty. Natt got called into a meeting with the coach. Only then did Sichting put on his uniform and smile for the camera.

By his third year in Indiana, Sichting had received some serious playing time and even started a few games. The following season, he played in 80 games, starting them all. In the 1984–85 season, he appeared in 70 games, starting in 25. What also intrigued the Celtics was Sichting's reliability: he shot 53 percent from the field in 1983–84 and 52 percent in 1984–85, excellent numbers. But Indiana was losing games, players, and money, and Sichting, like Walton, had had enough.

"I wanted to get out of Indiana in the worst way," Sichting said. "The team was so bad and I didn't think I was being treated fair, contract-wise. I would have given anything to be on a team like the Celtics."

After the 1984–85 season, Sichting became a free agent. A couple of days before the draft, Jan Volk called to officially confirm the Celtics' interest. He suggested Sichting call back after the draft. When Sichting saw the Celtics take Vincent, he didn't bother. A few days later, Volk called to reaffirm interest, a call that left Sichting both surprised and elated.

The Celtics and Sichting started talking, and it wasn't long before Volk and George Andrews, Sichting's agent, were able to come to an agreement. Nothing was signed, but the basic elements of the deal—four years at an average of $200,000 per year—were agreed upon, and Andrews told Sichting not to talk about it.

At the same time, the Celtics were also talking to Indiana about a deal for Quinn Buckner. On September 2, it was announced that the Celtics had traded Buckner to the Pacers, for a second-round draft pick. Sichting received all sorts of calls at his home in Indiana from Pacers writers and did his best to play Mickey the Dunce. "I told them it'd be great and there'd be more competition and all this stuff," he said. "In the back of my brain I'm thinking, when is this thing going to happen?"

Nine days after the Buckner trade, the Celtics finally announced they had signed Sichting to an offer sheet with the agreed-to terms. Under NBA rules, Indiana had fifteen days to match. During that time, the teams could also discuss a trade to facilitate the matter.

The Pacers waited the full fifteen days, which overlapped with the opening of the Celtics training camp. On the fifteenth day, Hurricane Gloria swept through the Northeast and the Pacers were unable to reach the NBA office in New York to announce they were matching the offer. The Celtics thought that meant Indiana was not going to match the offer, but the league considered the circumstances and sided with the Pacers, so the Celtics' offer became an Indiana contract. Sichting was hot.

"I think they were doing it out of spite," Sichting recalled.

Andrews called Sichting and told him to hold out and force a trade. The Pacers called and told Sichting to report to training camp. Sichting said he would not be there.

Three days later, a deal was struck. Key to the deal was the Celtics' agreeing to play an exhibition game in Indianapolis. The Celtics returned the second-round pick they received in the Buckner deal in exchange for a second-rounder in 1990. The preseason game, given Boston's fame at the time and the presence of Indiana legend Larry Bird, would be a guaranteed sellout for the then cash-hungry Pacers. Sichting flew to Boston, unpacked his bags at the Howard Johnson's Motor Inn, and headed over to Hellenic College, the Celtics' practice site, for a physical. But the exam had to wait; he was told to get onto the practice floor like everyone else. After all he had been through, that sounded just fine to him.

Eight days after the offer sheet was extended to Sichting, the Pacers and Celtics were again in the news. The subject this time was an even more valuable player: Boston's starting guard, Dennis Johnson, who, like Sichting, was also a restricted free agent. The Celtics had the right to match any offer, and they were never seriously worried they might lose Johnson.

Johnson, who had been in the league for almost a decade

and had just turned thirty-one, could have brought the young Pacers a veteran presence and some instant credibility. He was coming off a season in which he was chosen to play in the All-Star Game for the fifth time. His scoring average (15.7) and field goal percentage (.462) would turn out to be personal highs in his seven years with the Celtics.

On September 20, Johnson flew to Indianapolis to meet with the Pacers. The Celtics figured it was a little bit of posturing by Indiana, especially after the Sichting signing; and since Johnson was not accompanied by his agent, Fred Slaughter, they saw nothing sinister or ominous in the visit. While Johnson was there, however, he sat down with Pacers coach George Irvine, and before he returned home he had a lucrative offer to consider.

"I wanted the longevity and the security," Johnson said. "I honestly at that time didn't know where I was going to be. Indiana's numbers in the beginning were about the same as what Boston offered, but they went much higher in the last three years."

What was somewhat upsetting to Johnson was Irvine's very legitimate query as to why Johnson was even considering Indiana in the first place. Irvine told Johnson that there was nothing in Indiana that was better than the situation in Boston. He told Johnson the Pacers were young and rebuilding, and why would he want to finish his career in a situation like that and leave an NBA championship contender?

"I'm thinking, this is my tenth year, and it was like he was saying, 'You're coming here just for the money.' But every place I had been, we had won," he said. "The number of wins has always gone up everywhere I've gone. Maybe they were just playing me, I don't know. I told Fred to sew the thing up one way or another."

And Slaughter did. Four days later, Johnson and the Celtics agreed on a four-year contract. It wasn't as lucrative as what he turned down, but it doubled his previous salary of $400,000 and

kept him on a contending team. At this point, he referred to the
Indiana visit as a "courtesy call."

The Celtics now felt they had settled their backcourt troubles.
Danny Ainge and Johnson were back. Jerry Sichting and Sam
Vincent were new and valuable additions to the club. As for the
front court, Cedric Maxwell was gone, and while the Celtics
were confident that Kevin McHale and Scott Wedman could
handle the small-forward load, they kept looking for help in
that area as well. In early September, at the suggestion of assistant coach Jimmy Rodgers, the Celtics signed David Thirdkill, a
6-7 defensive specialist known as "The Sheriff." Then, later in
the month, they added another player to the mix. He was familiar to all New England basketball fans, both for his ability on the
court and his reputation off it. Basketball fans didn't call him
"The Sly One" for nothing.

On September 27, the day the Celtics were set to open training camp, they announced they had acquired Sylvester "Sly"
Williams, who had just been cut by the Atlanta Hawks.

It looked like a something-for-nothing deal for the Celtics.
The move not only brought Williams back to the area where he
had first achieved basketball notoriety as a star at the University
of Rhode Island, but it also brought him to the team that had
tried to sign him two years earlier when he was with the Knicks.

In 1983, Boston signed three Knicks free agents, including
Williams, to offer sheets in an effort to eat up the Knicks' room
under the salary cap and keep them from going after Kevin
McHale. The strategy worked, as the Knicks, unwilling to lose
three players (Williams, Rory Sparrow, and Marvin Webster),
matched the offer and left McHale alone.

After four inconsistent seasons, Williams was traded to Atlanta, where he was besieged by injuries, including what the
Hawks and other teams called an "intestinal illness"—which
was, in reality, an excruciatingly painful case of anal warts. The

pity was, he could really play: he was an exceptional passer, a good post player, he had it all. Anyone who ever coached him will admit to that.

Williams played in 34 games in 1984–85, and Atlanta, already blessed with a big, young, and healthy front line, released him, eating his $450,000 salary in the process. (The $450,000 was the amount Boston had offered him two years earlier as a free agent before being matched by New York.) Prior to releasing him, however, the Hawks' general manager, Stan Kasten, aware of Boston's previous interest in Williams, called Volk to see if the Celtics were still interested in him. Volk was somewhat wary; the two teams were Eastern Conference rivals (or so Atlanta liked to think) and the Hawks were seen as one of the real up-and-coming teams in the league. What was Kasten trying to pull?

"I had to assume that Stan wouldn't find Boston an attractive place to be for someone with talent," Volk recalled. "And I had to assume he went everywhere else first. But he suggested we give them [the Hawks] a third-round pick, sign Williams for the NBA minimum, and then pay Atlanta on a per-day basis for every day Williams was on the team."

The Celtics agreed to the deal. Williams first had to clear waivers, but given his high salary, neither Boston nor Atlanta was concerned. Volk and Williams's agent, Hartford-based Joe Moniz, then met to discuss Williams's future with the Celtics.

"We made it clear to Sly that this was going to be for the future, not for 1985–86," Volk said. "At that time, we saw the team as fairly well set. But we told him that in a year or two, there might be an opportunity. He said all the right things and the deal was done."

Despite Williams's reputation, the Celtics saw no downside. Although they were committed to paying Williams, none of the money was guaranteed. In their mind, he was the equivalent of a first-round pick, which in fact he had been at one time, getting chosen twenty-first overall in 1979 by the Knicks. He had six seasons under his belt, but was a "young" twenty-seven in that he had played in just 47 games the previous two seasons.

The Celtics had always enjoyed a reputation as a team that could revive supposedly moribund careers and turn bad boys into altar boys. Williams was merely going to be the latest, or so they thought. He seemed to think so, too.

"Ever since I was little, the Celtics were the greatest thing to me," he said shortly after signing. "And when you play with a great supporting cast, as they have now, that can only make you look better. It's definitely a shot in the arm and a step in the right direction for me."

Sly Williams, one of fourteen children, was one of the finest prep products to come out of New England in the 1970s. Until the ninth grade, however, his main sport was baseball. A southpaw, he was a terrific pitcher and might have been a Randy Johnson–esque prospect had he stuck with baseball after growing four inches before entering Lee High School in New Haven, Connecticut. With the added height, Williams turned to basketball and found his niche. He was, however, a reluctant participant at first, particularly when he discovered most of his friends weren't as gifted and thus couldn't make the varsity. So he would accommodate both the school and his buddies by playing on the varsity after class and shooting around with his friends after dinner.

Williams had a curious-looking shot, a left-handed delay pump, that he developed after watching the Knicks' legendary star Walt Frazier. "He had this great reach, as some left-handers do," said Dave Gavitt, the coach at Providence College when Williams was in high school. "He was a tough power forward; good body, good hands, solid rebounder."

By the time Williams was a senior at Lee, he was averaging 35 points a game. He was the latest in a number of high school stars from Connecticut who made their way to glory and fame; Calvin Murphy was from Norwalk, and the city of Bridgeport had sent a number of players to the pros, including Charles Smith, the slender forward for the Clippers, the Knicks, and the

Spurs, and John Bagley, the not-so-slender guard who played for a handful of teams, including the Celtics. Hartford also gave the NBA Rick Mahorn and Marcus Camby.

The college battle for Williams came down to two out-of-state schools: Providence and Rhode Island. He had connections at both. Providence featured Bruce "Soup" Campbell, who played high school ball in New Haven; and Rhode Island had Jiggy Williamson, another Connecticut product, who was the brother of former NBA and ABA star John Williamson.

"I think it was those close connections that made us the two favorites," Gavitt said.

In Gavitt, Williams had a high-profile suitor. He was the coach and athletic director at Providence, which, at the time, was arguably the top program in New England. In addition, Gavitt already had been selected to coach the 1980 Olympic basketball team. Williams got so carried away by the Providence interest that he called a news conference in May of 1976 to announce he had signed a letter of intent to attend the school. This stunned the folks down the road at the University of Rhode Island, for they had been given similar news by Williams, who later explained his contradictory remarks: "You don't want to say no to anybody."

Williams was acting without the advice of a father; his dad had died nine years earlier, so Williams was on his own in making this decision. And he had to deal with the rivalry. The bad blood that existed between the two schools only served to intensify the situation.

Unfortunately for Gavitt and Providence, Williams had signed only a school letter of intent, not a national letter. Neither school at the time used the national letter, which was used mainly for football schools. (Providence didn't have a football team, and Rhode Island was in the Division I-AA Yankee Conference.) And on the day that Providence was to start classes, Williams showed up downstate and registered for classes at Rhode Island. Gavitt was left in the dark, just like everyone else, and to this day the most ardent Providence alumni feel Williams was somehow "convinced" to sign in Kingston by Rhode Island officials.

"You could say I was a bit shocked," Gavitt said. "We thought we had him. But he enrolled at Rhode Island and they became appreciably better right away."

The Rams would go on to become an Eastern power in Williams's last two years there, but his freshman year was a learning experience. When he decided to play, Williams made Rhode Island a force. He averaged 20 points per game as a freshman (including a 32-point performance in a tournament in Providence at which he was jeered during introductions), and set a freshman single-season scoring record with 520 points.

But the Rams were only a .500 team, and coach Jack Kraft occasionally had to remind Williams that there were four teammates on the floor. Williams thought about transferring and started to skip practices and, eventually, games. He was a no-show for two easy matchups against Biscayne College and Stonehill, and Kraft, annoyed with his star player, finally sat him down and explained to him that being a player meant attending everything. The talk registered, at least temporarily.

In Williams's sophomore year, Rhode Island went to the NCAAs and nearly beat eventual runner-up Duke in the first round, losing 63–62.

By his junior year, Williams was the best player in New England. He averaged 25.6 points and 8.7 rebounds a game through January. He scored 44 points in a game against the University of Detroit en route to establishing a University of Rhode Island single-season scoring record of 693 points. That year, 1978–79, Williams was named Player of the Year by *Eastern Basketball* magazine. In 84 games covering three years, Williams averaged 21.2 points a game, and Kraft—who had Howard Porter, Chris Ford, Wali Jones, and Bill Melchionni while coaching at Villanova—said Williams was the best player he had ever coached, a period covering seventeen years.

But Williams's game tailed off badly over the final two months of his junior year. In what turned out to be his final game for Rhode Island, Williams got the ball on the break with his team leading by one point against Maryland in the first round of a National Invitation Tournament game. There were only 13 seconds remaining and Williams could have iced the game by simply dribbling out the clock. Instead, he drove to the basket, missed a layup, and was called for charging. It was his fifth foul. Maryland tied the score and went on to win in triple overtime.

Williams never played another college game, joining three others, including a sophomore from Michigan State named Earvin Johnson, as "hardship" entrants in the 1979 NBA draft.

The Knicks had three first-round picks that year, courtesy of a trade with the Celtics in which they had shipped Bob McAdoo to Boston. New York picked Bill Cartwright with the first pick, Larry Demic with its second, and Williams with the third (the penultimate pick of the first round).

After a slow start, Williams played three reasonably solid years for the Knicks. But after averaging 13.2 points a game in 1980–81, a season in which he started 50 games, he wanted to renegotiate his contract. New York didn't. Williams decided he needed a leave of absence to attend to his large family and was promptly suspended by the Knicks.

There were times when he was late for practices or missed them altogether, a situation that didn't sit well with the ordinarily benign Red Holzman. Knicks coach Hubie Brown had Williams for one year and quickly tired of it all. In 1983, the Knicks shipped Williams to Atlanta for Rudy Macklin. The Knicks also sweetened the deal with cash to get rid of Williams and basically forgot about Macklin, who appeared in eight games the following year and was never heard from again.

Injuries curtailed Williams's time in Atlanta. He broke a thumb and a foot in his first year with the Hawks, and then the warts set in and basically made it impossible for him to play. They could be burned off but they always seemed to return, and despite Williams's public assurances that all was well, he simply was unable to play basketball for any prolonged period of time. The Celtics knew about Williams's medical history, and decided he was still worth a shot. They were less fazed by the alleged personality issue; remember, this was a team that had gone through Marvin Barnes, Sidney Wicks, and Curtis Rowe.

"Once you get to know me, and it's all said and done, people will only have good things to say about me," Williams said. "I have gotten a lot of bad publicity and Boston knows that. They also know that three-quarters of it isn't true."

Red Auerbach, for one, was willing to look and listen. "When a guy is unhappy, as he was in New York and Atlanta, then he can do a lot of crazy things."

Little did Auerbach realize that Williams's crazy life would not end in Boston, though his NBA career would. As the Celtics prepared to open training camp, Williams was on the "untouchables" list—the players deemed to be certain to make the 12-man roster. There was the returning starting five of Larry Bird, Kevin McHale, Robert Parish, Danny Ainge, and Dennis Johnson, and a bench consisting of Bill Walton, Jerry Sichting, Scott Wedman, Greg Kite, Sam Vincent, and Sly Williams. A yet unknown lad would fill out the final roster spot as the Celtics headed into the 1985–86 season.

CHAPTER THREE

Training Camp:
Cuts and Cutups

The Celtics opened their training camp with seventeen bodies, but it was soon clear that the battle for the twelfth man would come down to three people: returnees Carlos Clark and Rick Carlisle, and a former Phoenix first-round pick, David Thirdkill. (Also on the roster was a writer for *USA Today*, David DuPree, who spent training camp with the team for a first-person story and actually played a minute in the exhibition opener against the 76ers before getting "cut.")

The last roster spot would be decided in practice and in the eight-game exhibition season, which had one unusual feature that year: four games against the hated Lakers. For two high-powered, high-profile teams that clearly did not like each other, this was both a fan's dream and a coach's nightmare. As the Lakers' Mitch Kupchak put it, "It's a little too early in the season to be this intense. Personally, I could do without it."

The bad blood between the two teams started to simmer in the third game. K.C. Jones was ejected and a total of eight technicals were called. In the fourth game, the bad blood was boiling. Robert Parish and Maurice Lucas got into a fight with six seconds left in the third quarter. Soon Bill Walton and Michael Cooper got into it, and Sly Williams, dressed in civvies, got in enough good licks to get ejected. Fines totaling more than $5,000 were assessed. Lucas was fined $1,000: $750 for fighting and $250 for getting ejected. Parish was fined $750 for fighting. He was not ejected. The rest of the players were fined $500 each for leaving the bench. In the announcement, the NBA noted that "Tom Kite" had been among those fined. Said Greg Kite, "He must have come out of the stands and hit someone with a sand wedge." Kevin McHale seemed to best sum up the four games against the Lakers: "Familiarity breeds contempt," he said. "Just ask my wife."

The fourth game against the Lakers ended the exhibition season and marked the beginning of a time of soul-searching for Jones. He had one roster spot available and three players worthy of serious consideration.

The twelfth-man story always dominated the last week of the exhibition season in those days. Here was a player who would become Mr. October in the eyes of the media and then, with few exceptions, return to oblivion for the rest of the season.

The previous year, Carlisle, a third-round draft pick, had beaten out top pick Michael Young and made the team. Now he was on the bubble again along with Clark, who had two NBA seasons under his belt, and Thirdkill, who had been in the league since 1982.

Clark's chances were slim from the start. He had made the mistake of not appearing at rookie camp, even though, like Cedric Maxwell, he was not a rookie. "That," Carlisle said, "was a huge mistake. If Carlos had come, it would have been tough for me to make it because he was a superior talent. The only advantage I had over him was that I could play both guard positions."

But Carlisle had another advantage over Clark, unbeknownst to him at the time. K.C. Jones thought Clark was lacking the fundamentals and determination to make a serious impact on the team. Carlisle, who did attend the rookie camp, also had an advantage over Thirdkill, in that he had made the team the year before.

"I knew David was good enough and I had some skills that he didn't have. But I had no idea what was happening," Carlisle said.

Two days before the October 25th regular-season opener, K.C. Jones made his decision: Clark and Thirdkill were released. Carlisle made the team. The Celtics figured Carlisle would get picked up by another team if he was released, while Thirdkill, who had been available all summer, would probably be available again should the need arise.

Thirdkill had been a big surprise in camp and remembered being crushed when given the news. "It was very disappointing," he said. "My first year in the NBA with Phoenix I had gotten to be friendly with Dennis Johnson, and he and I felt that I should have made the team. So did a lot of other guys. But it didn't happen. The NBA works in strange ways."

The release of Thirdkill created a very unusual racial mix on the Celtics: eight whites and four blacks. In a league where almost 80 percent of the players were black, this was almost unthinkable. There hadn't been a team with such a disproportionate mix since the 1969–70 Golden State Warriors, who also had eight white players.

While the greater Boston area has always had a well-earned reputation of being inhospitable to blacks—Bill Russell couldn't buy a house in one suburb because of his skin color—the Celtics themselves had always tried to go the other way. This was one team that didn't have to apologize to anyone for its racial history. The Red Sox, on the other hand, were one of the last teams to integrate and, in the 1950s, had an incorrigible racist as a manager.

In 1950, the Celtics broke the NBA color barrier by drafting Chuck Cooper. In the 1965–66 season they were, along with the Philadelphia 76ers, the first team to start five blacks—Bill Russell, K.C. Jones, Sam Jones, Willie Naulls, and Tom Sanders. They hired Bill Russell—the first black man to coach a professional sports team—to succeed Auerbach in 1966. Auerbach used to room whites and blacks together on the road.

The Celtics did not make their decision based on anything other than what was best for the team. Their games were sold out—fans waited four nights outside Boston Garden for the privilege of buying obstructed-view seats—and the only issue to management was assembling the best team.

"I had hoped it was something that wasn't going to be an issue," Carlisle said years later. "I didn't want to be kept on the team for the wrong reason. I've never seen anything like the buildup for that last cut. There's nothing like it anywhere. I understand it, though, because it is special. You just have to protect yourself and that's the way I went about it."

There was no outcry from the black players and it was hard to quibble with a lineup that featured Larry Bird, Kevin McHale, Danny Ainge, Scott Wedman, and Bill Walton.

"The guys who grew up and love the game like I do, those guys don't see color," Walton said. "All I see out there is movement. It had nothing to do with race. Heavens no! It had to do with people who could play good basketball. People who are not smart have racial problems. Intelligent people don't. And we had an incredibly smart bunch of guys."

Dennis Johnson admitted he had been hurt personally by the decision because he and Thirdkill had been friends. But he also knew Carlisle and what he could bring to the team.

"From the inside, sports is one of the best ways to attack racism," Johnson explained. "You know the makeup of the team. You're among a group of people and you have to come together if you want to win. I didn't have to like Larry or Robert or Bill. I respected them. And if you're giving the effort and no one thinks you're backsliding, then it doesn't matter if you're black or white. If I have a choice of passing the ball to Larry or David, I don't make the decision on black and white. I make it because Larry will probably make the shot.

"Yes, I thought David should have made the team, but on talent, not because he was black. I would never think that. God would have bopped me on the head. My thoughts are not who I want on the team because he is black or white. But I don't always have to agree with K.C. either. Basically, I thought David was better than Rick, but I also think Rick hustled a lot more for that position. And maybe David laid back too much and he might have thought it was easier because he had been on a team before."

The Celtics took no heat for the unusual racial mix, in part because of their history and in part because the white players on the team were all, with the exception of Kite and Carlisle, terrific. But having been a bench warmer once himself, Jones knew the value of having players who worked as hard as Kite and Carlisle always did. The race issue, then, wasn't really an issue at all, especially since the man who made the decision to keep the white player (Carlisle) over two black players (Clark and Thirdkill) was a black man. For someone who had grown up in Jim Crow country and experienced racism much of his life, the decision was a colorless one.

"That was nowhere near my thinking," Jones said. "I thought Carlisle was the best man for the team. The race issue was a non-issue. The only issue for me was winning."

You could look long and hard and not find anyone who has won more than K.C. Jones. He played for an NCAA champion. He was on the 1956 Olympic Gold Medal basketball team. He played for eight NBA champions. He was an assistant coach on two other NBA champions and the head coach of two more. He ran out of fingers for all his rings.

Skeptics point out that Jones's success could be directly attributed to Bill Russell, his teammate in college, the Olympics, and the pros. And, as a coach, he stepped into a situation in Boston in which the team's great players were entering the prime of their careers, and he merely had to provide the appropriate atmosphere. All of that was certainly true. He was either lucky or good, but whichever it was, he triumphed as a player and coach as no individual in NBA history had done before.

Jones got his basketball start in San Francisco. His family settled in the Bay Area when his mother, Eula, moved the family west from Texas, where they had bounced around during the Depression, living in Taylor, Corpus Christi, and Dallas. Eula and her husband, also called K.C. (the initials did not stand for anything), were getting divorced at the time, so the mother took the five children out west, where they settled into a segregated housing project in an area that would eventually become Candlestick Park.

The family immediately went on welfare and K.C., the oldest of the children, started honing his basketball skills in various recreation leagues throughout the area. By the time he entered Commerce High, he was a reasonably good shooter but a below-average student. He didn't start school in Texas until the age of seven and had trouble catching up. But his basketball was terrific and, although only 5-9, he was an all-regional selection. Still, he envisioned a career as a milkman until a high school teacher and friendly sportswriter intervened, changing his life forever.

The teacher, Mildred Smith, placed a call to University of San Francisco coach Phil Woolpert and suggested he take a chance on Jones. The sportswriter, Al Corona of the *San Francisco Chronicle*, then wrote a flattering article suggesting Jones was wanted by every major college in the area. Woolpert was forced to take action. Woolpert agreed to take Jones provided he gained admission to the university first, but Jones, who lived fifteen minutes from the campus, could not find the school the day he was supposed to take the entrance exam. Woolpert rescheduled the exam and made sure Jones got there the next day, and in the fall of 1951 K.C. Jones headed to USF.

In college, Jones grew four inches and lost his shooting touch. "I knew then," he said, "I should start to concentrate on defense." As a freshman, he was so upset with his game, his 7-14 team, and his family situation that he decided to leave school and get a job. Woolpert intervened, however, and helped land Eula Mae Jones a job as a chambermaid at the St. Francis Hotel. K.C. had new life.

The next year, Bill Russell arrived and ended up rooming with Jones. The varsity still struggled (Russell was on the freshman team) but by 1953–54, the prospects looked better. But Jones played only one game that season before undergoing an emergency appendectomy and losing twenty-five pounds. He almost lost more than that; doctors feared for his life because he had been complaining of stomach pains for weeks before the diagnosis. Things were so grim that Jones lost consciousness for four days and the university had a prayer service for him.

He eventually recovered, and over the next two years, with Bill Russell and a healthy K.C. Jones, San Francisco lost only one game and won two NCAA titles. Jones played both years and was a member of the 1955 championship team. (He was ineligible for the 1956 tournament because the NCAA ruled that he was technically playing a fifth season.) In 1956, the Celtics drafted him in the second round (Russell had been a first-rounder), but he didn't like his prospects so he joined the army.

He made a name for himself as a football player while stationed at Fort Leonard Wood in Missouri, particularly in the eyes of serviceman John Morrow, who also played center for the Los Angeles Rams. Jones ended up getting a tryout with the Rams and started three exhibition games at defensive back before developing a huge calcium deposit in his thigh. Told to keep practicing, Jones knew better and called Red Auerbach. Was there still a chance for him with the Celtics? There was. Could he get there in time for camp? He could. Jones abruptly left the Rams camp and flew east to join the Celtics for the 1958–59 season. By then, Russell was in his third season and the Celtics had won the first of what was to be eleven titles in thirteen years. Jones was around for eight of them before retiring at the end of the 1966–67 season.

His number 25 was retired in Boston and, after a brief and

unsuccessful fling in the insurance business, he went into coaching. He spent three years as head coach at Brandeis University, a year at Harvard as an assistant, and then joined former teammate Bill Sharman on the Los Angeles Lakers bench for the 1971–72 season. That Lakers team won 33 straight, finished 69-13, and won the NBA championship. Jones then accepted a head coaching job in San Diego in the ABA, but a year later he was back in the NBA as the head coach of the Capitol Bullets.

In his three years there, the Bullets never finished worse than second. They advanced to the Finals in 1975, but were swept by the upstart Warriors. During that series, Jones's reputation was forever sullied when a television camera showed him in a huddle giving way to assistant Bernie Bickerstaff. He lasted another year before getting fired.

"That was the low point for me," he said.

Bullets owner Abe Pollin paid Jones through 1977, but the money was only partial solace. Jones's life started to fall apart. His marriage was deteriorating. He could not get a job interview, convinced it was because he was black. The Chicago Bulls talked to him, but hired Ed Badger instead.

He eventually got a job in Milwaukee as an assistant to Don Nelson, but was basically ignored and let go after one unfulfilling season. He then left his wife and moved back to Boston where Tom Sanders, coaching a very bad Celtics team, asked Jones to come aboard. He remained an assistant even after Sanders was fired and successor Dave Cowens decided he would not continue. He stayed on when Bill Fitch was brought in for the head coaching position in 1979.

When the Celtics and Fitch parted ways after a turbulent 1982–83 season, Jones had no inkling he was next in line. Fitch, like Nelson, had all but ignored him. Jones distinctly recalled a practice where he was explaining something to Tiny Archibald: "As soon as I was finished, Bill yelled across the room, 'Come over here, Tiny, and I'll show you how it should be done.' You can imagine how I felt," Jones said.

The two came to blows after the draft one season. Jones had

not been invited to the predraft player-evaluation meeting, or even been told there was one. He went out and played golf instead. The following day, Fitch asked Jones why he hadn't attended the meeting and one thing led to another and the two men got into a fight. Jones got on top of Fitch and had to be pulled away by one of the office secretaries. The following day, Jones arrived at the Celtics office fully expecting to be fired, and went in to apologize to Red Auerbach. He was told to go see Fitch, and the two worked out an uneasy truce.

Auerbach saw the easygoing Jones as the ideal personality to succeed the abrasive Fitch. The players sympathized with Jones and several players, M.L. Carr and Robert Parish among them, openly supported him when the announcement was made.

Jones's forte lay not in X's and O's or in breaking down a team's defense on videotape, but in knowing what to say, exactly what the Boston Celtics needed at the time. In that regard he was the ideal head coach.

Did he fail later in Seattle when he really had to coach? Yes. Has he ever been seriously considered for a head job since? No. Did this quality hurt him as the Celtics grew more predictable in the late 1980s? Absolutely.

But the 1985–86 Celtics were like a collection of Ph.D. candidates. They didn't need to be told when they could go to the bathroom or how long they had to study at night. They needed the right atmosphere in which their tremendous skills could flourish, and Jones provided that.

"Sometimes, it's hard to judge a coach," Danny Ainge said. "It's the whole staff. [Assistant coaches] Jimmy [Rodgers] and Chris [Ford] were such a big part of that team. The greatest assets K.C. had were respect from the players and his lack of ego. He would allow and encourage input from other coaches and the players. With that kind of a team, it was a great combination.

"There are a lot of guys who know X's and O's and can't coach," Ainge went on. "But on a scale of one to ten, for that particular team and that particular time, K.C. was a ten. On another team, he might have been a seven or eight. The combination was perfect. Chris was the holler guy. Jimmy was the technician. And K.C. was the leader who commanded the respect."

Jones never let his ego get in the way. He never felt betrayed when Bird openly defied him on the floor, throwing up a three-pointer while the coach tried to call out a play. He leaned on his assistants, Jimmy Rodgers and Chris Ford, both of whom would eventually follow him as coach. He didn't try to coach; he tried to manage.

To this day, Walton ranks Jones as one of the finest coaches he has ever played for, in the same breath with the venerable John Wooden. Jones didn't waste time at practice, or bring in any meaningless sets and schemes. You reported to work, did your job, and the coaching staff tried to inspire you, not intimidate you. While Walton reveled in the freedom he had off the court, he was all business on it. He liked everything just so when he was playing. Jones provided that. With K.C., there was order and structure, and the time expended was on meaningful things.

And now the team was complete. Jones had made his decision and Carlisle had survived another October. Carlisle had been through it the year before, so this was nothing new to him. He was neither shocked nor surprised to have made the Celtics again. He had made a career of proving people wrong.

Rick Carlisle was used to challenges. The one in October 1985 was only the latest in a long line dating back to his prep school days in northern New York. But at each step along a circuitous road to the NBA, the same thing invariably happened to Rick Carlisle: he was an excellent fit for every team on which he played.

He was the oldest of three children raised in the small town of Ogdensburg, New York. Carlisle's father, Preston, was an attorney and occasional recreational basketball player who raised his family on a 185-acre horse farm. His mother raised the horses, conducted a riding camp, and ran the household. Preston Carlisle settled into private practice after spending time as a district attorney.

Basketball became more than just a game to Rick as he made his way through Lisbon Central School, which had grades kindergarten through twelve. He devoured every basketball magazine he could find. He played for four coaches over four years at Lisbon Central, and he was the tallest player and best ball handler on the team. By the end of his senior year, Rick Carlisle made a decision that would wholly influence his life: he would dedicate himself completely to basketball.

"By the time I graduated, basketball was the only thing that I cared about," he said. "The only thing."

He had some work to do. He was from Nowheresville, USA, he had no consistent coaching in high school, and he was viewed as a typical slow white guy who played a position (point guard) that was not made for slow white guys. No Division I school showed any interest even though Carlisle felt he could play at that level.

Rather than accept an offer to play at Division II American International College in Springfield, Massachusetts, he and his father decided to scour the region's prep schools to see which one had the best basketball program. They settled on Worcester Academy, a school that had already won a string of New England prep titles. In Carlisle's year there, they would add another.

"His father called me and said that he truly believed his son would be a great college player and a pro," said Tom Blackburn, the Worcester Academy coach. "He said he was from a small high school and needed the exposure and the challenge. I mean, you hear that all the time from the fathers. Then, his father said, 'I don't know much about prep schools. Is there TV?' I said, 'No.' He asked if Rick could have a car. I said, 'No.' But he came anyway. And Rick had to pay the full tuition, then about $8,000, because scholarships were based on need."

Carlisle wasn't crazy about the facilities in Worcester. They were old and run-down. "Everything was all grubby," he said. He did, however, manage to skirt the rules and found a place behind St. Vincent's Church to hide his car. And he did like Black-burn's approach.

"He told me that Worcester Academy gets the best because they know they'll play against the best. I figured if I couldn't play there, I couldn't play Division I. It was sink or swim," Carlisle said.

But after a fine year and a championship at Worcester, only one Division I school offered Carlisle a scholarship: the University of Maine. Carlisle accepted, spent two years there, but came to the inescapable conclusion that he could do better.

He decided to transfer, and by then he at least had some exposure to big-time competition. Maine would occasionally make a foray out of their conference to play at Duke or Kentucky, and back then the coach at Boston University, another conference school, was a young whippersnapper named Rick Pitino. Jim Larranega, the coach at AIC who had tried to recruit Carlisle out of high school, was now an assistant under Terry Holland at the University of Virginia. Larranega thought Carlisle was a player in the Jeff Lamp/Jeff Jones mold and would be a good fit. Providence was also interested in Carlisle.

One night, Preston Carlisle called Larranega to ask, point blank, if his son could play at Virginia. Jim Larranega was on the road, but Liz Larranega did an admirable job substituting for her husband.

"Jim wouldn't be recruiting him if he didn't think he could play here," she said. "He would take Jeff Jones's spot."

"You know," Preston mentioned, "he has a chance to go to Providence."

"Well," Liz Larranega shot back. "You say your son wants to step up a level? Then he should come to Virginia. Or he should stay at Maine. Providence is not a step up." This was a strange comment coming from the wife of a former Friar who had been a stalwart at Providence in the late 1960s and early 1970s. But it was accurate at the time.

Carlisle transferred to Virginia and had to sit out his first year. Though ineligible for games, he could practice, and coach

Terry Holland noted that Carlisle was always in demand when the team held its intrasquad scrimmages. During his transfer year, Carlisle taught himself to play piano, a skill he maintains to this day. There were many times on a Celtics road trip when he'd settle into a piano at a hotel lounge and play a quick tune before catching the team bus.

The University of Virginia was big-time and unlike anything to which Carlisle was accustomed. They had Ralph Sampson at center. Their games were always on television. And they were considered a legitimate national power. In Carlisle's first year there, the team beat Patrick Ewing's Georgetown in a wildly anticipated game, and then made a trip to Japan where it dismantled a very good Houston team featuring Akeem Olajuwon.

On the way back from Japan, the Cavaliers stopped for some R&R in Hawaii. At the time, they were 8-0, ranked No. 1, and scheduled to play a tiny school called Chaminade. They had soundly beaten the team in two of the previous three years, taking advantage of a cream-puff opponent and the lure of a Hawaiian break. But this time they were beaten, 77–72, in one of the greatest upsets in college basketball history.

"Everyone on the team was devastated except Rick," Larranega said. "He felt that we lost one game, that it wasn't that big of a deal. But everyone else realized it was big. Every time we lost, it was big news."

Carlisle was still in the green stage of his college career. Everything was a novelty to a kid who was never used to the spotlight. "I really didn't know what it was all about at that level," he said. "It was something I had never been through before."

That team represented Sampson's final chance at an NCAA title. It finished 29-5, but was upset in the regional finals by eventual champion North Carolina State, a team it had beaten twice in the regular season. Sampson crumpled to the floor as the buzzer sounded, knowing he would never get what he had come to Virginia for: an NCAA championship. In fact, in Sampson's four years there, the Cavaliers made the Final Four only once.

"That loss to N.C. State was hard. Real hard," Carlisle said. Thirteen years later, after the Celtics had defeated the Rockets to win the NBA title, a championship won over a team that featured a highly inconsistent Sampson, Kevin McHale turned to Carlisle on the bus ride out of the joyous Boston Garden and said, "After seeing Ralph Sampson, I'll never again ask you why you didn't win a championship at Virginia."

But Carlisle knew he had an excellent opportunity to win one in Boston. That would be the easy part. The hard part, he knew, would be staying on the team. He had been through it once before and he knew what lay ahead. In his own manner, Rick Carlisle understood the subtleties of basketball as well as anyone. At the end of the season, Carlisle would still be around to collect his championship ring.

While the roster may have been set, no one was immune to the customary, good-natured hazing that affected all newcomers. Sichting was one of the first to discover how different it was being a Celtic, how different it was being on a team whose best and most valued player also happened to be its premier prankster and practical joker.

Larry Bird and Jerry Sichting had their Indiana heritage as a unifying force in their relationship. The two were a year apart, and Sichting's high school was larger and his basketball team much better. Bird played in southern Indiana at tiny Springs Valley High School and was left off the Indiana high school all-star team because voters didn't think he played against top-notch competition.

"I wish I had played against Larry in high school because my team would have kicked his butt," Sichting said. "But every time I played against him in any kind of all-star game, it seemed like he'd win. The year after he graduated from high school, I was on the Indiana all-star team and we were on our way to Kentucky (to play high school all-stars) when we stopped to play a tune-up game in Mitchell, Indiana. Larry was on the other team.

He'd been out baling hay all day, or something like that, and he still hit us for about 40. He was something then. I didn't know him that much but when I got to Boston . . ."

A few days into training camp, Bird played the "concerned host" role and asked Sichting if the newcomer had any plans for the night. Sichting shook his head. Bird suggested they get together and watch the baseball playoffs at a bar near the hotel where Sichting was staying. Sichting said that sounded fine to him. Bird chose the place, a bar called Ramrod.

"He said it was a good place and told me to meet him there because he'd be just a little late," Sichting said. Bird then enlisted the help of Rick Carlisle, Sichting's roommate. With Sichting present, the two pranksters staged a phone call allegedly agreeing to meet at the bar.

"I asked Rick to come because I was new to Boston and I didn't know anything about the city," Sichting said. "He told me he had to make a phone call; and that he'd be right over. So I go there and there's no name on the door. I walk in and there's two guys at the bar. I walk around to see if there's anyone watching the game. There isn't anyone, but they have the TV on so I figure it must be the place. I went to the bartender and asked if Larry Bird had been in there. The bartender looked at me like I was crazy."

Sichting stayed for about fifteen minutes and then decided he was in the wrong place. He went back to the hotel and found Carlisle and told him that he either had the wrong place or that Bird was not coming. But Carlisle told Sichting he had just gotten another call from Bird saying that he was on his way.

"I'll be right over, too," Carlisle promised, "as soon as I make this phone call."

Sichting still had not caught on to the gag. He returned to Ramrod and after a while realized it was a gay bar. He flew back to the hotel where Carlisle was on the floor with laughter. The next day at practice, coach K.C. Jones took Sichting aside and, feigning seriousness, said, "If I had known you were like that, we never would have traded for you."

So Sichting got hazed like everyone else, but as the season drew near, no one seemed more excited about playing than he did. This was, he was certain, going to be one long, strange, but rewarding trip.

When the season opened, the Celtics were, at worst, the second-best team in the league. Second-best didn't count, of course, but it wasn't a bad starting position either. The only factor that could jeopardize the season and all the careful summer planning was an injury to a key player. And as the season opened, one key player, *the* key player, wasn't feeling 100 percent.

CHAPTER FOUR

October–November:
Slow Beginnings

In the summer of 1985, Larry Bird went home to southern Indiana, as he did every off-season. French Lick was the one place where he could be one of the guys, have a few beers, play some softball, and stay out of the limelight. It was a sanctuary he guarded zealously at all times.

That summer, Bird planned on building a fence around his home. Despite his considerable wealth, Bird never lost his appreciation for the value of a dollar or his unshakable belief that money should never be expended for such mundane physical tasks as fence building. So he tried to do it himself, and while shoveling gravel for the post holes, he hurt his back.

He had had back problems before, dating back to college, but the pain had always gone away. This time, the pain wouldn't go away and Bird needed to find out why. He skipped rookie camp in August to see a Michigan back doctor, but when training camp opened a month later, the back was still bothering him.

The first public sign of trouble came in the third game of the exhibition season when Bird developed back spasms and played just nine minutes against the Lakers. The team physician, Dr.

Thomas Silva, termed the setback "one more problem in the Larry Bird saga." Bird played only 11 minutes in the next game against the Bullets and did not make the trip to Portland, Maine, for a game against the Nets.

Getting information on Bird's back and the severity of the injury was about as easy as getting the CIA to divulge its list of covert operatives. Bird wouldn't talk. The Celtics publicly downplayed the injury, but coach K.C. Jones admitted the obvious: "If we can't get him healthy, it's going to be a long season."

The Celtics knew that any championship hopes would be wiped out without a healthy Bird, and as their new season was about to begin, Larry Bird was not healthy.

"There's an old saying," Alan Cohen said, remembering the concern over Bird's back. "If someone sneezes, the world catches cold. Well, when Larry sneezed, everyone on the Celtics worried about the flu. Anything bothering Larry was cause for great concern. We were all concerned. One of the crazy things about being an owner is that so much of your dream can go up in smoke if there's just one misstep. It's a horrible thing, but it's true. You like to think that we live in a rational world in which rational plans produce rational results. In the sports world, things are different; the physical elements of the game can take control away from rational planning."

The Celtics' next game was at Indiana, and favorite son Bird went along, but he played only nine minutes and never even came out of the locker room for the second half. The Celtics decided to send Bird back to Boston as the rest of the team headed west to Los Angeles for the last two exhibition games.

"I don't know what's going to happen," Bird said. Dennis Johnson felt Bird shouldn't have made the trip in the first place, and Jones admitted that had it been any other venue, the Hoosier legend would have remained home. One trip, however, that received no attention but meant a lot to those who made it, was a journey Bird, Quinn Buckner (then with Indiana), and Bill Walton took to French Lick.

"We talked K.C. into letting us go down there," Walton said, "and when I got to Larry's house, I took out a jar and scooped up some dirt from the driveway court where Larry used to play as a kid. I carried it in my gym bag all year long and then, when the season was over, I went to my parents' home and sprinkled it over the court I played on as a kid and stomped it in. That ground is now sacred."

When the team returned to Boston, Bird's plight was finally brought to the attention of physical therapist Dan Dyrek. The two would need two months to get the pain under control and Dyrek, as much as anyone, deserves credit for getting Bird ready to play the season.

It began when Dyrek got a call from the Celtics' orthopedic surgeon, Robert Leach, who told him it was time to pay a visit to Bird. Dyrek, whose specialty was dealing with spinal pain, had done some work on former Celtics Cedric Maxwell and Rick Robey while at University Hospital, where Leach practiced. Dyrek had just opened a private practice and was about to land a very important patient.

Leach and Dyrek met at a gas station and then drove over to Bird's house in Brookline, where they conducted an examination in the family room. Dyrek was stunned by the extent of the inflammation. Bird already knew.

"Larry knew this wasn't a little backache," Dyrek said. "He wasn't going to seek care for a minor problem. We got him down to the office and started treatment right away. When I saw him, I couldn't believe he was even practicing, let alone playing. His attitude was that if he kept playing, it would go away. It was an element of his attitude. Of his upbringing."

Toughness was a Bird family trait. Bird never forgot the sight of his father trying to put on a shoe over a painfully swollen foot so he could get to work. His upbringing had not been an easy one by any stretch of the imagination. His father, Joe Bird, had a drinking problem, a scattered employment history, and eventually shot and killed himself while talking to his wife, Georgia, on the telephone.

The town of French Lick, Indiana, where Bird was raised, is located in one of the least affluent parts of the state, but Bird never considered himself deprived or his family as anything other than economically normal. There were mouths to feed—there were four brothers and a sister—and Larry often spent time with his maternal grandmother. Bird never thought of his family situation as anything other than typical; most of his friends were in similar economic straits.

"There were very few rich families where we lived," said Bird's childhood friend Tony Clark. "Everybody had the same thing. You appreciated what you had and always worked to do better."

French Lick had a population of about 2,000 but a noted history, mainly for its warm springs. Several resort hotels catered to wealthy visitors in the early twentieth century, among them, or so the legend says, Franklin D. Roosevelt. Joe and Georgia Bird usually worked, sometimes holding down two jobs, so the boys were often left to their own devices, and in Indiana that almost always meant two things: playing sports (usually basketball) and hunting mushrooms.

Larry Joe, the fourth of the six Bird kids, followed his big brothers around and, like them, developed a passion for basketball. He came under the tutelage of Jim Jones, a former baseball star at the University of Indiana who ran the town's "Biddy Ball" program and who had as much influence on Bird's basketball life as anyone. Jones stressed fundamentals and the only way to develop sound fundamentals was to practice, practice, and practice.

"Jim had this way of making sure you were always working," Bird said. "He'd stop by and see you practicing and he'd say, 'Keep working at it. I'll be back later.' You didn't want to not be there when he came back so you kept practicing. Half the time, he never did come back."

Clark, who often would practice with Bird, remembers Jones

in reverential terms. "He is one of the best teachers of funda-
mental basketball that I have seen to this day. He can really develop players. He keeps them willing to play and he's still doing
it today."

By high school, Bird had survived a broken ankle to become
one of the top players in the state of Indiana. While missing
much of his sophomore year with the ankle injury, he would still
practice, leaning on a crutch. Clark thinks that that single exercise helped to develop Bird's incredible passing skills. Jones,
who coached Bird in high school, agrees.

"His passing and his understanding of the game was just so
far above everyone else's," Jones said. "And the same for his rebounding instincts. What kid gets 38 rebounds in a high school
game? Larry did."

Players of his stature in the state of Indiana invariably draw
the interest of Bobby Knight, who, at the time, was in the
process of assembling one of the greatest college teams ever at
the University of Indiana. Knight visited Bird on three occasions, saw him play, and offered him a scholarship. Bird was hes-
itant.

Georgia Bird wanted her son to stay closer to home and attend Indiana State in Terre Haute. Joe Bird, a big IU fan, hoped
his son would go to Bloomington. Purdue was a long-shot third
choice. Bird had already ruled out anywhere outside Indiana,
having been snubbed by Joe B. Hall at Kentucky, who refused to
recruit him. Louisville coach Denny Crum challenged Bird to a
game of Horse and, if Crum won, Bird would come down and
see the campus. Crum lost. "I really busted him," Bird said years
later.

In the spring semester of his senior year, Bird finally committed to Indiana. When it came time for him to make the trip
north to Bloomington, he arrived on campus with $75 in his
pocket, one pair of tennis shoes, and one large set of wide eyes.
He lasted three weeks before returning home.

Basketball ability had nothing to do with his quick exit. Bird
had played in a few pickup games with some members of the In-

diana team—a veritable all-star squad that included Kent Ben-
son, Quinn Buckner, Scott May, Bobby Wilkerson, and Steve
Green—that would lose only one game over a two-year stretch.
Socially, however, Bird felt out of place, intimidated by the size
of the university, the number of students, and the wardrobe of
his roommate, Jim Wisman, who, incredibly, had more than one
pair of sneakers and several pairs of pants.

It all felt like a bad dream and the only sure way to end it was
to hitchhike home to French Lick and look for work. Bird eventually took a job with the town, driving a garbage truck on occasion. He loved it; he was with his buddies, hanging out, drinking
beer, and feeling that he probably would never set foot on a college campus anywhere again.

Although there was some sense of betrayal in French Lick—
it wasn't often that one of theirs made it to the big time at IU, as
Bird had—Bird did not look back and never explained his reasons to Knight. And although Knight wonders if Bird would
have done anything more than warm the Hoosier bench as a
freshman, Bird saw enough on the court to believe he could
have helped. In fact, Indiana's only loss that year came in the
NCAA tournament, when forward Scott May broke his wrist.
Who better to pick up the slack?

"My game," Bird said, "was coming along at that time."

Knight said, "It was a very difficult transition from French
Lick to IU and I didn't help him at all. But, no matter. I don't
think anyone could have stopped him. He left two weeks before
we even started practice and I thought to myself, 'If I wouldn't
chase a [Scott] May or a [Quinn] Buckner, I'm not going to
chase this kid.'"

In retrospect, it seems Bird may have acted in haste, but if so,
it was a rare and uncharacteristic event. He rarely, if ever, does
anything without considering all the angles, and once he's
made a decision, he sticks with it.

It was that same trait—some would call it stubbornness—that
brought him and Dyrek together in October 1985. Had Bird
simply hired someone to build his fence, the two might never

have met; had Bird simply not tried to play through the injury and allowed nature to heal his back, there may have been no reason for therapy.

"I knew I was in trouble when I sat down with Jan [Volk] and [trainer] Ray Melchiorre and discussed the rigors of basketball and what the workouts were like," Dyrek said. "Then I asked Larry how many minutes he wanted to play. He said, 'Forty-eight, of course. Hell, that's not even an hour.'

"His problem was too localized for stretching and it involved a lot of specific, hands-on manual treatment. I don't know if he understood all that, but he was as focused a patient as I've ever had. He never even asked for an appointment card and I'm thinking to myself, 'Everyone wants a chunk of this guy. How is he possibly going to keep track?' I asked him that and he told me, 'Dan, I've got two things to worry about, basketball and staying healthy.' At first, I saw him four days a week. By December, he was playing well again."

Dyrek helped Bird through his problems and he was soon on his way to another great season. Like their star player, however, it took the Celtics a while before they, too, got going.

The Celtics opened the season that year in the charnel house in New Jersey now known as Continental Airlines Arena. Their opponent was the New Jersey Nets, a team that annually had enormous hopes but unfailingly fizzled as the season wore on. The franchise's glory days, as a member of the defunct American Basketball Association when Julius Erving was their star, were long gone.

Bird was available for the opener and started, but was clearly feeling the effects of his bad back, missing 10 of 15 shots. He still managed a triple-double with 21 points, 12 rebounds, and 10 assists; he also had eight steals. To compensate for the loss of Cedric Maxwell, Bird and Kevin McHale combined to cover the opposing forwards, with McHale getting the tougher assignments. Bird never was an accomplished one-on-one defensive player and the Celtics always had him guarding the least threatening front-liner on the court, even if the individual was a center.

"I would always make sure I would run my guy right into Robert [Parish] or Kevin or Bill [Walton]," Bird admitted. Normally Bird, a small forward, would have to match up that way at the other end, but the Celtics could use the more mobile McHale and his tremendous wingspan to stop the devastating small forwards of the league. It worked.

Or at least it did on most occasions. The Celtics, however, beat themselves in their first official game of the 1985–86 season. They committed 28 turnovers. They squandered a 19-point third-quarter lead, missing 14 of 17 shots in the fourth quarter. Dennis Johnson, normally a dead-eye free throw shooter, missed two attempts with the Celtics leading 99–97 and 10 seconds remaining. Robert Parish and Kevin McHale fouled out, Sly Williams never got off the bench, and the Nets went on to win, 113–109, in overtime. After the game, Nets forward Buck Williams announced that things had changed in New Jersey because in previous years, the coaches would have given up on the team. Not so this time, he said. Dave Wohl—a former Lakers assistant in his first year as the Nets' head coach—had his team prepared.

As for the Celtics, this clearly was not the way they envisioned starting the season, and among the longest of the many long faces in the locker room was Bill Walton's. No one on the team had been looking forward to this game more than Walton. He was finally about to experience a lifelong dream, and then he went out and played an atrocious game. In 19 minutes, he had four points, five fouls, and an appalling seven turnovers. In the locker room, Walton looked as though he had just been told that he was heading back to the Clippers. Some of his teammates even suggested such a move, starting what would become a season-long trend of using Walton as their human dartboard.

"I was so embarrassed and the guys really got on me. 'Why did they bring you here? Where's Cedric Maxwell when we really need him? What are you here for, you have no game,'" Walton recalled. "I couldn't catch the ball. I couldn't jump for the ball. I couldn't block my man off the boards. I was a total disgrace to the game of basketball."

The Celtics then flew to Cleveland for the second game, left coach K.C. Jones behind at the hotel (he missed the bus before it turned back to get him), and barely survived, winning, 105–100. The Cavs had lost none of their feistiness from the year before, when they battled the Celtics almost evenly in the first round of the playoffs. And had Cleveland not missed nine free throws in the fourth quarter, and 14 of 33 in the game, the Celtics might well have returned home with an 0-2 record. They settled for a split.

It was apparent that this team was going to take some time to gel. Walton and Sichting, two key players, were newcomers. Bird was hindered by his sore back. But the Celtics, more than any team other than the Lakers, knew it was a long season, and unless your sport was baseball, October was not the month to hit your peak.

Walton, who hadn't played a meaningful NBA game since 1978, understood this as well as anyone. He was in Boston for one reason: to win an NBA championship. That championship is determined in June, not October, and the Celtics, unlike most other teams, had played in June the year before and the year before that. "If we had set any other goal except winning a championship, we might have won even more games than we did," Walton said. "But it was difficult for a team like the Celtics, especially in that era, to start at a perfect pace when you knew you were going to play for the championship. It's very important to get a little bit out of shape and to rest and to relax. Basketball players are not machines that are on all the time. Teams like the Celtics need time off in the summer because they have been playing through June. And I think we played our best basketball that year as the season went on and at the end."

Still, the victory over Cleveland started the Celtics on an eight-game winning streak—so much for Walton's slow-start theory. Big Bill was given a thunderous ovation in the Boston Gar-

den opener against Milwaukee and he simply pursed his lips until the noise went away. There was no acknowledgment or wave.
On game days, Bill Walton was all business.

On practice days, the phone would ring at his house in the
Avon Hill section of Cambridge (where he lived at the suggestion of author and friend David Halberstam) and McHale, Bird,
or Danny Ainge would be on the line, predicting imminent ruin
when the team gathered for workouts. But on game days, even
Walton's beloved Grateful Dead had to take a backseat.

"After breakfast on game day, I was simply incapable of having a conversation," Walton said. "The phone would get un-
plugged. The stereo would go off. Nothing. You try to develop a
personal rivalry to help you play better. I could never do what
Magic Johnson did and go kiss [Isiah Thomas] before a game. I
stay in my hotel room and think about how I am going to beat
them. I don't want to talk to them. I don't want to shake their
hand. I just want to beat them."

Walton's hunger for victory and his fierce competitive drive
were not on display solely for NBA fans. After winning the
championship in Portland in 1977, Walton honored a commitment to friend Phil Jackson and showed up at an Upward
Bound program in South Dakota run by Jackson, which was attended primarily by Oglala Sioux kids at the Pine Ridge Reser-
vation.

Jackson congratulated Walton on winning the championship
and told him the true mark of a good team was repeating. Walton shot back, "We want to do that. We are not a flash in the
pan. We're very serious about that."

The guest list of counselors at the program were the kind of
people Jackson called "kindred spirits." Jackson's former Knicks
teammates Willis Reed and Bill Bradley showed up. So did Neal
Walk. Walton certainly qualified as a kindred spirit then, but
what Jackson was unprepared for was the fire that resurfaced
once the games began.

"Bill was unbelievably competitive," Jackson said. "He was
showing kids all these sophisticated defensive moves, like

putting your hand on a back to knock someone off balance. We hooked up together in a game and he did everything to win and I think the final score was 15–5. He wanted to win. At everything."

Over the first nine games, the Celtics did practically that. They weren't winning by large margins or dominating opponents, and three times at home they were pushed to the limit before emerging with a victory. But they were winning nonetheless, and despite their serious approach, sometimes the games weren't always the most interesting event.

Less than two weeks into the season, Walton turned thirty-three. As usual, the Celtics reported for practice at Hellenic College that day, and Walton even brought along longtime friend and Grateful Dead drummer Mickey Hart to watch the practice. The Dead, Walton's favorite band and occasional cohorts, were in nearby Worcester, so Hart got a limousine to take him to practice.

What Hart and everyone else saw that day was something that doesn't usually happen at your average NBA practice. After a spirited workout, Jones called the team to midcourt and brought out a chair for the birthday boy. Instead of wheeling out the traditional cake and candles, a woman came out with a tape player. She put the machine on the floor, turned on some lounge music, and began to disrobe. The striptease lasted about ten minutes. Mormons Greg Kite and Danny Ainge tried to look the other way, and Walton, embarrassed and predictably frazzled, tried to stop his complexion from matching the color of his hair. The whole thing had been planned in advance by Susan Walton, Bill's wife, who had gotten approval from K.C. Jones.

"Ah, that stuff has no place in basketball," said Walton, ever the purist. "But it was quite an experience, I'll say that. But basketball is about passing and shooting and rebounding. You have to have a coach like K.C. Jones to even think about doing something like that. That's why we loved the guy. It also pointed out something else. Obviously, I made the right decision and joined the right team."

Walton was glad to be there, and the Celtics were glad to have him.

The Celtics were in the midst of a five-day break between games, so Walton had plenty of time to recover from his practice ordeal. They hosted the Phoenix Suns on November 8 and ran away with the game, winning, 125–101. The Suns committed 36 turnovers as they unsuccessfully tried to employ an uptempo game.

That year, the Suns featured a twenty-five-year-old forward by the name of Georgi Glouchkov, a seven-year veteran of the Bulgarian National Team and one of the better players in Eastern Europe. At the time, this was a revolutionary development in the NBA, since Eastern bloc players were off-limits. Today, players such as Vlade Divac, Dino Radja, Toni Kukoc, and Sarunas Marciulionis are NBA fixtures. In 1985, however, there was no glasnost or perestroika and there was still an Iron Curtain and a domineering Soviet Union. The Suns had selected the 6-8 Glouchkov with a seventh-round draft pick the previous June, the 148th pick overall, and then paid the Bulgarian Basketball Federation $100,000 for his release. Glouchkov was paid $175,000 by the Suns.

Against the Celtics, Glouchkov had eight points and 11 rebounds in 21 minutes. He also had five fouls, three turnovers, and missed all four of his free throws. As it turned out, this would be his one and only appearance in Boston Garden. After one season with the Suns, he went back to Bulgaria. He simply didn't have an NBA game. In the fall of 1986, he signed with Caserta in Italy. His NBA career consists of 49 games that season with a team that won only 32 games. It would be four more years before Divac, Marciulionis, Alexander Volkov, Zarko Paspalj, and Drazen Petrovic started the first wave of former Eastern bloc players to the NBA.

The Suns game was followed by the Celtics' first visit to Detroit since their six-game series the previous spring. That series, the first of four between the two teams in the 1980s, marked the beginning of a mutual hatred that always surfaced whenever the two teams met, even in the regular season.

The Celtics thought the Pistons were showboats and wimps. They detested Bill Laimbeer, who they (along with many others) thought was out to hurt them. The Pistons (along with many others) thought the Celtics were arrogant and imperious. Although the rivalry would intensify in the next few years with the maturation of the Pistons and the arrival of players like Dennis Rodman, the seeds of antipathy had been sown in 1985.

"They don't like us," McHale said, "and we don't like them."

As if to drive home their point, the Celtics jumped to a 30–12 lead in the first eight minutes, putting a noticeable chill on the 25,148 at the Silverdome. The game was never close and the Celtics won easily, 124–105. McHale, who had scored 56 points in one game against the Pistons the season before, had 28, prompting Detroit coach Chuck Daly to moan, "I spent all summer trying to think of a way to stop Kevin McHale, but I didn't come up with anything. He's still too tall."

The game wasn't without the obligatory histrionics. McHale and Earl Cureton had to be separated, and Dennis Johnson and Laimbeer were ejected for fighting. Sam Vincent, meanwhile, almost didn't make it to the floor. He was stopped by security as he tried to enter the Celtics' locker room after all the other players were already there.

The next game, in Boston against the Indiana Pacers, took on added significance, given the Pacers' ill-fated and ill-conceived run at Dennis Johnson over the summer. The Celtics guard decided he would remind Indiana what they were missing just in case they had forgotten. Johnson went out and played 37 minutes, registering 30 points and six steals; he committed no turnovers. With the game tied 91–91 in the fourth, the Celtics went on an 11–2 run with Johnson scoring nine of the points and assisting on the other two, a dunk by Robert Parish. It was a classic "I told ya so" performance by Johnson, another indicator of his enormous pride and his incredible talent.

"I loved DJ," said Danny Ainge. "He'd lose it a couple of times over the course of the year and there would always be four or five games when you didn't want him to be on your team. But in the fourth quarter of every game, you wouldn't want anyone else. That's the way he was."

The Pacers got revenge three days later, beating the Celtics in Market Square Arena, 111–109, on a buzzer-beating tip-in by Clark Kellogg. The basket set off a wild celebration in the building and, in many respects, typified the few defeats the Celtics suffered that season. Of their 15 losses, only five were to teams that had winning records; the average margin of defeat was five and a half points and only one of the losses was by more than 10.

"That year, we would win eight straight games and then we'd get a little complacent. That's the way it was," McHale said. "We could have won 70 that year if we weren't that way."

The Celtics did not lose again for the remainder of the month. During that stretch, they beat Philadelphia—still their most feared Eastern Conference opponent—twice. The first victory came without Dennis Johnson, who missed two games to attend his grandmother's funeral. The Celtics then went on to beat the Pistons with Bird scoring 47 points, but it wasn't Bird who was the subject of postgame talk after that victory. It was Detroit's Vinnie Johnson, who had come off the bench and, in a style that came to be quite familiar, hit the Celtics for 35 points. Boston had been similarly blitzed by Johnson in the playoffs that previous spring, and here he was doing it to the Celtics again.

"I'll tell you what," said Ainge, unaware that he was about to make basketball nickname history. "If that guy in Chicago [William Perry] is called the Refrigerator, then you gotta call Vinnie the Microwave. He really heats up in a hurry."

And so the Microwave was born on that November night. Not only was it fitting, it was equally appropriate that the man who coined the nickname was Danny Ainge. He later would provide nicknames for Kevin "Oscar" Gamble, Pervis "Out of Service" Ellison, and Kevin "The Black Hole" McHale (so named for the regions of superstrong gravity, because once the ball went in to McHale, it never came back out). To those who knew Ainge, it came as no surprise. He nicknamed himself once, too.

The name was Amo Wong. To this day, Danny Ainge doesn't know how he decided on such a name, only that he actually posed for a high school yearbook photo using that alias. He simply parted his hair differently and put on a pair of glasses. The yearbook editor wasn't fooled though, and Amo Wong never made the printer's version, though Danny Ainge did.

He also said he used the name in college while playing intramural football so he wouldn't get caught by the basketball office. The story has, like the fish that got away, grown larger and more impressive over the years. Ainge said the disguise worked until a classmate tipped off the basketball office that he was, in fact, playing intramural football. Frank Arnold, the Brigham Young basketball coach, scoffs at such a suggestion. ("Intramural football wouldn't bother me," he said. "Now if he had gone skiing, that might have been different.")

Ainge was always into nicknames, pranks, or practical jokes. He followed his big brothers David and Doug around everywhere, absorbing abuse, learning to cope, and, like Larry Bird, getting the best from his older siblings. His older brother Doug was a terrific athlete, all-state in two sports. David Ainge, a late-bloomer, was tough, determined, and tenacious.

"I got Doug's athletic gifts and David's intensity," Ainge said. "I'd be in awe of Doug's skills and how David got by on sheer hard work and hustle. We'd have these games and they'd always, always, end up in a fight. Then I'd make the last shot, run into the house, and lock the door."

The Ainge children were raised in Eugene, Oregon. Don Ainge, the patriarch, moved there and became a three-sport athlete in high school. He went to the University of Oregon on a football scholarship where he was a teammate of Southern Cal coach John Robinson, but a knee injury prevented Don Ainge from playing in the 1958 Rose Bowl. As an adult, he became good friends with Bobby Doerr, the great second baseman for the Boston Red Sox in the 1930s and 1940s. Don Ainge, in fact, had attended a Red Sox tryout camp when he was eighteen. Among those scouting the wannabes was Doerr, then retired. He told Don to go to college. Later, Doerr would scout Danny while working for the Toronto Blue Jays.

It didn't take the Ainges long to realize that they had something different in young Daniel Rae Ainge. The family took a bus trip to Salt Lake City for the purposes of formally converting to the Mormon faith. On the trip, four-year-old Danny sat next to a young, twenty-something man and struck up a conversation. When the bus arrived in Salt Lake, Don Ainge went to retrieve Danny, only to hear his son say, "You are not my daddy. He's my daddy."

"People looked at me like I was some kind of kidnapper," Don Ainge recalled. "And the other guy was blond so he could have been the father. Finally, we get Danny and he's crying and screaming and making a scene and we get him out of the bus depot and he stops crying and starts laughing. He thought that was the funniest thing he'd ever seen."

He soon got an appropriate nickname from the incident: Squirrel. The reason? He was always doing "nutty" things. That passed for humor in those days, and Danny Ainge did nothing to dispel the notion that he was, well, nutty.

His high school coach, Barney Holland, recalled the time that Ainge showed up to drop off his date, a woman who happened to live across the street from Holland. The coach had a curfew—violators had to do extra running—and Danny Ainge was out after curfew on this particular night. After saying good night to his date, Ainge walked quietly back to his car and, so as not to disturb the important neighbor, drove away without putting on his lights. Holland was soon awakened by a loud crash. He looked out his window and saw a figure running from the scene. He recognized the car.

"The next day was Sunday and we had practice," Holland said. "I got a phone call from Danny, who told me he couldn't make it because he wasn't feeling well. The next day at school, he showed up and said his shoulder and arm were sore. I asked him what happened and he made up this story. I asked him again, telling him it wasn't a good idea to lie to the coach, and he said, 'Well, you know what happened.'"

It was impossible to stay mad at Ainge for long. He was Ricky Nelson, the pesty but lovable little brother. Larry Bird always used to compare Ainge to his own little brother, Eddie, saying, "One minute he's your best friend and then he does something that makes you want to beat the crap out of him." Holland agreed.

"Danny enjoyed his life. Whatever we had to do, he tried to make it fun. To him, everything was both a challenge and a game," Holland said.

There were times during games when Ainge, who loved to shoot free throws, would go to the line even though someone else on his team had been fouled. He could not understand why his teammates would view that as an insult. Wasn't he the best free throw shooter on the team?

There were other times when he would pitch quarters in the locker room or plug up the shower drains to create a waterslide. He called the slides worm dives. They lasted until one day Holland noticed water coming under his office door. He opened the door to see a stark-naked Ainge sliding on his stomach on a sheet of shower water.

Danny Ainge was a sensational high school athlete. He made the all-star Shrine teams in baseball, basketball, and football. As a wide receiver and free safety on the football team, he was good enough to be recruited by big-time programs like Notre Dame and Michigan. When it was time to choose a college—and he had plenty of choices—Ainge didn't know what to do. He wanted to play two sports, and a football-baseball split seemed like his best chance.

"A lot of people said football was my best sport in high school," Ainge said. "But I was six feet four and kinda skinny, and I thought there was too much risk for injury if I played in college. So I told the football recruiters I wasn't going to play in college."

The San Diego Padres, who had scouted Ainge, wanted to make him their first pick in the 1977 amateur baseball draft but had been told in advance that Ainge wouldn't sign for less than $100,000. The Padres were only willing to spend $80,000. The Blue Jays, who used the same scouting service as the Padres, then drafted Ainge in the fifteenth round.

While he would continue to play baseball and eventually turn pro in college, Ainge had decided he would attend college on a basketball scholarship. He was a hot item. Eugene North High had gone 51-1 in Ainge's last two years, winning the state title each year. Dick Harter, then the coach at the University of Oregon, lusted after Ainge, and Don Ainge, a former Duck, was a big booster.

"Danny was an absolutely sensational high school player," Harter said. "I never saw a kid, at that level, with a better feel for the ball. I just loved his game. I haven't seen five better high school players, and that's hard to say about a guard."

Ainge had grown up a Pac-8 fan and liked to pretend he was Lucius Allen or Mike Warren, former UCLA guards, when he played in his driveway. But UCLA never entered the picture. Then-coach Gene Bartow told Don Ainge that he didn't think Danny was quick enough to play for the Bruins, and that Kiki Vandeweghe, a snail by comparison, was getting the last scholarship.

Ainge narrowed his choices to Oregon, Oregon State, and Brigham Young. BYU seemed like a long shot. He knew little about the Mormon school, the coach, or the program. He knew both Harter and the Oregon State coach Ralph Miller well, and had frequented many OU practices as a high-schooler in Eugene. Brigham Young coach Frank Arnold never saw Danny Ainge play in a regular season high school game, but he had enough interest to send an assistant to watch him, and then to visit the Ainge home himself, delivering what turned out to be a most persuasive pep talk.

"I told him that I already had recruited this kid from Provo who could knock his block off. And that we had Steve Craig coming back from a mission and two other guys, too," Arnold said. "I told him he'd be the twelfth man if he came and to not expect to play much."

And that was all the competitive Ainge needed to hear. He visited the school and discovered he liked what he saw and who he met.

"At first, I really had no intention of going there," Ainge said. "When I went to Oregon and OSU, there were all these parties with booze and pot and I didn't feel comfortable. BYU was different. I was around guys like me, guys who wanted to have fun, guys who were wild and crazy but didn't need drugs to have a good time. It was a lot easier for me to be who I wanted to be. And it turned out to be the best decision I ever made."

Once he decided, there were two tough phone calls to make. Ainge told Harter and OSU assistant Jimmy Anderson that he was headed to Brigham Young. "It would have been a lot easier for me to call Frank Arnold, who I didn't know very well, and say, 'I'm not coming.' It was a difficult decision."

It was a blow to Harter, who really wanted Ainge. "It wasn't a happy moment and it was a phone call we didn't want to get," Harter said.

Back home in Eugene, Don Ainge started to feel the heat from his Oregon friends.

"You could not believe the hate mail I got," he said. "There were eggs on the front door. Phone calls. At the Eugene Country Club, my friends wouldn't even talk to me."

Soon after that, Don Ainge and his family moved to the San Jose, California, area. He would carefully guide his son's athletic career over the next several years, playing an instrumental role in getting him both a professional baseball contract and a shot at making the Celtics.

After Ainge had been drafted by the Toronto Blue Jays in the summer of 1977, he ignored all the mail he received from them. He was going to Brigham Young to play basketball; he was not going to Utica, New York, to play minor league baseball for some expansion franchise.

"I threw them all away," he said of the letters. "I knew I was going to college and I wasn't going to Utica for five hundred dollars a month."

Ainge then played in a regional baseball tournament in Yakima, Washington, and old family friend Bobby Doerr, then a scout for Toronto, showed up to watch him. Ainge played well, and the Blue Jays decided it was worth some creative risk-taking to get him to sign.

Toronto general manager Pat Gillick offered the following proposal: what if Ainge did both and got paid for one? The Blue Jays would sign Ainge and he wouldn't have to report until school was out. He could then return to BYU in the fall, and play for Toronto as his summer job.

That sounded great to Ainge.

"I'm thinking, heck, it won't interfere with college. It won't interfere with basketball. I might as well get paid by the Blue Jays than play for the BYU baseball team," he said.

The NCAA had recently instituted a rule allowing college athletes to play professionally in one sport while retaining their eligibility in another. What the NCAA did not allow, although neither Ainge nor BYU knew it, was for an athlete to be paid by a professional team and to be on athletic scholarship at the university.

It wasn't until two years into his career at Brigham Young that the Ainges discovered the discrepancy; and they found out in a rather unusual fashion. The father of prospective University of

Pittsburgh quarterback Dan Marino called Frank Arnold to inform him that his son, having been drafted by the Kansas City Royals, wanted to do the same thing. Marino had checked with the NCAA and learned that his son could not do that and accept a football scholarship to the University of Pittsburgh.

Arnold quickly checked with his athletic director, who in turn checked with the Western Athletic Conference commissioner, who decided that BYU was doing nothing wrong. A week later, however, the NCAA called and said the rule had been misinterpreted and Ainge would have to repay the university for his schooling. Fortunately, it wasn't a significant sum (around $1,500 a year), and the money from Toronto was more than enough to cover it, but in retrospect it could have been much worse. The NCAA could have cracked down mercilessly on Brigham Young, forfeited their games, and declared Ainge ineligible. That they did not was a recognition that it was an honest misreading of the bylaw. It might never have been uncovered had not Marino inquired about it two years after Ainge entered BYU.

It was perhaps understandable that, in 1981, the Blue Jays were more than a little upset to learn that Ainge wanted to abandon baseball and play professional basketball. Ainge had managed to crack the major leagues in 1979, playing 87 games for the Blue Jays. He played 124 games for them primarily as an infielder over the next two years, finishing with a .220 batting average.

It was always Ainge's public posture that baseball was his job and basketball was his avocation, and that once his college career came to an end, he would devote himself entirely to professional baseball.

What Ainge did not contemplate was a senior year in which he would win the John Wooden Award as the Player of the Year, singularly destroying UCLA in the NCAA tournament, and beat Notre Dame with an unforgettable, end-of-the-game, coast-to-coast dash to the basket.

Ainge averaged 24.4 points a game as a senior and led BYU

into the NCAA tournament with a 22-6 record. In the first round of the NCAA regionals, BYU faced Princeton, the Ivy League champion. The morning of the game, Ainge could not get out of bed. Brent Pratley, the BYU team physician, reading about Ainge's problem in the *Los Angeles Times,* hopped a plane, and got to Providence in the afternoon. By that time, Ainge had already been to three doctors and was on Percodan to relieve the pain.

Coach Frank Arnold and Pratley visited Ainge in his hotel room and saw for themselves how bleak the situation was. Pratley placed a call to famed Los Angeles doctor Robert Kerlan, who advised Ainge to get some rest. Pratley agreed, telling Arnold, "If you want to destroy his career, let him play." Arnold said Ainge would not play, but acceded to Ainge's request to accompany the team to the game.

"I didn't even bother to bring my uniform," Ainge said.

One thing led to another, and Ainge soon began to feel better. He watched the Georgetown–James Madison game and his adrenaline started to flow. When it was time for BYU to shoot around, he went out and discovered his back wasn't all that bad anymore. Ainge took another Percodan and had the trainer massage his back. Eventually, Ainge reported that he was fine and that he wanted to play. Arnold mulled over the situation and let him.

"He went out and scored 21, played all but three minutes, and did a heckuva job," the coach said.

Then came the UCLA destruction, witnessed by Celtics president–general manager Red Auerbach. The UCLA game was an absolutely stunning victory. Ainge outscored the entire Bruin team in the first half and finished with 37 points, as BYU routed the Bruins, 78–55. It was amazing that Ainge was able to play at all, after his painful back spasms just forty-eight hours before. After the game, Ainge continued to stress that his athletic future was on the baseball diamond even though Auerbach made it clear to reporters that Ainge was so good "He could fill in the numbers on the check."

"I tried to use that later in negotiations," Ainge said. "Red said he was misquoted."

A week later, the BYU team was in Atlanta for the regional finals against a strong Notre Dame team that included John Paxson, Kelly Tripucka, and Orlando Woolridge. Brigham Young trailed 50–49 after a late Tripucka basket when, with eight seconds to play, Ainge broke free from a press, took an inbounds pass, and went through the entire Notre Dame team for a layup. BYU won, 51–50.

"To this day," Ainge said, "people still come up to me and tell me it was the greatest play they've ever seen."

But BYU's joyride ended two days later when Ralph Sampson and the Virginia Cavaliers defeated the Cougars, 74–60. Ainge rejoined the Blue Jays, where he had experienced only occasional success. It was the first time in his athletic life that he wasn't terrific at what he was doing. The Blue Jays were willing to wait, but Ainge was starting to have second thoughts.

Auerbach had already called him, advising him to play basketball. In the summer of 1981, Ainge was a .187-hitting third baseman, so Red's advice was hard to ignore. On the morning of June 9, the day of the NBA draft, the Blue Jays were in Chicago playing the White Sox. Ainge got a call from Auerbach at his hotel room. Had any team called Ainge to say they were going to draft him? No, said Ainge. Auerbach then said the Celtics were seriously thinking of drafting him with their first round pick (twenty-third) or their early second-round pick (twenty-fifth). The Celtics also had the thirty-first pick that year.

Ainge decided to attend the Chicago Bulls' draft-day "party" to monitor the event. He and Blue Jays teammate Garth Iorg took a cab to the hotel and watched the proceedings from the back of the room. Ainge didn't like what he saw.

In the first round, the Celtics chose Charles Bradley of Wyoming. With their first pick in the second round, they selected Tracy Jackson of Notre Dame. Disconsolate, Ainge left the room, only to find out later that the Celtics had taken him with the thirty-first pick. When Ainge returned to his hotel, Auerbach was on the phone again.

"He told me I was a basketball player and to forget about the Blue Jays," Ainge said. "I was pretty impressed, but I didn't tell Red anything different. I told him I wanted to play basketball but that I didn't think I could under the circumstances."

Over the next two days, Ainge met with both Pat Gillick and Blue Jays president Peter Bavasi and told them he had changed his mind and now wanted to play for the Celtics. He was willing to return the $300,000 bonus the Blue Jays had paid him as part of a three-year, $525,000 deal signed the previous September. According to Ainge, neither Gillick nor Bavasi said they would object.

"Peter basically told me not to worry about the commitment, that you have to do what you have to do to be happy," Ainge said. Gillick had similar thoughts, telling Ainge that no contract should restrict a person from doing what he wanted to do.

Encouraged, Ainge called Auerbach to say the Blue Jays were going to let him out of the deal. The following day, Ainge was summoned to a meeting with Gillick and Bavasi and handed a letter. It said, in effect, that Ainge was under contract to Toronto, that the contract had a clause prohibiting him from playing basketball, and that he would be sued if he attempted to breach it.

Ainge broke down and cried.

"I looked at Pat, who was a friend, and I could tell he had nothing to do with it," Ainge said. "Peter was working for the owners."

Auerbach shot back prophetically, "This is just a money thing."

He was right.

In the summer of 1981, major league baseball players went on strike. Ainge returned to BYU to help Frank Arnold with basketball camps and, even though he was still under contract to Toronto, started negotiating with the Celtics. He had taken the initial words of Bavasi and Gillick to mean that he had permission to negotiate with Boston. The Celtics did, too, citing the doctrine of oral recision—that Toronto had verbally agreed to let him out of his contract.

Over the Fourth of July holiday, Danny and Don Ainge, along with their family attorney, traveled to Boston to meet with Celtics management to discuss a contract. The original discussions were, to say the least, unproductive. Ainge & Co. asked for a deal that started at $600,000 and escalated to $800,000, a salary that would have made Ainge the highest-paid player on the team. The Celtics thought that something around $200,000—what Kevin McHale was making—was more appropriate. Though they never articulated their offer, the Celtics were prepared to offer a five-year contract with three years guaranteed at $220,000, and two more years at $300,000 and $500,000. The Ainges' demand caught them off-guard.

"If that's what you feel you need," team owner Harry Mangurian told the Ainges, "then I'm not going to insult you with what we think it should be because, frankly, it's quite a bit different."

The Celtics wanted to get the deal done during the strike because the Blue Jays' attention was elsewhere. Ainge's original demands made that impossible. Finally, baseball returned and, in September, just before the Celtics were about to open training camp, the Blue Jays sued the Celtics, charging them with trying to breach a contract. Ainge, who had not said anything publicly to that point, broke his silence in a New York courtroom, telling a federal judge that he no longer wanted to play for the Blue Jays and that he had filed papers with the players association to retire. The judge gave the two sides nine days to settle or face a trial. The Blue Jays' asking price to settle was $1 million; the Celtics said no thanks.

The trial lasted three days. The Blue Jays had a written, binding contract on their side. The Celtics had an uninspired third baseman on theirs. Using Ainge's honest belief that he had been given permission to negotiate with Boston, the Celtics hoped to tug on the heartstrings of the six-member jury. (To no avail; the jury sided with Toronto, taking only two hours to deliberate.)

During the trial, Ainge testified and restated his position that, regardless of the outcome, he was finished with baseball and the Blue Jays. He then watched in amazement as others took the stand.

"Peter Bavasi is on the witness stand saying that he and I are like father and son and that me leaving would be like him leaving his wife for some blonde floozie," Ainge recalled. "I'm laughing as I listen to this. I had met the guy twice and I didn't like him either time." At one point in the trial, Bavasi came in and sat next to Ainge, putting his arm around him as if he were a close friend. Ainge got up and moved.

Ainge also found Red Auerbach's testimony enlightening.

"Red wasn't any better. I'm thinking, my gosh, where is the integrity? Everything I said was true and both sides agreed to that. But all they cared about was money. It's not their life, it's just about money. I understand it more now. Players are assets. But they're people, too. It woke me up. Pat had told me that I would be able to play basketball, but that we had to go through all of this first."

After the decision, a jubilant Bavasi lit up a victory cigar, tweaking Auerbach, and ripped the Celtics for their arrogance and pomposity. He said he would have nothing more to do with Auerbach and felt confident that Ainge would return to baseball the following spring. Ainge again said he would do no such thing and returned to Provo, Utah, to coach the Brigham Young junior varsity team.

Months later, after the matter had been settled, Ainge got a letter from a man who had been in court all three days of the trial. Ainge remembered the man because he was wearing a

Brooklyn Dodgers baseball cap. The letter presented an interesting twist to the proceedings: Peter Bavasi's father, Buzzie, a Dodgers executive in the 1950s, was still mad at Auerbach for taking Bill Sharman from the Brooklyn Dodgers organization. In the fall of 1951, the Dodgers called Sharman up as a fill-in outfielder, anticipating an early clinching of the pennant. But the Giants overcame a huge deficit and won the pennant and Sharman never got into a game. Sharman planned to focus solely on baseball at that time—and in fact played five years of minor league ball while also playing for the Celtics (1950–53 and 1955). But in 1951, his basketball rights were owned by Fort Wayne and he had no intention of playing there. Auerbach appeared on the scene, reminding Fort Wayne owner Fred Zollner that he (Auerbach) was owed a player from a previous trade. Zollner quickly agreed to make it Sharman, convinced that he would never play basketball anyway. Boston didn't sound a whole lot better to Sharman than Fort Wayne, so he went in and asked for what was then a huge salary ($12,000), confident the Celtics would turn him down. They didn't, and he joined Bob Cousy in the backcourt.

So was this trial a payback for something that had happened thirty years earlier?

"It made sense," Ainge said, "because there was a hatred there before we even went to court. I sensed it. I just wonder whether Peter Bavasi would have taken the same stand if I had been drafted by Cleveland."

Ainge probably would have stayed in baseball had he been drafted by Cleveland, but the Celtics were a lure. They had Larry Bird, Robert Parish, Kevin McHale, and Cedric Maxwell— the Big Three and a Half as Maxwell liked to call them—and they were now making a strong bid for a player who, if not encumbered by the baseball contract, would have been one of the top three picks in the draft. They also happened to be the defending NBA champions.

Auerbach was accustomed to getting what he wanted and, more important, he knew that Ainge wanted to play in Boston.

Despite the loss in court, he felt he had won in the court of public opinion and that the whole mess would eventually be settled.

With things dragging on, the Blue Jays in November decided to try and bring closure to the episode, giving the Celtics two weeks to work out a deal with Ainge. The window ended on November 30. Over the Thanksgiving weekend, all the principals gathered at the Ritz-Carlton in Boston, the Blue Jays occupying one fourth-floor suite, the Ainge contingent another.

The chances for a settlement improved when Bavasi unexpectedly resigned the day before Thanksgiving, leaving matters in the hands of Gillick and the Jays' attorney. Two deals had to be worked out: Ainge's release from Toronto and Ainge's contract with the Celtics.

The Blue Jays agreed to a $500,000 buyout paid by the Celtics, freeing Ainge to sign with Boston, but the Ainges and the Celtics were still far apart. At one point during the negotiations, Auerbach complained to owner Harry Mangurian that the Ainges were holding up the deal.

"This is bull," Auerbach said with characteristic bombast. "Three or four thousand is holding this thing up."

Don Ainge promptly noted that the figure was actually close to $100,000.

"Yeah, but look at all the taxes," Auerbach said.

"I don't think we're in the 97 percent tax bracket," Don Ainge replied.

"Maybe we should give him a boat, like we did with [John] Havlicek," Auerbach said.

Don wasn't biting.

The two sides stayed up until three A.M. before Ainge essentially accepted what the Celtics had in mind the previous July. Over the next year, he wondered more than once if he had done the right thing as he struggled to adjust to a new team and a new league.

By November 1985, however, Danny Ainge was firmly entrenched as a Boston Celtics regular, a starter on the best starting five in the game and, needless to say, an occasional irritant and pest. As December dawned, the Celtics were comfortably in first place but were about to face their most difficult stretch of the season. They were also about to experience their only roster move of the season. Sly Williams was acting up again, and the Celtics had had enough.

CHAPTER FIVE

December:
Coal in the Stocking

The first Sly Williams "episode" occurred when the team returned from Cleveland after its opening weekend road trip. That following Monday, the club gathered at Hellenic College for practice, and Williams did not show. The Celtics said Williams was suffering from hemorrhoids and that his absence was unrelated to the "intestinal ailment" that caused him to miss 48 games the year before. Williams went along with the ruse.

Had this been anyone else, the situation would have been uneventful. But Williams had a history of broken alarm clocks, flat tires, and missed planes, and it seemed like nothing, not even the prospect of playing for a gifted Celtics team, was going to change him. He returned to practice the next day and played six minutes in the next two games before missing a Saturday night game in Washington, failing to tell K.C. Jones that he couldn't make the trip.

The situation was getting ridiculous. If there was one thing this team did not need, it was erratic behavior from someone who didn't even figure in their immediate plans. The Celtics thought Williams might eventually replace Scott Wedman, who was nearing the end of his career, but for the 1985–86 season, Williams wasn't considered an integral part of the team.

Williams returned the following Wednesday and went six minutes in a victory over Indiana. Two nights later, he played three minutes against the Bullets in Boston. He would never play another NBA game. Over the next two weeks he had no communication with the team, suffering from what the Celtics dubbed a bad case of hemorrhoids. Finally, on December 2, 17 games into the season and sixty-seven days into his Boston career, the Celtics released him.

The Celtics feel the same now as they did the day they cut him loose: the guy was blowing the chance of a lifetime.

"A wasted talent," said Alan Cohen. After having seen Williams play for the Knicks, he thought the Celtics could do wonders for him. "I know he had incredible problems with his backside, but he just wasn't into the game anymore. I think he thought he wanted to [get back into basketball], but he was unable to do so, for whatever reasons."

What happened to Williams was anybody's guess. The Celtics have their suspicions and some players say they heard some wild stories, but Williams simply disappeared without telling anyone.

"There simply was no reliability or consistency and we didn't need the distraction," Jan Volk said. "As good a player as he could have been, he's no good if he's not here, so we cut him. His agent was as perplexed as we were. It was not done without an attempt to see what was happening. But there was no information that could have provided an explanation for his unreliability. We simply couldn't tolerate it while we were putting a team together."

K.C. Jones didn't have to be persuaded to release Williams; he, too, was tired of the whole thing. He, as much as anyone, knew the team's track record for rescuing wayward souls, rehabilitating bad guys, or simply resurrecting waning careers; he had seen it firsthand with the likes of Willie Naulls, Bailey Howell, Wayne Embry, and Don Nelson. But Sly Williams would join the group of players for whom even the Celtics had no answer, a group that included Sidney Wicks, Marvin Barnes, Curtis Rowe, Bob McAdoo, and Ray Williams.

"Sly? He was bad," Jones said. "He'd go away and not say a word. He was upset about this and that and playing time. I just said 'Screw him' and put him at the end of the bench to see what would happen. It was a write-off."

Williams may have left, but his memory lingered. Players joked about a certain part of the bench in the Hellenic College locker room because it was the spot where Williams always sat. Don't sit there, Walton would tell his teammates, or you'll disappear, just like Sly. Danny Ainge and Kevin McHale took it one step further, putting a piece of tape on the spot with the words "Sly's Spot" on it. No one sat there the rest of the year.

The release of Williams created a roster opening, and the obvious choice to fill it was David Thirdkill. As the team had anticipated, no one had signed Thirdkill in the six weeks since he was cut. Thirdkill had remained in the area—he was in attendance at Boston Garden for the home opener against Milwaukee—and was planning to play with the Bay State Bombardiers in the Continental Basketball Association to stay sharp. He was in Maine with the Bombardiers when he got a call from his agent, Joe Napoli, informing him that the Celtics wanted to sign him. He caught the first plane to Boston, was picked up by Sam Vincent at the airport, and soon checked in at the team's training camp hotel near Fenway Park. He eventually found an apartment in the Hyde Park section of Boston not far from the Celtics' practice site. And he certainly didn't need any introductions the next day at practice.

"The guys all thought I should have made the team the first time around," he said. "But it didn't happen. Things happen in strange ways, I guess. But in the long run, this was the best thing that happened because they brought me back."

David Thirdkill had plenty of personal history to draw on in those disappointing days following the Celtics' decision to cut him seventy-two hours before the season opener. He had been waived by Detroit, Milwaukee, and San Antonio in three seasons, yet he had always managed to find an NBA address, if not a lot of playing time, from November to April in those three years. Patience was one thing Thirdkill had come to understand. It was something he had learned well even before he came into the NBA as the first-round pick, fifteenth overall, of the Phoenix Suns in 1982.

"David Thirdkill," said Dick Versace, who coached Thirdkill at Bradley University, "is one of the most interesting guys I have ever known, let alone coached. He was bright, headstrong. His emotions ran the gamut. He also was one of the most intimidating players I ever coached. When we did defensive drills, he was like the werewolf of London. I finally started calling him the Sheriff—when he guarded you, he locked you up."

The intimidation was compounded by a noticeable scar on Thirdkill's face, just under his right eye. It was ugly and looked like the result of a serious knife fight or brawl.

"Nothing like that," Thirdkill said. "When I was eighteen months old, my brother and I were playing near a radiator. I fell out of bed and hit the radiator. It has been with me ever since. It's like a part of me."

David was the youngest of the nine children born to Willie and Dorothy Thirdkill, who still live in the house in the west end of St. Louis where they raised all their children. Willie Thirdkill was tall, 6-4. He told his skeptical sons that he was a pretty good high school player back in his day, and he must have been right because two of his four sons went on to play professionally. David's brother, Johnny, had a brief stint in the CBA, but David was clearly the best. "I guess everything they did got handed down to me," he said. "I learned a lot from them."

David played his high school ball at Soldan High School, the public school in his district. He didn't make the team as a freshman and was a reserve as a sophomore. He then cracked the starting lineup as a junior and led his team to the city championship for two straight seasons. He counts among his biggest basketball disappointments the team's inability to win a state title.

"We just didn't play well enough when we got there," he said.

Once out of high school, Thirdkill was uncertain about his basketball future. He was torn by the conflicting desires to stay close to home and possibly attend St. Louis University, or to cut the family ties and head elsewhere, somewhere he might be able to play. But since he didn't have the grades to qualify for a scholarship to a Division I school, he decided to head elsewhere and play basketball at a top-notch junior college program for a year while he raised his grades enough to qualify for a Division I scholarship.

The place he chose was and still is a junior college power-house located twenty-four miles from the Nevada border in the town of Twin Falls, Idaho. If he had deliberately set out to find somewhere diametrically opposite St. Louis, he could not have chosen a better spot. It was, as Dick Versace likes to say, "Fifteen minutes west of nowhere." But Southern Idaho was exactly where Thirdkill belonged. Under the stern guidance of Coach Mike Mitchell, Thirdkill would really improve his game.

"How do I put this?" Mitchell recalled. "There are two sides to David. On one hand, he is very, very competitive and a very intense player. On the other, he's very emotional, and we butted heads. I think I was the first coach he ever had who asked him to do things he either wasn't used to doing or didn't want to do. It was just a matter of him getting to accept reality. I'm sure there were times when he hated me. With David, every two weeks you had to establish who was running the show."

Mitchell never saw Thirdkill play in high school, although he was aware of who Thirdkill was and the probability that Third-kill would go the JUCO route. After successfully recruiting him, Mitchell met him at a summer camp at the University of Colorado, where Mitchell would soon end up as an assistant to future NBA head coach Bill Blair. Mitchell saw Thirdkill as the

prototypical swing man, and it wasn't long before he knew he
had a player.

Southern Idaho won the regional JUCO title that year, but
was eliminated in the national tournament. Thirdkill averaged
22.8 points a game, earned All-America honors, and also made
the national JUCO All-Tournament team. Mitchell played him
on the wing offensively, where Thirdkill had great success hitting the medium-range perimeter jumper. It was a shot he could
never master in the NBA, however; had he been able to, he
might have had a very long career.

"I thought with repetition and maturity, he would develop
into a good shooter," Mitchell said.

After one year at Southern Idaho, there was intense competition for Thirdkill. His grades had improved and he was being
courted by several Big Ten teams as well as New Mexico and Colorado. UNLV was also in the hunt, but Thirdkill decided at the
last moment not to visit the campus, leaving Coach Jerry
Tarkanian waiting at the airport (or so Thirdkill likes to say).
Bradley University, another suitor, started to look like the best
prospect. It was closer to home and it was a place where, like
Southern Idaho, Thirdkill could hit the ground running. Plus,
Bradley had a P.T. Barnum–ish head coach in Versace, who, as
the saying goes, could talk a dog off a meat wagon.

Yet Versace left the Thirdkill home in St. Louis convinced
that his recruiting pitch had fallen on deaf ears. The two had
talked about many things on the front porch, and Thirdkill had
finally given the news to Versace, that although he wasn't entirely sure, he didn't think he was going to Bradley. Versace said
he wanted a yes or no answer and, as he got up to leave, told
Thirdkill that if he didn't hear a yes by the time he reached his
car, he would assume the answer was no. Thirdkill said nothing
as Versace pulled away.

On the long drive back to Peoria, Versace cursed his fate but
figured that something good might happen because of their
long talk. And, of course, it did: Thirdkill had gone back into

his house, thought for a moment, and then called the Bradley basketball office to let them know he was coming. Versace got the news when he arrived in Peoria hours later.

Thirdkill did not hesitate when the Celtics called in December 1985. Three days after Williams was waived, Thirdkill was signed for the remainder of the season. One night later, he was in uniform for the Celtics' home game against the Portland Trail Blazers. He must have wondered about his sense of timing. Not only did the Celtics get crushed, 121–103, but the defeat turned out to be their worst of the season and their only one at home.

Heading into the game, Portland looked like the last team on the planet capable of inflicting the first home loss on the Celtics. The Trail Blazers were on one of those dreaded eastern swings and had already lost to Washington and Atlanta. Not only had they dropped three straight and eight of 12, but they arrived in Boston without their leading scorer, Kiki Vandeweghe, who had been sent back to Portland to nurse a bone bruise. The Celtics, meanwhile, had met what everyone figured was a challenge of sorts by beating Milwaukee and New Jersey on successive nights on the road. Those two teams had been a combined 15-1 at home and Milwaukee had won 24 straight in the MECCA. The Celtics had now won nine straight and had a 17-2 record.

The venerable Portland coach, Jack Ramsay, wasn't concerned so much about the Celtics' alleged invincibility as he was by the infuriatingly woeful play of his own team. After getting blown out of Atlanta, he told the ailing Vandeweghe to return to Portland; he then went out for a beer with his old friend Kevin Loughery, who was doing broadcasts for the Hawks at the time.

"I've never seen a team of yours play that bad," Loughery told Ramsay. The Blazers coach could not disagree.

"We're struggling," he said.

"Are you headed back home?"

"No," Ramsay said, "we're going to Boston."

"Too bad, they're playing great," Loughery said, adding insult to injury.

Ramsay knew his team. He knew that after an embarrassing loss like the one to Atlanta that they needed to hear some strong words, so he read them the riot act. He also knew that the Celtics probably did not feel threatened by the appearance of a reeling Western Conference wannabe.

"I don't think they expected anything from us," Ramsay said. "It probably was logical for them to think they could win one without working too hard."

With Vandeweghe out, Ramsay elected to start second-year flyer Jerome Kersey at small forward. It was the first start of Kersey's career and he made the most of it. The Blazers used their speed advantage, relying on the swiftness of Kersey, Steve Colter, and Clyde Drexler to beat the Celtics down the court.

"We were a team of young, energetic guys, and it kinda wore them down," Colter recalled. "We had no idea what we had done then, but now, well, it's kinda special when you think about it. We did something no one else was able to do that season. It's something we'll be able to talk about for eons."

Portland led virtually the entire game, pulling ahead by double-digit margins only to see the Celtics rally and get close. Boston led only once in the game, 75–74, following a three-point play by Larry Bird, who was a horrendous 9-of-26 from the field. Kersey, who had 22 points, then sparked an 11–2 run and the Blazers poured it on in the fourth quarter, extending the lead to as many as 23 points.

It was hard to pick exactly where the Celtics went awry; there were so many culprits. Dennis Johnson fouled out in 23 minutes. Neither Robert Parish nor Bill Walton could neutralize Sam Bowie, who had 18 points and 13 rebounds. Frustration over the way the game was called—and the way the Celtics played—led to four technical fouls, two resulting in the first ejection of the season for K.C. Jones.

Afterward, Jones simply told his players to take a shower and wipe off whatever it was they had on them. Down the hallway, Blazers quote machine Mychal Thompson said the team's miserable outing two nights earlier in Atlanta had done for them exactly what Ramsay had hoped.

"Looking terrible when you lose is doubly tough," Thompson said. "But the Celtics are human and people tend to forget that. But I won't say they were off. My few rules in life are these: don't cheat the IRS, don't curse the dead, and don't get Larry Bird mad."

The defeat snapped a nine-game Celtics winning streak. And Portland? The Trail Blazers were so rejuvenated by the showing that they lost by 12 the following night in New Jersey.

The Celtics did not play again for four days; they then made the first of three regular season visits to Hartford, Connecticut. They did so partly to protect their television base from the lure of the New York teams, but also because the Civic Center cut them an attractive deal—as much as $100,000 more than what they made in Boston Garden.

To the players, however, the Hartford games were nothing more than an annoyance. Yes, they wore home uniforms and the crowd was generally pro-Celtic, but the bus trip took as long as two hours—Bird hated the fact that the sun was always in his eyes the whole way down—and the locker room was cramped. No one could tell the coaching staff or the players that this was a home game under these conditions.

The opponent in Hartford was Atlanta, a good, solid team trying hard to challenge the Celtics in the East with its mixture of young, athletic types, like the acrobatic Dominique Wilkins, and its role-playing bruisers, Wayne "Tree" Rollins and rookie Jon Koncak. But even if the venue was Hartford, the Celtics weren't about to lose two in a row at "home," and they didn't, beating the Hawks, 114–100. K.C. Jones milked the starting five dry, getting 104 points from the unit.

At this point, one-quarter of the way through the season, Jones still had not really settled on a regular rotation. There were times when the bench played and made big contributions, and there were nights when it did little. On some nights Jerry Sichting was the first guard off the bench; on other nights it was Sam Vincent or Rick Carlisle.

Part of Jones's inconsistency was the result of the new mix of players, but part of it was also the coach's near phobia about relying too much on his reserves. One of the reasons the Celtics fell short in 1985 was that their starters were exhausted for the NBA Finals. It's hard not to keep players like Larry Bird, Kevin McHale, and Dennis Johnson on the floor, but the acquisition of Walton and Sichting, in addition to giving rest to the starters, was also supposed to create a more regular and consistent flow to the game. With the way Jones was using his bench, however, playing time varied widely. It stayed that way throughout the month, and the Celtics responded with several erratic performances. If the Celtics were to play consistent basketball throughout the season, Jones would have to settle on a regular rotation.

While the team was in Hartford, another development arose that warranted attention: Larry Bird spoke publicly for the first time about his sore back. Prior to the season, it had been revealed that Bird was involved in an altercation in a Boston bar in which he may or may not have injured his hand. That he was involved was indisputable and he later paid an out-of-court settlement. Whether or not he was hurt was something else, and the intensely private Bird was so furious about media reports of the incident that he stopped talking to Boston reporters at home.

But Hartford was, to Bird anyway, a road game as far as the media was concerned and he always had a sense of noblesse oblige when talking to out-of-towners. He opened up in Hartford and admitted what everyone already knew: he was hurting and he wasn't playing up to the ultra-lofty standards to which he and everyone else was accustomed.

"There's no question I'm struggling," he said that night. He was averaging "only" 22.9 points a game—a 20 percent drop from 1984–85—and he was shooting poorly from the field. "But

if I was averaging five rebounds, two assists, and 35 points, nobody would be saying anything. But since I'm not shooting the
ball like I have in the past, everybody gets all excited. I'm not
moving well because of injuries. But I'm giving the effort and
I'm playing just about as well in other aspects. Just as soon as my
back feels better, I'm going to have a great year. But I have to
work on every aspect of my game to stay at the top and I haven't
been able to do that."

The Celtics also received some unhappy news that day: the
NBA required their presence in New York on Christmas Eve because of their Christmas Day game with the Knicks. The team
had hoped to come down Christmas morning, but the league
rejected that suggestion. The league did offer to pay the bill for
the families to come down, but those with families still didn't
think that waking up Christmas morning in the Summit Hotel
(affectionately known as the Slumit) was any consolation.

The next few days were filled with some more unexpected de-
velopments. A pounding of the Sacramento Kings on December 12 was tarnished by a potentially serious thumb injury to
Dennis Johnson. The Celtics, fearing the worst, were relieved
when the X-rays showed that the injury was only a hyperexten-
sion; instead of missing up to eight weeks, Johnson would miss
only a couple of games.

The following day, Danny Ainge put his John Hancock (and
not his Amo Wong) on a six-year extension, telling reporters,
"The last two guys who signed extensions [Cedric Maxwell and
Gerald Henderson] got traded. I hope I'll stick around for a
while." Ainge then cracked that he thought he was heading
back to baseball. "Maybe I'll go back as a relief pitcher."

On the night of December 14, the Celtics traveled to Cleveland
and lost to the Cavs, 109–99. Dennis Johnson missed the game
as he rested the sore thumb, and the Boston backcourt came
out firing blanks all night, shooting only 37 percent from the

field. Afterward, coach George Karl of the Cavs summed up the Cleveland game plan in almost embarrassing simplicity.

"You don't have to worry about any of their guards. I mean, they are NBA guards, but who are you going to let beat you?"

His message was clear: if the Celtics guards could shoot, the outcome of the game was a foregone conclusion. Someone needed to make the outside shot if the Celtics weren't running (which they weren't) and if their post men were being double-teamed underneath (which they were). They needed an outside element to their inside game. At this time of the season, their best shooter was ineffective. As good a team as they were, the Celtics were struggling with their halfcourt game and they needed Larry Bird to make it all come together.

The loss to Cleveland was the first of three defeats in a five-game, eight-day stretch. In only one of those games—a 20-point home win over Dallas in which Danny Ainge shot 9-for-13, and the team registered a franchise record 46 assists—did the Celtics play well. They lost games in Chicago, where Orlando Woolridge scored 37 points, and in Philadelphia, when Jones's lack of a set rotation came into play—Scott Wedman was on the floor for just two minutes, and Larry Bird, bad back and all, went 47. The loss to Philadelphia, their first of the season to their hated rival, dropped Boston to 21-6 as the team headed home to prepare for the Christmas Day game in New York.

In most cities, 21-6 would be a cause for celebration, but not in Boston in 1985. Incredibly, there was genuine concern over what was ailing the Celtics. They weren't running. They weren't rebounding. There was no consistent rotation. The three R's.

On the morning of December 24, *Boston Globe* columnist Bob Ryan addressed the issue of presumptive greatness that stuck to the team like a barnacle to a rock.

"If they started a seven-game series with the Lakers tonight, and all seven games were in the Garden, they might win one. But make Larry healthy and I'll take it all back."

At the time, the Celtics were three games behind the 24-3 Lakers for the league's best overall record. On Christmas Eve, the Celtics reluctantly boarded a plane for New York City. Most saw the Christmas game as a concession to CBS and grudgingly accepted that they'd be the afternoon entertainment. No one wanted to play that day—well, almost no one. The irrepressibly hyper Walton simply loved to play and didn't care where, when, or against whom.

"For me, playing on the holidays is the biggest thrill of all. I prefer to play on the holidays," he said. "Basketball players have the summer off. It's an honor. Everyone is home watching. And if you're playing on that day, it's like you're something special. I don't have any trouble with that."

Kevin McHale did. He also had no intention of waking up Christmas morning anywhere but at his own home.

While his teammates were in New York, McHale rose in time to see the look on his children's faces as they saw the inevitable bounty under the tree at their Weston, Massachusetts home. He then took the nine A.M. shuttle to New York and made it to Madison Square Garden with time to spare.

"I'd do it again," McHale said years later. "And it's interesting that a couple of years later, I noticed that Isiah [Thomas] and Bill [Laimbeer] did the same thing.

"People lose perspective on the family and holiday part of Christmas. Yeah, it's fun to see the kids open their presents, but it's also a special time to be together as a family. And that's what I wanted to do. I knew it was wrong from the team perspective, but I knew that I would not miss the game and I got there in plenty of time. I think people do focus too much on the gift-giving part of Christmas and not on the family-religious part of it. If there was a game on the Jewish high holy days, do you think David Stern would show up? Of course not. So I don't see why it was such a big deal."

The Celtics didn't think so either. They said publicly that McHale would be fined, but Red Auerbach later said there would be nothing of the sort. In retrospect, no one should have been the least bit surprised. McHale never, ever allowed himself to be consumed by the game. It was his job. It was demanding.

He was very good at it. But it was also just a part of his life, not all of his life. One of the best assessments of McHale came from his coach in junior high school, Terry Maciej. "Kevin," Maciej said, "got the fun and the work out of everything."

Terry Maciej was one of many coaches who helped shape a rapidly growing Kevin McHale as the youngster went through the public school system in the northern Minnesota mining town of Hibbing. The town itself boasts an inordinate number of celebrities for its size (18,000) and location (three hours north of Minneapolis). Bob Dylan, Roger Maris (who soon thereafter moved to Fargo, North Dakota), Vincent Bugliosi (the man who prosecuted Charles Manson), and Gus Hall (the founder of the American Communist Party) were all born in Hibbing.

Kevin was one of four McHale children. His father, Paul McHale, worked the mines for more than four decades without ever taking a sick day. His mother, Josephine, whose Croatian heritage is believed to be responsible for her son's height, guarded the home front. Kevin and his older brother, John, were born sixteen months apart, which led to ferocious battles at home over just about anything.

McHale's basketball game was developed by several local coaches, all of whom saw in him the proverbial "diamond in the rough." He was tall and gangly, but well-coordinated. He enjoyed some early success as a Hibbing hockey player, but owing both to the demands on his body and the rigors of Hibbing winters, he gave up the sport. The town of Hibbing is one of many on the Minnesota Iron Range, an area that gave the United States some of the players on the 1980 gold medal–winning hockey team. One town on the range, Eveleth, is the home of the United States Hockey Hall of Fame.

But Hibbing also has a hoop history as well, sending local product Dick Garmaker to the National Basketball Association in the 1950s and 1960s. He is memorialized in Hibbing in a perverse way: the end-to-end sprints that high school players do during practice are referred to as Garmakers.

Hibbing High School is a magnificent five-story brick structure that was built in 1920 by the local mining company for $4 million, a staggering sum then. The school has classroom doors made of oak, a cut-glass chandelier, and a Barton pipe organ. But it did not have then, nor does it have now, a gymnasium that can accommodate enough fans to watch a high school men's basketball game. Kevin McHale had to play his high school games in a junior high school gymnasium.

As a sophomore, McHale was called up to the varsity. As a junior and senior, he became the state's most dominant big man, leading Hibbing to the state quarter finals his junior year and to the finals as a senior. But, despite being named the state's Mr. Basketball his senior year, he could not lead Hibbing to the state title. His Blue Jackets lost in the finals to Bloomington North, but not before McHale had showcased his talents and proved to many that he was good enough to earn a scholarship to the University of Minnesota.

Ironically, only one other school showed any real interest in Kevin McHale: the University of Utah, which went so far as to send an assistant coach to Hibbing almost every week. McHale, however, wanted to go to the U, which is what everyone in Hibbing calls the University of Minnesota. He had grown up watching their games, it was close enough for his family to still watch him play (and they did, oftentimes not arriving home until four A.M.), and it was in the Big Ten. He would go to the library and read about former Minnesota stars Dave Winfield and Jim Brewer and Ron Behagen and could see himself in maroon and gold.

Minnesota, however, wasn't as interested in McHale as McHale was in Minnesota. "I think they knew I wanted to go there so they didn't spend a lot of time on me," McHale said.

At the time, the University of Minnesota was on probation

due to recruiting violations committed while Bill Musselman was the head coach. The basketball program was limited to three scholarships over a three-year period (1976–79), so they had to recruit wisely.

The Big Ten was then, as it is now, a physical conference. After seeing McHale play in high school, Indiana assistant Bob Weltlich felt McHale would not be able to survive the rigors of a Big Ten schedule. Minnesota coach Jim Dutcher was given the same information by one of his assistants. McHale was put on the proverbial back burner, and Dutcher says now, "Had Hibbing not made the state tournament, we would never have had a chance to see Kevin, and we would not have recruited him."

Utah, meanwhile, was putting the full-court press on McHale, getting him to visit the campus and treating him to a helicopter ride over Salt Lake City. Jim Marsh, the dogged Utah assistant who spent more nights in Hibbing than any other college recruiter, had become so attached to McHale and the family that he was a regular diner at the house. Dutcher, on the other hand, was holding on tightly to the last of his three scholarships when McHale called and laid his cards on the table.

"We really didn't know much about him," Dutcher recalled. "But we knew he had an offer from Utah and that Kentucky was showing some interest. I gave him the last one I had."

McHale knew Minnesota's history going in, but the lure of the U was too strong to pass up. He never once thought about transferring even though he would not have lost a year of eligibility. He was having too much fun and the 1976–77 team, with Mychal Thompson and Ray Williams, was as good as any in the country.

"Kevin never overstated the importance of basketball in his life," Dutcher said. "At times that can really get to a coach, but when it's time to play, he takes it very seriously. You just learn to accept that in him."

McHale had many chances to transfer and he believes, from a basketball standpoint, a switch would have been helpful. The players who entered the school with him did transfer, and by the time he was a junior, he was starting alongside four freshmen. His senior year, he just "kinda played," as no one on the team helped complement his game.

"It goes back to the whole loyalty thing," he said. "I wasn't going to leave. I thought it would be a cop-out. It's easy not to play when you're hurt. It's hard to stick it out. I had role models who stuck it out."

Minnesota finally got off probation in time for McHale to play in the NIT as a senior, but the Gophers lost to Virginia in the finals. McHale was outplayed by freshman Ralph Sampson, and his draft prospects, which had been high until that point, dipped. But McHale rebounded with superior performances in all-star games that elevated him to one of the elite in the draft class of 1980.

Red Auerbach, who went to watch McHale play at the University of Minnesota's Williams Arena, came away impressed. The Celtics had the No. 1 pick in the 1980 draft thanks to a series of shrewd moves that had started with the signing of free agent M.L. Carr in 1979 and ended with the trading of Bob McAdoo to Detroit for two first-rounders in 1980. Detroit finished with the worst record in the East that year, and the Celtics won the coin flip to get the first pick.

Auerbach played it cagy. So did coach Bill Fitch. Publicly, the Celtics lusted after Joe Barry Carroll, the center from Purdue; privately, they wanted McHale, but wanted to somehow work a deal where they wouldn't draft him first overall. McHale was good, but he wasn't that good.

That Auerbach and Fitch were able to get McHale with the third pick, and also get Robert Parish in the same deal, ranks as one of the most lopsided trades in NBA history: the Celtics traded their No. 1 and No. 13 picks for Parish and Golden State's No. 3 pick. Golden State took Carroll with their No. 1 pick. Boston chose McHale. At the time, it didn't seem like a major Boston heist. But by 1986, it was already in the record books under the title: Grand Larceny, NBA Style. By then, Parish and McHale had two championship rings. Their third was on the way. But on Christmas Day 1985, the Celtics looked anything but title bound.

•

Virtually everyone associated with the 1985–86 Celtics lists the Christmas game as the turning point of the season. It woke up the players, alerted the nation to the shaky status of Larry Bird, who went 8-for-27, and made everyone take a second look at the big picture.

The Celtics lost the game, 113–104, in double overtime. It was their fourth straight defeat on the road, traditionally an area where the Celtics excelled. Boston had led the Knicks by 25 points in the third quarter and then completely collapsed. New York cut the deficit to a manageable 10 after three quarters while rookie Patrick Ewing sat on the bench in foul trouble. Ewing returned in the fourth with 9:28 to play and basically took over the game, scoring 16 points in an eight-minute stretch.

New York tied the game 86–86 on two Rory Sparrow free throws with 34 seconds left, igniting the 17,480 at Madison Square Garden into an almost uncontrollable frenzy. The Knicks were not a very good team. The Celtics were the best in the East, even though they weren't playing like it. "I know half of America turned us off at the half," said Hubie Brown, the Knicks coach. "But those who hung around witnessed a staggering comeback."

The game remained tied at 86 at the end of regulation. The Celtics led 97–92 with 69 seconds left in overtime, but Ewing, who finished with a then–career best 32, scored on a drive and then Trent Tucker, coming off a screen with 11 seconds left, drained a three-pointer to tie the game.

The Celtics would be burned repeatedly by three-pointers all season; at least five of their 15 losses were directly related to three-pointers that either won the game or sent it into overtime. They had seen Micheal Ray Richardson do it on opening night.

They would see it again in consecutive March games in Washington and Dallas and in Philadelphia in April. And they were seeing it again that afternoon.

Boston missed a chance to win it at the buzzer when the 6-5 Ernie Grunfeld blocked a shot by McHale. In the second overtime, the Knicks simply took control and built the lead to 11 and won going away. The Celtics shot 34 percent in the game, their worst of the season, with Bird and McHale (7-of-21) hitting little all day. Danny Ainge and Dennis Johnson combined for 12 points in 88 minutes. Bill Walton played only 13 minutes, Scott Wedman 15. The starters simply got tired and were worn out by the Knicks, who seemed to gain strength as the game went on. Had it gone another overtime, New York would have won by 20.

Celtics owner Alan Cohen, who lived in New York, sat in the stands completely befuddled. This wasn't just a loss; it was a national television loss to a bad team and it was embarrassing.

"That was a humiliation," Cohen said. "I distinctly remember feeling so good at halftime. I think we felt full of ourselves. Hubris is what it was. It was terrible. You constantly learn lessons in life and that was one I learned. As the game wore on and the Knicks won, all I could do was sit in the stands and think, 'What have we done? Am I wrong about all this? Is it not going to work out?' Because at that point, we just didn't know."

No one knew. Bird's back was still sore. K.C. Jones still hadn't determined a set rotation and there was a real feeling that the problems of the year before, when the starters had suffered meltdown against the Lakers, were starting to reappear.

"That day K.C. decided that the second string was not going to play and that he was going to go with the first string," Walton said. "And people got tired. That was a dark day. All of us that day learned something new about basketball: that when you have a three-point lead and they have the last shot, foul them. Make them shoot it from the line."

Jones said he came away from the game with a "better look at what we should be doing. You lose a 25-point lead and the game, it's hard to describe, but it was a totally embarrassing disappointment to me."

The team flew back to Boston that night. The following night they would leave for Utah and a short, two-game western run. Bird and Jerry Sichting went to Bird's home and shook their collective heads over a few beers. Sichting had sent his wife and children home to Indiana for the holidays, so he was alone. Bird was, too. They still could not believe what had happened.

"It was just a pathetic performance," Sichting said. "Everyone was so pissed off about it. It turned the whole season around."

It wasn't a total loss for Sichting. A couple of Brookline policemen who watched Bird's house when he was away saw the lights on and stopped by. Sichting got to know them well enough to get preferred parking the following summer for pro tennis matches at the nearby Longwood Cricket Club.

The Christmas loss dropped the Celtics to 21-7. They now had lost two straight games for the first time; they had gone into April the previous year before losing consecutive games. They still were four games ahead of the pack in the Atlantic Division, but they had lost 2½ games off their lead in seven days. And, having lost four in a row on the road, the last thing they needed was to go across the country to play an improving Jazz team that had taken them to overtime in Boston a month earlier.

Utah represented the antithesis of the Celtics in so many ways. Coach Frank Layden shuffled players in and out to the point where no one played more than 30 minutes a game. He had a talented, second-year point guard named John Stockton who was backing up Rickey Green. He had a bruising rookie power forward from Louisiana Tech named Karl Malone who inexplicably had slipped all the way to No. 13 in the previous draft, prompting a puzzled Layden to wonder aloud, "Does he have AIDS or something?"

This was not an easy game at this point of the season for the then-struggling Celtics. Inevitably, there were questions about

the team's personnel, a group that had been so carefully constructed over the summer and fall. Was it still the right mix? K.C.
Jones thought so, saying, simply, "I like what I have." General
manager Jan Volk, in a remark that would prove to be
prophetic, said, "I think this team does have enough depth and
it will show." The question was, when?

The Celtics, sensing the need for a big performance, led for
most of the game. Both Bird and McHale had found the range;
each would finish with 24 points on identical 10-of-16 shooting
from the field. Jones involved the bench more, with Sam Vincent getting 12 minutes. But the guy who sealed the victory was
the same guy who, years earlier, devastated many of these same
fans when they were down the street cheering for the University
of Utah and he was down Interstate 15 playing for Brigham
Young: Danny Ainge.

Boston needed Ainge because it blew a 13-point lead in the
fourth quarter and trailed, 106–105. Adrian Dantley, en route to
a 39-point explosion, was torching any Celtic who dared guard
him. But then Ainge, who finished with 17 points in only 28
minutes, hit a huge three-pointer to give the Celtics a 108–106
lead. After Utah tied the game, Ainge hit another jumper and
the Celtics sweated out a Karl Malone miss to escape with a
110–108 victory. No team played the Celtics much harder that
year over 101 minutes than Utah, and the Jazz came away with
two disappointing losses.

The Celtics then flew to Los Angeles to face the Clippers; it
would be Bill Walton's first appearance against the team that
had placed their hopes on him—and then traded him after six
frustrating seasons.

Walton's old team fell to 11-21 after losing 125–103 to his new
team. The Celtics outrebounded the Clippers 65–37 with Walton collecting 13 in just 17 minutes. Big Bill also had nine points
and a blocked shot. The Celtics led by 22 at the half and by 32
after three before emptying the bench.

The game also marked a reunion with Cedric Maxwell, the
player whose inability or unwillingness to correctly read the

Celtics' pulse that previous summer resulted in his banishment to Clipperland. The Celtics had even paid some of Maxwell's salary to facilitate the deal. That night, he had six points and 10 rebounds but he was his usual wise-guy self after the game when asked if he was after revenge.

"Revenge? How can you be seeking revenge against a team that's still paying you?"

CHAPTER SIX

January:
The Turnaround

As 1985 ended and 1986 began, the Celtics were still in control of both their division and their conference. They were 23-7, leading the Atlantic Division by four games, and heading into the new year with a modest two-game winning streak, with both of the victories coming on the road.

After the victory over the Clippers, they did not play again until January 2 at Indiana. K.C. Jones gave his players a little time off with instructions to rendezvous in Indianapolis for a New Year's night workout.

Walton immediately made a dash for Oakland, where the Grateful Dead were playing their annual New Year's Eve show at the Coliseum. Walton was, by now, almost a member of the band; he had toured with them through Egypt and played drums in the shadow of the Pyramids during a lunar eclipse. He had attended his first Grateful Dead concert in 1969 and was not only a certifiable Deadhead, but so close to the band that he attended Jerry Garcia's funeral in August 1995. He was going to be a cable television commentator for the New Year's concert.

Larry Bird and Jerry Sichting, the Celtics' Hoosier twosome, took a red-eye back to St. Louis and then changed planes for a flight to Indianapolis. Bird went on to French Lick to celebrate New Year's while Sichting met his family in Martinsville.

Throughout their pro careers, neither Bird nor Sichting ever forgot he was a Hoosier at heart. They both starred in high school and went to college in the state. At Martinsville High, Sichting was coached by Sam Alford, a legendary figure in Indiana prep basketball. Alford's son, Steve, would later go on to stardom under Bobby Knight at Indiana, but, in the mid-1970s, Jerry Sichting was the undisputed star of Martinsville hoops.

"Jerry was Steve's first childhood idol," Sam Alford said. "Steve followed him around everywhere. Steve wore his number. Steve was Jerry in imagination games. Of course, Jerry also locked Steve in a locker room locker once. But Steve still idolized him anyway."

Martinsville lost only twice in Sichting's senior year, once in a holiday tournament and then to Columbus North in the second round of the state tournament. Martinsville had beaten North three straight times, but the game was in Columbus because it had a larger gym. "It was a real low moment," Sichting said.

Sichting had several college opportunities available to him. Bobby Knight visited his house. "He was larger than life even then," Sichting said. But Sichting paid close attention to the recruiting battles in Indiana, and when he learned that another guard had committed to IU, he looked elsewhere. Cincinnati and Alabama also showed interest, but Sam Alford still felt that Louisville would prevail.

"We went down there for a visit, had a great time, and I remember telling my wife that he was going there," Alford said. "The next time he called me, he said he was going to Purdue."

Purdue had been in the picture all along. When it came down to Louisville and Purdue, Sichting was told by Knight to go to neither. "He told me to go to Miami of Ohio," Sichting said. "That's when I really decided it should be Purdue."

He promptly got caught in a logjam. Kyle Macy, Indiana's Mr.

Basketball that year, was already there, although he would eventually transfer to Kentucky. One of the two returning guards was Eugene Parker, a four-year starter who later went into the sports agent business and now has Deion Sanders and Charlie Ward as clients. Bruce Parkinson was there, too, as a medical redshirt who played Sichting's sophomore year.

In his four years at Purdue, Sichting did not miss a game. He moved into the starting lineup as a junior and was named co-captain as a senior. His scoring average increased steadily from year to year, finally reaching 13.6 points per game.

In his junior year, the Boilermakers, with Joe Barry Carroll as their star, were ranked No. 1 in some early polls. But they finished the season a disappointing 16-11 and Fred Schaus, the former L.A. Lakers coach who had recruited Sichting, left the head coaching position after six years at the helm.

Lee Rose, who had just taken North Carolina-Charlotte (with Cedric Maxwell) to the Final Four in 1977, succeeded Schaus and Purdue won more games (27) and drew more fans than at any other time in the school's history. The team finished in a three-way tie for the Big Ten title with Michigan State and Iowa, but, because of the rules at the time, only two teams from a conference could advance to the NCAA tournament. Purdue lost out—they were 1-1 with MSU and 0-2 against Iowa—and accepted an invitation to the NIT instead. (The two-school rule was changed in 1980 and Purdue, which finished third in the Big Ten that year, advanced to the NCAA Final Four.)

"You look back at the Big Ten and it might have been the greatest conference ever at that time," Sichting said. "Look at all the guys who played at that time and went on to have long NBA careers: Mike Woodson, Eddie Johnson, Ray Williams, Mychal Thompson, Rickey Green, Kevin McHale, Phil Hubbard, Magic. The list just goes on and on. It seemed like every guard I played against was a future pro."

Purdue made it to the NIT Finals that year (as Minnesota and McHale would the following year) and lost to Indiana, 53–52, on a late basket by Butch Carter. With little time left, Purdue called time and set up a play for Sichting. He got a good look and got off a good shot, but he missed at the buzzer.

"It was probably a blessing," he said, referring to getting humbled. "I had been talking so much trash in the papers about [Bobby] Knight and IU. But that loss, and getting beat in high school [by Columbus North] were the two most heartbreaking losses I ever had."

Larry Bird also experienced heartbreak in his final college game—a game that was watched by a then-record number of college basketball television viewers. He had led an otherwise ordinary Indiana State team to an undefeated season in 1978–79, having already been drafted by the Celtics. Bird had decided to go back to college after his one-year maintenance sabbatical with the town of French Lick. For two weeks he attended Northwood Institute, a junior college in nearby West Baden, before deciding he'd rather have money in his pockets than books on his desk.

At this time, Bird also became a father. His former wife—the two were married only eleven months before divorcing—gave birth to a baby daughter, Corrie. Mother and daughter never reentered Bird's life and he has remained estranged from both. When his number was retired in Boston Garden in an elaborate ceremony in February 1993, Bird did not invite his daughter, although she had written asking to be included. He also rejected her request for him to attend her high school graduation in 1995.

The ill-fated marriage wasn't the only problem going on in Bird's life at that time. In 1975, his father committed suicide. "All I can hope for," said Bird, "is that we'll meet up again." The suicide prompted Bird to seriously think about college again. Indiana State had a new coach named Bob King, who quickly made Bird his top priority, and King soon got the commitment he wanted.

At Indiana State, Bird brought instant recognition to a program that had had no prior success and was regarded with ill-disguised contempt by most basketball-wise people in the state. In his first season there (he had sat out 1975–76 as a transfer), ISU went 25-2 and finished the season ranked No. 16 in the country. The Sycamores, who had just joined the Missouri Valley Conference, were ineligible for the conference title and an automatic NCAA bid; they went to the NIT and, in a first-round game, lost to an Otis Birdsong–led Houston team, 83–82, at Hofheinz Pavilion.

The following year, Bird graced the cover of *Sports Illustrated*'s college basketball issue as the college game's best-kept secret. Two ISU cheerleaders were brought in for the photo shoot—they posed with their index fingers to closed lips. This was the pictorial equivalent of Yogi Berra's line: "That restaurant is so crowded no one goes there anymore." Bird was no longer a secret; after that issue, he was a phenom. As he put it, "That picture changed my life."

Indiana State went on to win its first 13 games (including a victory over Sichting's Purdue team) but tailed off badly and finished 22-8. Again they went to the NIT, and this time they lost to Rutgers in the second round.

By then, Bird was acknowledged to be one of the best players in the country. Because he would have been in the class of 1978 had he stayed in college at IU, he was eligible for the NBA draft. Taking advantage of the situation, the Celtics chose Bird with their first pick, the sixth overall, even though he had made it clear that he would return to ISU to get his degree and play some more basketball. The Celtics could hold his rights for a calendar year, and Red Auerbach felt the risk was worth it; the Celtics were coming off a terrible season and needed an overhaul.

What Auerbach did not know was that the club would be sold the following month, that several players would be part of the unique deal (it was actually a franchise swap), and that Larry Bird could just as easily have begun his career as an L.A. Clipper had the Clippers owner, Irv Levin, been convinced he could sign him. Five other teams had made similar judgments on draft day, refusing to risk a high pick on someone they might never be able to sign. Boston risked it because of Auerbach's willingness to do so, because the team was in trouble, and, most important of all, because they also had the eighth pick, so they could afford to take a chance.

Indiana State was more popular in Boston than the Celtics during the 1978–79 season. And for a good reason; the Sycamores won more games. (The folks in Terre Haute still refer to this season as the "Dream Season.") In Boston, Bird was making hoops fans salivate, leading ISU to a 33-0 record before losing to Magic Johnson's Michigan State team in the NCAA Finals. Bird, who played in the NCAAs with a fractured thumb, didn't play particularly well in the championship game as ISU lost 75–64. Three months later, just days before his name would go back into the draft, he signed a five-year deal with the Celtics. The negotiations had been nasty and gave Bird his first look at the underside of professional sports. But it was a decision he never regretted.

"Everyone else plays for all these other teams and they make a lot of money," he said. "And they always say they're very proud. But if you don't play for the Boston Celtics, you never played professional basketball. This is what basketball is all about. This is what every player in the world wants, whether they admit it or not. You want to be part of a family. You want to be part of a team. And the only way you can get that is to play for the Celtics. Not for a year. Or two years. But for a whole career."

He could get an argument from many today. But in 1985–86, there weren't any better places to call home if you played in the NBA.

When the Celtics reconvened in Indianapolis on New Year's night, K.C. Jones put them through a brisk workout. Sichting had gone out for an afternoon jog to shake the cobwebs, but even he was still huffing and puffing during the practice. This was January, and they knew they shouldn't feel like this. So Sichting, Bird, and others made a pact that day: no more beer for the rest of the season. There was one exception—a Super Bowl party hosted by Walton. The Patriots were in the Super Bowl that year.

The Indiana game once again showcased Dennis Johnson in a spectacular performance. He scored 29 points against the team that romanced him the previous summer. Bird had 27. The Celtics pulled away in the fourth quarter and won easily, 122–104, despite losing Danny Ainge with a sprained ankle and Walton with a fractured tooth after he was whacked in the mouth by Steve Stipanovich.

Two nights later, Bird played a marvelous game, recording 29 points, eight steals, and 10 rebounds as the Celtics beat the Nets in Boston, 129–117. Ainge watched from the bench, nursing his ankle sprain, but Walton was back, going 22 minutes. Sichting, given a start and by now the unquestioned third guard in the rotation, responded with 17 points, his season high, making eight of nine shots from the field. He also had six assists.

It was becoming increasingly clear that Bird's back problems were pretty much resolved and that he basically had bottomed out on Christmas Day, along with the team. At that point, he was shooting 44 percent from the field as compared to his previous career average of 50. He would have a couple of other regrettable shooting nights the rest of the season, but they were rare.

The victory over the Nets made it four straight for the Celtics as they headed to Detroit for another showdown with the hated Pistons. Ainge was back, but not 100 percent. He hobbled around for seventeen minutes, having no impact on the outcome of the game. Robert Parish was ejected 16 minutes into the game for taking a swing at Bill Laimbeer. The game went down to the wire and the Pistons led 111–109 when Bird hit an apparent game-tying shot.

Out of nowhere, however, referee Jess Thompson called a blocking foul on Kevin McHale, who was trying to establish position for a rebound. "I felt like I got hit by a truck," said the overly dramatic Kelly Tripucka, the alleged victim of the McHale block. McHale, enraged, chased Thompson all over the court, pleading his case to no avail. Years later, when reminded of the play, McHale said, with a touch of smugness, "You'll notice Jess Thompson isn't around anymore." He wasn't. But he was there that night and he was not going to change his mind, either. The Pistons hit three key free throws down the stretch to seal the victory.

The following night the Celtics returned home to play the Cleveland Cavaliers. Before the game Cavs coach George Karl was asked by reporters for his view on the call on McHale.

"It was, without a doubt, one of the worst last-10-seconds calls I have ever seen," he said.

Ainge and Walton (who had the tooth pulled and some bridgework done) were both unavailable for the Cavs game. It didn't matter. Cleveland had lost a lot of its spunk from the year before and the Celtics, still mad about the Detroit game, took it out on Karl & Co., defeating them 126–95—the Celtics' largest victory margin of the season. It was Cleveland's twentieth straight loss at Boston Garden. Bird, continuing his "comeback," scored 25 points.

While January was the month that the cloud lifted over Bird, it was also the month that Boston fans got to see the best of Bill Walton. Through the Cleveland game, the thirty-fourth game of the season, Walton had three games where he managed 10 or more rebounds. In the next 17 games, he would have five. In the last three weeks of January, there were three particularly significant games for the Celtics. They won them all. And Bill Walton was huge in each one of them.

The first game was January's version of the Christmas game, only this time, the Celtics played the role of comeback spoilers. The Celtics had won four straight since the Detroit game and were headed to Atlanta for a meeting with the Hawks. Atlanta, desperate for respect, clearly regarded this game with extreme importance, drawing the largest crowd in the history of the franchise and even importing the mascot of the hated Lakers, Dancing Barry, to gin up the proceedings.

As Barry put it beforehand, "The people of Atlanta need me. I'm 6-2 lifetime against the Celtics."

For a while, it looked as though Barry would be 7-2 when he returned home to Los Angeles. The Hawks, energized by their crowd, bolted to an astonishing 70–47 lead in the second quarter. As they built their lead, they began to talk trash nonstop. What other public disgrace could befall Boston? First, the dreaded Lakers mascot; now, the contemptible Eddie Johnson slinging insults at them?

The deficit was 22 at the half. Walton remembers the locker room was totally silent. No one had to say a thing. "Everyone was mad," McHale said. The Celtics were mortified at what had happened in the first half, and the only solace was that there were still 24 minutes left to play.

"K.C. didn't say a word," Walton recalled. "He literally did not say a word. Then, when it was time to go, he said, 'Okay.'"

The Celtics went out for warmups and Bird approached one of the referees who happened to be standing in front of the Boston bench. His message was simple: "We're not going to quit. Make sure you don't quit, either."

Bird then set the tone for the second half by scoring 17 in the third quarter. Scott Wedman also came up big, scoring 21 as the Celtics cut the Hawks' lead to eight by the end of the third quarter. In the fourth, the Celtics took the lead. Atlanta regrouped and regained the lead, but, with the game tied at 112–112, Dominique Wilkins went to the line with 66 seconds to play. Shortly before shooting, he saw Bird give him the choke sign. He missed them both and the game eventually went into overtime.

Walton, who matched his season high of 28 minutes, was huge in the overtime, breaking the final tie on a tip-in and then blocking an Eddie Johnson shot on the Hawks' next possession. He finished with 11 points, eight rebounds, and four blocked shots. Bird, who scored 41, clinched this most rewarding victory with four free throws. The Celtics had now won nine out of

10 since Christmas and had a few days to not only savor this special one, but also to get ready for the next game. And the next game was most definitely not just another game: the Lakers would be making their only regular season visit to the Boston Garden. Few expected the Lakers not to be back in June, but in mid-January 1986, a Celtics-Lakers matchup was as good as it got.

The Lakers and Celtics watched each other throughout the season. "We kept an eye on them," Magic Johnson explained, "just like they kept an eye on us. They thought they were better than us. We thought we were better."

In January, it was hard to make a case that either one had an edge. The Lakers had broken from the blocks looking like they would easily defend their title, winning 24 of their first 27 games. Ennui, not any team, appeared to be their biggest enemy. Even later in the season, when they won their sixtieth game, Clyde Drexler noted that "they looked bored stiff."

Coach Pat Riley worked hard that year to fight the complacency he saw setting in as the Lakers, without a serious threat in the Western Conference, mowed down the competition. "Anytime you stop striving to get better, you're bound to get worse," he wrote in his book, *The Winner Within*. "There's no such thing as simply holding on to what you've got."

Los Angeles entered the Celtics game with a 32-7 record. The Celtics were 30-8. The Lakers arrived with a full complement of bodies, but Kareem Abdul-Jabbar was missing his jersey; he had to wear No. 50 instead of his customary 33.

Abdul-Jabbar might have had a different number, but he was still Kareem. That was important to Walton, who has always spoken glowingly, almost reverently, of Abdul-Jabbar. To play well against him was one of Walton's fondest wishes. To be recognized by Abdul-Jabbar for what he was and what he had been would also have been nice, too.

"When I think of Jabbar, I mean, that was always my man," Walton said. "I spent my whole life trying to beat that guy, no matter what I was doing. He would always be on my mind. The night before we played the Lakers, I went to bed early and dreamed I was going to kill him. I just knew I had to play my best all the time if we were going to have a chance to win against them. And I loved to play those games. Kareem just plays his game. He's the best I ever played against, by far. And everything I did when I played basketball was so that I would be able to beat him."

Abdul-Jabbar never understated Walton's basketball abilities or was dismissive of him as a basketball player. Kareem felt, however, that the adulation Walton received was based in part on his race. He also felt that that praise diminished *his* own basketball accomplishments.

In his 1983 autobiography, *Giant Steps,* Abdul-Jabbar praised Walton's game, calling him "a Great White Hope that was legit, a white man with the chance to show the niggers how to play basketball." Later, he added, "What I found offensive was the way our relative talents were treated. I knew that white players got better press—that was obvious everywhere—but I was angry when, in order to exalt Bill Walton, the media started knocking me. If he played well against me, I was over the hill; if I excelled against him, it was no big deal. . . . I resented people using him to knock me. When he started playing well, the television commentators and newspaper columnists were tripping all over themselves saying, 'Forget Kareem, it's Bill.' They could promote Bill all they wanted; he deserved it. But I had been Most Valuable Player four of the last six years—one trophy would be the highlight of most players' careers—and I wanted the respect I had earned."

Walton was supposed to be the difference this year, the player who would push the Celtics past the Lakers in June. But he apparently decided January wasn't a bad time to do it, either, and he delivered a memorable performance that night against L.A.

The instant Walton stepped onto the floor at the Garden, one could sense that he was ready. He blocked an Abdul-Jabbar shot. He quickly got two rebounds. And on that night, he would

cram 11 points (on 5-of-6 shooting), eight rebounds, four assists, and seven blocked shots into only 16 minutes of play. Talk
about impact! When he was removed from the game with 7:55
to play, the Celtics had the game well in hand (the final score
was 110–95) and the Garden exploded.

"It's about time he did something," Robert Parish deadpanned. "He hasn't been playing for three years."

The ribbing never, ever stopped on the Celtics. It wavered only
in its viciousness, or, as Walton knew, its feigned viciousness.
Every Celtic who regularly engaged in Bill-bashing—the main
culprits being Bird, McHale, and Ainge—also knew how critical
he was to their season. But that didn't stop them from abusing
Walton relentlessly. And Walton loved it. He also understood it.

"That goes on on every team," he said. "What was so nice
about the Celtics was that you could do it in the media as well.
You have to be careful about doing that stuff publicly if
the other players don't have confidence in their abilities. The
camaraderie and friendships you have on the team are so special, but the danger of it being in the media is so devastating
that it can destroy a team if the guys don't realize it's all in fun.
A lot of guys are bothered by somebody saying something bad
about them. But it didn't bother me. I could care less. It was fun.
And few people have as quick a wit, or as creative a wit, as Larry
Bird or Kevin McHale. Those were unique circumstances."

Ainge, who before Walton's arrival was the target of most of
the barbs, now gloried in his new role as a verbal dart thrower.
Walton, Ainge suggested, looked a lot like Rocky Dennis, the de-
formed child in the movie *Mask*. McHale teased Walton about
everything from herbal teas to drugs to radical politics. Walton's
age was a frequent topic as well, McHale said he vaguely recalled
seeing Walton on a grainy, black-and-white television picture.
And Bird, always the sensitive one, got on Walton one day in
practice for stuttering.

"You and I have something in common," Bird told him.

"What's that?" Walton asked.

"We both need therapists. I need a back therapist. You need a speech therapist."

McHale later said if he could do it all over again, he would re-assemble the 1985–86 team and play year after year and never tire of the companionship. Ainge concurred.

"It was," Ainge said, "as loose as any team could possibly be. There was just so much confidence and fun. Everyone got along. Everyone liked each other. I think that looseness allowed us to win a lot of games along the way. It helped us get through the season. You need to have fun to get through a long season."

The Celtics were greeted everywhere like rock stars. Fans—the Green People—waited for them in hotel lobbies and sur-rounded the team bus as it left for the games. Fans would be waiting for the bus when it arrived at the arena. The Celtics fans in the stands, especially those in Western Conference cities, where the Celtics only made one visit a year, often outnumbered those of the home team. Even in the Los Angeles Forum, there was a sizable Celtics contingent.

Virtually every game they played was sold out. They were on national television as often as possible, darlings of the network for their ability to attract viewers. The Celtics had always been an institution in the NBA, but in the 1980s they were something more. They were icons.

"We had a following that was not seen by many teams," Den-nis Johnson said. "People would bring their little kids to games just so they could see us. We'd walk down the stairs and people would be waiting for us at the hotel. We were one of those teams that loved to be hated. Danny and Kevin were picking on Bill. I've never been big on [team as] family, but this team was. It hung together."

The outlet for their competitive zeal was practice. The ses-sions often bordered on the ferocious. The five starters played the reserves, then known as the Green Team, and careful ac-counting was taken of the results. Insults abounded. McHale, for instance, would block a shot by David Thirdkill, control the ball, and then turn around and hand it back to the surprised player: "Here David, try again. Let's see something better than that weak stuff." The taunting infuriated Thirdkill, but it was typical of the way the team practiced.

"Practices were a lot of fun and real competitive," Greg Kite said. "We took a lot of joy in beating the first team and yelling at Chris Ford [the referee] when he made a bad call. We would keep a running tally and the Green Team would always be ahead until Larry, Kevin, and Danny would start cheating. We all joked around and got on each other's case, but we were serious when we played."

Scott Wedman recalled a post-scrimmage game of one-on-one he had with Bird. Usually, Bird would control the game and he would never hesitate to let Wedman know that. But on this day, Wedman, arguably the team's best pure shooter, was ahead. Before he could close out the game, a camera crew came into the gym to film a little of the practice. Inspired, Bird turned to Wedman and said, "You're in trouble now." He proceeded to make five straight shots. Game over.

"You never wanted to leave the floor if you were losing, so you would think of other things," Johnson said. "You'd say, 'C'mon chump, let's play one-on-one. I'm going to get something out of this.' It was stuff like that that kept us together."

Sichting said, "When I look back on that year, even more than the winning, it was the practices that we had that stand out in my mind. They were so competitive and we used to keep a tally. And the second team had an advantage after games because the starters were still a little tired. Bill would accuse K.C. of giving the starters a break on calls and stuff. Meanwhile, Bill's kids would be running all over the place, Kevin would be yapping with Danny about what was in the paper. It was wild. The next year, no kids were allowed. But that year, it was anything goes."

As long as they continued to win, the goofiness was tolerated and even encouraged. "It was," McHale said, "honestly just about as much fun as you can have playing basketball."

A younger, hipper Bill Walton in his early days with the Portland Trail Blazers. His signing by the Celtics in the summer of 1985 solidified an already impressive team.

1

2

The man Walton replaced: forward Cedric Maxwell, whose falling out with Red Auerbach led to his bitter departure.

4

Sly Williams, whose ailments and disappearances proved a pain to the team and to himself.

3

The addition of Jerry Sichting gave the Celtics a solid backcourt player off the bench.

5

The Celtics' first-round draft pick in 1985 was Sam Vincent of Michigan State. Although he had hoped to make an impact on the team as the season progressed, Vincent found himself watching more than playing.

6　K.C. Jones *(at right)* provided the direction that would lead the Celtics to their sixteenth championship.

7

The man behind the whole operation:
Red Auerbach.

8

One-half of Boston's awesome back-court: Dennis Johnson could beat you with both explosive offense and smothering defense.

Danny Ainge, Dennis Johnson's back-court mate, showing just one of the ways his style of play frustrated opposing players, coaches, and fans alike.

The Big Three:
Larry Bird *(right)*,
Kevin McHale *(below left)*,
and Robert Parish *(below right)*.

When Walton wasn't listening to the Grateful Dead, he was all business on the basketball court. His contributions to the Celtics that year earned him the Sixth Man Award.

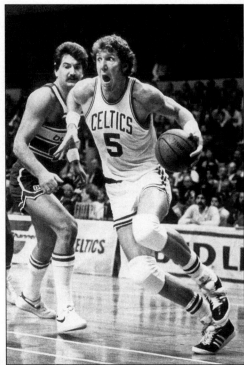

13

14

When McHale briefly struggled with a strained Achilles tendon, K.C. turned to Scott Wedman to help out the team.

15

For Rick Carlisle, October was his month to shine. He edged out Carlos Clark and David Thirdkill for the twelfth spot on the Celtics' roster.

16

Sly Williams's early departure made room for David Thirdkill. The scar under Thirdkill's right eye only bolstered "The Sheriff's" reputation as a tough defensive specialist.

17

Hard-working Greg Kite, exhibiting the fierce determination that kept him employed in the NBA for twelve years.

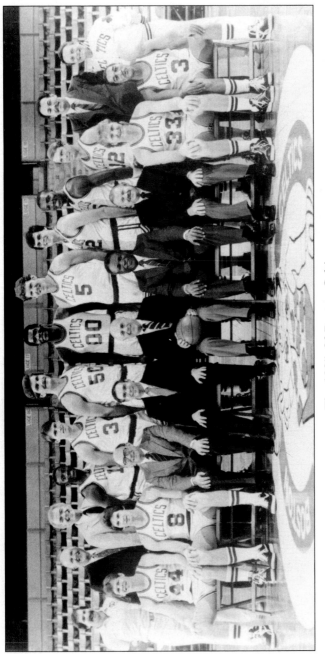

The 1985–86 Boston Celtics.

Front row (from left to right): Danny Ainge, Scott Wedman, Alan N. Cohen (Vice Chairman and Treasurer), Jan Volk (General Manager), Red Auerbach, K.C. Jones, Don F. Gaston (Chairman), Larry Bird, Dennis Johnson.
Back row (from left to right): Wayne Lebeaux (Equipment Manager), Dr. Thomas F. Silva, Jim Rodgers (Assistant Coach), Sam Vincent, Rick Carlisle, Greg Kite, Robert Parish, Bill Walton, Kevin McHale, David Thirdkill, Jerry Sichting, Chris Ford (Assistant Coach), Ray Melchiorre (Trainer).

The fun for McHale was about to end for a while. Two nights after the big victory over the Lakers, he was unable to play against the Warriors. He had been suffering from a sore left Achilles tendon and had shot an uncharacteristic 3-of-14 against the Lakers. He had missed only three games in the prior five seasons and had continued to play, hoping things would improve. "I guess they didn't," he shrugged.

The Celtics could never hope to replace McHale in the long run; he was simply too valuable a player and, in Walton's opinion, was en route to a possible MVP season. But the beauty and strength of the 1985–86 Celtics was their depth and variety. With McHale out, K.C. Jones turned to Scott Wedman, a proven veteran and former All-Star forward who quietly had learned to live with his role. It was a process that did not come easily to Wedman, but with him in the lineup, the Celtics hardly missed a beat. He could not duplicate McHale's inside scoring, but he gave the team another deadly shooter from the outside. It was exactly why he was there.

It took Scott Wedman some time to get comfortable in Boston. He had been an All-Star in Kansas City, a highly touted free agent who signed for big money in Cleveland, and now, ten years into his pro career, he was strictly a backup player. What made it even more difficult was that the player ahead of him on the depth chart at small forward was Larry Bird. (Bird moved to power forward when McHale was injured.)

"My first year there [1982–83], Larry was relentless, he really was," Wedman said. "I don't know if he'd ever admit it, but I don't think he was too thrilled about my making more money than he was. I had never been around a team that talked trash like they did and it was constant from Larry. He would score on me in practice and then say, 'He's too slow. He's too short. He can't guard me.' I was absolutely stunned. It was a very tough year."

By nature, Wedman was not a super-aggressive individual. It

was a character trait he struggled with throughout his career. "I had to work on having a kick-butt attitude. It was not always on the surface with me and it was the biggest problem I had."

Scott Wedman was almost always laid-back. He was raised on a 100-acre farm in Harper, Kansas, and learned how to shoot baskets by hanging a rim on the family barn. "You don't go in for too many layups when the rim is hanging on a barn," Wedman said. His father, Tom, worked for Boeing as an engineer in Wichita. Scott and his big brother, Mike, were members of the 4-H Club, drove tractors, and learned how to milk cows. The family moved to Denver, briefly moved back to Kansas, and then resettled in Denver by the time Scott was in the sixth grade. His midget basketball team won the city championship. At Mullen High in Denver, Wedman tried out for football. He was 5-6, and during a scrimmage with the varsity, he was taken down hard by a linebacker.

"He rang my bell. I saw stars," Wedman said. "I switched to cross-country after that, but basketball was still my main thing."

He was a late bloomer. He was a reserve on the B team as a freshman in high school, a junior varsity reserve as a sophomore, a junior varsity starter as a junior, and, finally, a varsity starter as a senior. He averaged 19 points a game as a senior and made the all-state team.

Only two colleges offered him scholarships, Wyoming and Colorado. The Wedman family wrote a letter to Kansas State but never got a response. Wyoming was interested in him mainly because Wedman's high school coach, Rick Egloff, had played football there. Wedman visited Wyoming, where the recruiting pitch included a fishing trip with the head coach. He liked Wyoming, but he wanted to join his brother, an accomplished pole vaulter, at Colorado.

The University of Colorado wasn't exactly Basketball U. It had little history of postseason achievement, something that still holds true today. Occasionally, a bona fide NBA player will surface from Boulder—Wedman is a prime example—but the

list of CU alums in the pros barely covers a page in the basketball media guide, and that includes bios, pictures, and stats. The
coach at the time, the venerable Russell "Sox" Walseth, had a
hard time recruiting good players because the school had terrible basketball facilities. "But it was a beautiful campus and we
tried to sell that," Walseth said. "Still, it was hard."

Walseth and Wedman had met at a summer basketball camp
prior to Wedman's senior year of high school. On the last day of
camp, as the parents were coming in to pick up the children,
Wedman asked Walseth to work with him. All of a sudden, every
shot went in. Over a five-minute span, Wedman could not miss.

"It was incredible, but everything clicked at once," Wedman
recalled.

Walseth agreed, but added, "I think he always had it. I don't
think I had anything much to do with it."

That was a defining moment in Wedman's life. He now had
the confidence he lacked in high school. He had read John
McPhee's book about Bill Bradley, *A Sense of Where You Are,* and,
like Bradley, shot 300 balls a day. He was offered a scholarship
that Walseth admitted would not have been offered if Wedman
had not lived in Colorado.

Wedman enjoyed his years in Boulder, but the basketball
team was horrible. In his three varsity seasons, the best Colorado
could muster was a 13-13 record in his junior year. It was after
that year, when Wedman had tied for second in scoring in the
Big Eight, that he started to hear about interest from NBA
teams. He continued his strong play as a senior, but the Buf-
faloes were 9-17, and he missed the last three games with an ankle injury.

Two weeks before the 1974 NBA draft, the Kansas City Kings
flew him in for an interview and for a medical evaluation of his
ankle. They were also interested in Keith (later Jamaal) Wilkes,
Bill Walton's teammate at UCLA, but passed on him, selecting
Wedman with their first pick, No. 6 overall. (Wilkes went to the
Warriors at No. 11.) Wedman gladly returned to the Midwest, ig-

noring overtures from Memphis in the American Basketball Association.

In his first year in the NBA, Wedman was named to the All-Rookie team, averaging 11.1 points a game. He also became a vegetarian. Ever since he could remember, his mother had been a health food fanatic, serving the children a strange concoction every morning.

"It had molasses, wheat germ, eggs, orange juice. That was the root of my health food concerns," Wedman said.

He is still a vegetarian today and his Boston teammates were merciless at times in kidding him about his dietary habits. Walton, for one, said nothing. He once had been a vegetarian, but by 1986 had done a 180 degree turn, to the point where he was doing commercials for a Boston steak house. But the others had their fun.

"We would always kid Scotty that he had an advantage over us," McHale said. "After games, we'd go out and eat and have a few beers and he would go home and do his yoga and then go to sleep. So when he beat us in practice, we'd always say there had to be an asterisk because it wasn't fair. Larry would tell him, 'I'd like to see you come out with us after a game and drink as much beer as we do and then be able to practice like that.'"

Wedman brought his own bottled water on the road. When he was with Cleveland, he would not practice in a particular gym until he was convinced there was no asbestos in the walls. He ate at health food restaurants—the Good Earth was a particular favorite—but he never proselytized. He just went his own way.

"He was just so different from the rest of us, but truly a great guy," McHale said. "I remember going out to eat with him once and the waiter mixed up our orders. He got a chicken burrito and halfway through it, he figured it out. I offered to switch with him, but it was too late. He was so upset that he had eaten a piece of chicken.

"So we're on the bus to practice later and I told him I didn't think he looked so good. I'm teasing him the whole time and he got so mad we almost got into a fight in practice. He actually took a swing at me. I said, 'Whoa, Scotty, I'm just kidding. But no more meat for you. It turns you into a killer.'"

Wedman had been a killer of sorts in Kansas City. He spent seven seasons with the Kings and, with the exception of a 1979 auto accident in which he was thrown from his Porsche and spent five days in the hospital with a bruised lung and separated shoulder, he has nothing but good memories of the team and his years there. The 1981 team made it to the conference finals despite injuries to Phil Ford and Otis Birdsong. Wedman and Ernie Grunfeld had to man the backcourt, but the Kings lost to the Rockets, who would later lose to the Celtics in six games in the 1981 NBA Finals.

That summer, Wedman was a free agent, and Kansas City was strapped for money. Both Birdsong and Wedman got huge offers to leave the Kings. Birdsong went to New Jersey and Wedman struck a five-year deal with the Cavaliers worth $700,000 a year. The Kings could not afford to keep him and Wedman, reluctantly but a lot richer, left Kansas City.

"I did it for the money," Wedman said. "I had no desire to leave Kansas City and I would have stayed if they had offered me $400,000. But the owners had trouble making up their minds and Jeff Cohen [the Kings' GM] had his hands tied."

Before taking the Cleveland offer, Wedman called Kings coach Cotton Fitzsimmons for his advice. His response was go for it. "In five to ten years, you won't regret it," Fitzsimmons told him. Wedman went, but very soon he did regret it. Cleveland was utter chaos.

In his only full season with the Cavs, 1981–82, Wedman played for four coaches and had 23 different teammates. The Cavs were owned by Ted Stepien, who spent wildly and mindlessly, and then wondered why his team didn't play better. The Cavs soon became a laughingstock around the league and, even worse, by 1983 were on the verge of bankruptcy. Enter the Celtics.

Boston had been eyeing Wedman for some time. Owner Harry Mangurian was a big Wedman fan and coach Bill Fitch thought Wedman could help a team that was starting to unravel. After talking with Cleveland, Mangurian and general Manager Jan Volk believed the Cavaliers were a week away from going belly-up. The Celtics agreed to front Cleveland the money they owed Wedman for the rest of the season; they got Cleveland to defer the rest of the pay until later; and then got Wedman to redo his contract so that he would cost the Celtics only $400,000. "I never heard a word about the trade until it happened," Wedman said. "I thought I was doomed to Cleveland for five years."

"I think economically it saved them," Volk said. "They were on the verge of bankruptcy and were quite desperate."

The Celtics sent Darren Tillis, their seldom-used, oft-forgotten first-round pick in the 1983 draft to the Cavaliers for Wedman. Tillis had gone to college at Cleveland State, so it was sort of a homecoming for him. He was also a lot cheaper. Once Wedman agreed to redo his deal, he passed a physical at the Cleveland Clinic and drove with Volk to the Coliseum. By sheer coincidence, the Celtics and Cavaliers were playing there that night. There, trainer Ray Melchiorre painted Wedman's sneakers green and gave him jersey No. 20. He hit everything in warmups, and felt good going into the game, but he never got to play. Even worse, the Cavaliers beat the Celtics.

The last few months of the 1982–83 season were difficult for Wedman. He rarely played and the Celtics were on a downhill slide. He had trouble fitting in, getting accepted, and at times wondered why he was even there.

"It was the first time I had not played," he said. "I thought the team was tight and, with Larry, it was almost like a hazing. Everything he did was good-natured, but it was at my expense. He was having a good time. I wasn't. Finally, one time we were in Atlanta discussing the labor situation [there was a potential strike looming] and I fried Larry. We had to have a vote to see if we would strike, and Larry wouldn't raise his hand. He said he wanted to talk to his agent first. I said, 'What's the matter, Larry? Can't you think for yourself?' He never said a word, but on the way out of the meeting, Rick Robey came up to me, and Larry called to him, saying, 'Don't talk to him, he's not our friend.'

"The next year, I started to figure out how it all went. And I started to talk trash back. We would go at each other in practice and he'd throw out a compliment every six months or so. From him, that was pretty good."

With McHale out, Wedman made the most of his chance against the Warriors in his first start, scoring 21 points and grabbing 13 rebounds. The Celtics won easily, 135–114, and David Thirdkill came off the bench to score 20 points and collect eight rebounds in 20 minutes. McHale watched it all from the bench, unaware that his absence was going to last almost a month. But even though his Achilles was slow to improve, the same could not be said for the Celtics. They were starting to find their groove, losing only once all month. After their big comeback against the Hawks and their convincing win over the Lakers, Boston's third big game was a Super Bowl Sunday matchup with the 76ers.

On most any other occasion, this would have been big news in Boston. But on this day, everyone's attention was in New Orleans, where the Patriots were playing the Chicago Bears in Super Bowl XX. Not even a Boston-Philadelphia game could make a dent in the hysteria sweeping the region. Two days before the game, when asked who he thought would win the Super Bowl, Greg Kite deadpanned, "Who's playing?"

Philadelphia had won 17 of 19 games when they arrived in Boston Garden that Sunday afternoon. The 76ers were no longer a strong rival to the Celtics in the East, as had been the case in the early 1980s. Philadelphia's nucleus had grown old while the Celtics were just reaching their prime. But they did have largemouth Charles Barkley, and he always made for an interesting game. They also had some pretty good players and would go on to win 54 games that season, but they weren't the

Sixers of old and the Celtics would prevail after a hard-fought game.

The Sixers led by 13 in the third quarter when Bird made three big three-point baskets, including a 35-footer to end the quarter. That hoop climaxed a 21–4 run that gave the Celtics an 82–78 lead heading into the fourth. The Sixers reclaimed the lead but the Celtics pulled it out at the end, winning, 105–103. It was to be their closest call at home over the final three months. Walton had another great game, chalking up 19 points, 13 rebounds, and two blocked shots in just 25 minutes. Bird finished with 28, despite woeful (9-of-25) shooting.

Philadelphia, which now trailed Boston by five and a half games, was not willing to make any concession speeches after the game. Far from it. The voluble Barkley wanted everyone to know the score.

"They cannot beat us. They cannot beat us," he said. "I honestly think they know they cannot beat us. One through 12, Cleveland has more talent than Boston. Anyone who knows basketball knows that." The Celtics were already 3-1 against Philadelphia to that point, so the Celtics (and everyone else) were a bit amused by what Barkley had to say.

"Tell Charles to keep yapping," Danny Ainge said.

In the same locker room, the estimable Julius Erving was asked to assess the talent on the Celtics. "They've had stronger teams," he said. "But they may make a liar out of me yet."

The Celtics finished the month of January with a 97–88 victory at Washington. Wedman started his fourth straight game and had 24 points, prompting the Bullets' sage, Jeff Ruland, to note, "The way Wedman was shooting, we wished McHale was back." Bullets coach Gene Shue observed that when the Celtics go to their bench, "There are no weaknesses."

The following morning, a Washington newspaper led its story of the game with the headline "Wedman Leads Celtics to Victory." Larry Bird walked by and saw Wedman reading an account of the game. Noticing the headline, Bird pointed to it and told Wedman, "Enjoy it while you can, because that will never happen again." Bird was back at last, both on the floor and as the consummate needler. He would hit full stride in February as the Celtics headed west, but before doing so, he wanted to make a little history, and deepen his already deep pockets, by doing something that came naturally to him: shooting three-pointers.

CHAPTER SEVEN

February:
The King and His
Courtmates

In the fall of 1985, the NBA decided to liven up its All-Star proceedings with a new event for its Saturday program. They already had a Slam Dunk contest and a "Legends" game, both of
which had been successfully introduced in Denver in 1984. The
following year, however, the league decided that there should
be another contest: the Long Distance Shootout. To everyone
else, it was known as the Three-Point Shot Contest.

The contest was the brainchild of Rick Welts, at that time the
league's vice president of communications. The NBA arranged
to have the contest format tested at two CBA games and was
pleased with the crowd reaction. Larry Bird was among the first
to be invited. Once invited, Bird practiced with a fury, salivating
over the prospect of winning the inaugural event and the
$10,000 that went with it. At the time, Bird was earning $1.8 mil-
lion a year and hundreds of thousands more in endorsements,
but the sheer prospect of picking up $10,000 for shooting three-
pointers was like found money to him.

Bird was an obvious choice for the competition. He had
made the first three-pointer in All-Star Game history and was

among the league leaders at the time in three-point attempts and percentage. But there also was a touch of irony in his selection because Bird was never an enthusiastic supporter of the three-point basket, although he rarely hesitated to use it to his advantage. He always felt that if you were up two at the end of a game, you shouldn't lose to a basket.

And while Bird was the perfect team player, the prospect of individual competition fired him up even more. "I definitely want to win and do my best," he said. Kevin McHale added, "Once I heard that Larry could win ten grand for shooting basketballs all afternoon, I knew it was over."

But before Bird got his chance, the Celtics still had some business to take care of prior to the All-Star break. They won three games in four days to push their winning streak to 13 games and their record to 38-8 before the break. They began with a 114–101 home win over Seattle, a victory that took on a bit of added importance since the Celtics had previously acquired the SuperSonics' first-round pick in the 1986 draft in a deal for Gerald Henderson. Anything the Celtics could do to make the pick a lottery pick would be a big help in the long run. Boston got off to a terrible start, trailing by 21 in the first half before rallying to win going away. Two nights later, McHale made a brief return (12 minutes) and went 6-for-6 from the floor against the Bucks in a 112–93 victory in Milwaukee. The Celtics shot 61 percent from the field and had a team total of 33 assists.

Afterward, McHale lamented about his injury, "It's just not healing as quickly as it's supposed to be. I don't know." Even without McHale, Milwaukee coach Don Nelson could not figure out how to contain the Celtics. "I don't know how to play this team at this point," he said after the loss. "I consider myself a bright coach, but I'm out of ideas if they play like that. They made us look like a high school team and we're not. The Celtics are just awesome."

McHale did not play the following night at home in a routine dispatching of the Bullets. Instead, Walton stepped up his game, collecting 13 points and 17 rebounds in only 28 minutes.

The 17 rebounds constituted a season high for Walton, but he saw it as nothing unusual. The year before, he had led the NBA in rebounds-per-minutes, and he wasn't far off the lead in 1985–86, solidifying his claim as perhaps the game's greatest defensive rebounder.

"You've got to figure out how the ball's going to come off the rim and move to it. You can't wait for it to come to you," Walton said, explaining his rebounding theory. "You can tell where the ball is going. That's how you get it. You see the shot, you know exactly where the basket is, and you tell yourself, 'Okay, that ball is short or that ball is going to hit the rim.' You can tell by the arc, spin, and by the guy's motion where it's going to hit and where it's going to bounce.

"I like to shag for guys in practice. I watch the shots and figure out where the ball is going. When the ball is on the floor, you go to the floor and get it, don't you? It's the same thing with rebounding. You move to the basket area. It also helps if you have large arms."

And it helps if you're seven feet tall. Or taller. Walton always referred to himself as 6-11, even though he towered over Robert Parish, who was seven feet, in the Celtics' team picture. It was just something he never, ever wanted to officially recognize. He thought people viewed seven-footers as freaks.

"I am 6-11," he said unconvincingly. "How do I know that? Because the last time I was measured, I was 6-11. That was my sophomore year at UCLA. I never went back to the measuring table."

At one point in the 1985–86 season, someone remarked to Walton about the size of Tito Horford, then playing in college at Louisiana State University. "He's huge. He's as big as I am," Walton replied. Then, before he could be caught, Walton added, "Yeah, he's 6-11." Horford was a legitimate seven-footer.

"It's not how tall you are," Walton said. "It's how tall you play. Kevin was 6-11 and played 7-5. And anyway, everyone under 6-10 is the same size—short."

There was nothing short about the Celtics' winning streak,

however. After the Washington victory, much was made about the 13-game streak, already the longest in the league that season and the fifth longest in team history (their best was 18 in 1982). There wasn't much else to talk about; the Celtics had all but clinched the Atlantic Division title, now leading second-place Philadelphia by 10 games in the loss column. The streak featured wins over the Lakers and 76ers and two games (Seattle and Atlanta) in which the Celtics rallied from deficits of more than 20 points. Six of the wins had come without McHale as Scott Wedman stepped in and averaged 19 points a game while shooting 52 percent and committing just two turnovers in 199 minutes.

On Thursday, February 6, the Celtics went their separate ways for the All-Star break. They would reconvene four days later in Sacramento to play the Kings. The coaching staff, by virtue of having the best record, headed to Dallas to coach the Eastern Conference team. That team featured Bird, selected as a starter, as well as McHale and Parish, who were chosen by the coaches as reserves. For McHale, the trip represented an opportunity to test his still-sore Achilles. For Parish, who would have rather had the time off, the All-Star Game was a necessary evil. And for Bird, the trip presented an opportunity to add to his already substantial cash flow, something he was ready, willing, and eager to do.

The NBA had selected eight participants for the first Long Distance Shootout, held in Reunion Arena, one of Bird's favorite buildings (or, as he called them, gyms). Each player had 60 seconds to shoot 25 balls that were stationed around the three-point arc in five ball racks. Bird had already been practicing his rhythm after practices, helped (and needled) by Scott Wedman and Danny Ainge.

"Scotty and I both felt we were better three-point shooters than Larry," Ainge said. "We were razzing him because of his name and that was the only reason he was going to be in the contest. But he really was the third best three-point shooter on our team. And we gave him a hard time about it."

Bird was the only pure forward in the contest, although Dallas's hometown favorite Dale Ellis occasionally played the position. The other six contestants were Sleepy Floyd of Golden State, Craig Hodges of Milwaukee, Norm Nixon of the Clippers, Trent Tucker of the Knicks, Kyle Macy of Chicago, and Leon Wood of Washington. Bird began working them over verbally as soon as he put his bag down in the locker room.

Wood, who spent a lot of time practicing three-pointers before games, was Bird's first target. Wood had mentioned to Bird that he thought the old ABA balls, the ones colored red, white, and blue, were hard to handle. (The last ball in each five-ball rack was like the old ABA ball and it counted for two points instead of one.) Bird said he couldn't agree more and wondered aloud how either one of them could expect to compete, much less win, if they had to shoot such slippery balls. He also reminded Wood constantly about Wood's shooting slump. Predictably, Wood faltered and lost in the first round.

Then Bird stood up and announced that everyone else in the room was competing for second place. Did anyone care to be the runner-up? No one answered. Several players laughed. Bird shot back, "You're all playing for second place because I am going to win."

Bird's first-round opponent was Sleepy Floyd. Bird had been concerned about getting off 25 shots in a minute, but had no problem doing that against Floyd. Bird beat him 16–13, and was just starting to warm up. In the second round, Bird, still in his warmup jacket, eliminated Trent Tucker to advance to the final round. He then watched Dale Ellis and Craig Hodges go into overtime; by the time Hodges prevailed, he was already feeling tired.

The final round wasn't even close. Bird, who by then had taken off his warmup jacket (at the suggestion of John Havlicek, who was in town for the Legends game), missed his opener and then made 11 straight, finishing with a score of 24, double that of Hodges.

Bird was cocky and jubilant after winning. He strode triumphantly into the interview room and proclaimed, "I am the new Three Point King! And the ones who didn't think I could win can go to hell. My teammates got me pumped up. They didn't think I could do it."

Asked what he would do with the money, Bird responded that he would make another donation to his favorite charity: the Larry Bird fund. (The year before, the players had donated their All-Star earnings to famine relief in Africa. A year later, there was still famine in Africa but the All-Stars kept their money this time.)

"Hey, this is better than the Slam Dunk contest because everyone can jump but not everyone can shoot threes," Bird said. "I'd rather win the MVP, but this is more exciting. I'm on Cloud 9. I'm going to shoot threes all day tomorrow."

He shot four in the All-Star Game, making two. He ended up with 23 points, eight rebounds, five assists, and seven steals in 35 minutes as the Eastern team won, 139–132. Parish, getting his wish from coach K.C. Jones, played only seven minutes and did not attempt a shot.

But the big news for Celtics fans that day was that Kevin McHale went 20 minutes, his first basketball activity in five days. McHale had six points and 10 rebounds and it seemed that the unexpected performance marked an end to his enforced idleness.

"I really didn't think playing in the All-Star Game was going to be that big of a deal," McHale said years later. "It didn't bother me at all that day. I played, what, 20 minutes? And it was fine. Plus, I really wanted to get an idea of what it was like to be running again."

No one thought much about it until the following day. The Celtics gathered in Sacramento to begin their annual February swing, a seven-game, ten-day trip that would take them in and out of California on three separate occasions. Bird continued to brag about his Saturday triumph, making him even more insufferable than usual. "He was pretty tough to take," Ainge said. "But we just kept reminding him that he didn't compete against the best." But that night, as the team started to work out the kinks from the All-Star break, Kevin McHale reinjured his Achilles.

"I really went hard because I thought it was fine, and then it started to hurt and I said, 'Uh-oh, I better not do that anymore,'" McHale said. "And that was that. I had to wait until it felt completely, totally better again. And it took some more time."

Instead of sending McHale home, the Celtics kept him on the trip where he served as unofficial tour guide and jokemeister. While K.C. Jones took the conservative approach and suggested a 4-3 trip was fine with him, McHale said flatly, "Anything less than five wins is unacceptable." Had he been able to play, he might have been able to back up his own words.

Sacramento was then in its maiden season in the NBA, having relocated from Kansas City the year before. The Kings, despite a 20-30 record, were seen as celebrities in the city. It was the first and only major league sports team in town. They had a small arena that was a converted warehouse and boisterous sellouts were already the norm. Bird got a long, standing ovation when introduced, temporarily stunning him. He wasn't used to that anywhere but in Boston.

The Celtics certainly did not play as if they were in Boston. They played in the ozone and saw their 13-game streak come to a crashing halt. A 12-point third quarter, during which they shot 4-for-27, sealed the Celtics' fate. They trailed by 21 heading into the fourth quarter and fell just short after staging a furious rally and trailing by only three points with less than a minute to go in the game. With 42 seconds left, Bird was fouled and went to the free throw line. He had already missed two free throws in the game; he then missed these two, much to the delight of the crowd. The Celtics did get to within two points and still later had a chance to tie it with a three-pointer, but ended up losing, 105–100. The rustiness was evident. Boston shot 35 percent, with Danny Ainge starting the trip by going 1-for-8. Robert Parish missed 12 of 18 shots. It was such a major happening in Sacramento that Joe Kleine, their rookie center, continued to refer to it as his best NBA memory years later.

"It was huge," Kleine remembered. "Being a rookie, I didn't realize the magnitude of that team, how good they were, the aura they had. Later, that's what really impressed me. We had a lot of veterans on our team, but it was still gratifying to beat them. The only thing comparable would have been beating the Lakers. But the Celtics were special."

Added then-coach Phil Johnson, "Everyone thought we had won the world championship. But I knew what had happened. We had caught a team coming off the All-Star break. That was a great time to catch a team like that because we, obviously, had no one in the All-Star Game."

Bill Walton made no excuses. "That was another disgrace to the sport of basketball," Walton recalled. "You just forget how hard it is that you gotta finish. They got rolling, got pushed on by their crowd, and we couldn't do it."

The Celtics had a day to let the unusual sting of defeat settle in and by the time they arrived in Seattle, no one was in a particularly good mood. There was one exception: for Dennis Johnson, this was a return to the city where he won his first NBA ring in 1979. He still had a home in the area and did not mind returning at all.

The Dennis Johnson who arrived in Seattle in February of 1986 was quite different from the one who had touched down ten years earlier after the SuperSonics picked him in the second round of the 1976 draft. In 1986, Dennis Johnson was regarded as one of the top guards in the game. A decade earlier, he was an almost feral, high-strung, determined young player. And prior to that, he was just another Johnson, one of sixteen children, who grew up on the mean streets of Compton, California. That he

was even in the NBA, let alone an unquestioned star, made his
story one of the more remarkable ones on a team full of remarkable stories.

•

Compton is one of many communities that form the greater Los
Angeles area. There is no Mezzaluna restaurant in Compton, and
Benetton isn't planning on relocating its corporate headquar-
ters there anytime soon.

When Dennis Johnson was born in September 1954, there
were already six other Johnson mouths to feed. His father was a
cement mason, his mother a social worker. If the house got
crowded, as it often did, some of the kids would hop the bus to
San Pedro and stay with Dennis's grandmother.

"We were just like everyone else," Johnson said. "My mom
had a car. My dad had a truck. We weren't rich, but I wouldn't
call us poor, either. I guess you could say we were scraping by,
just like everybody else. I know sometimes I'd ask for a quarter
and my mom would give me one. I'd get some candy, go home,
hide it, and eat it later. Sometimes I had pants with a hole in the
knee. Around Christmas, my father worked a little longer and a
little harder and we'd have some money to buy presents. You
might get a new pair of Chuck Taylors, pants, shirts, whatever. I
was set. I mean, it wasn't like I needed fifteen pairs of pants. You
don't find that out until much later."

His sport as a kid was baseball. He played second base, and
stayed with baseball throughout his years at Roosevelt Junior
High School, where, at 5-4, he was too small to make the basketball team. After being cut in seventh and eighth grade, he didn't
even bother to go out for the basketball team in ninth grade.

High school hoops at Dominguez High wasn't any more
rewarding. He made the C team as a sophomore and the junior
varsity as a junior. As a 5-9 senior, he languished on the bench as
a tenth or eleventh man. His job was taken by someone who
eventually ended up in jail. In his junior year, he lost playing
time to future major league baseball player Kenny Landreaux.

"My whole time in high school was spent as a bencher. I might have played three minutes a game, here or there, when I was a senior," he said.

When he left high school in 1972, Dennis Johnson figured he had as much chance of playing professional basketball as he did of being an astronaut. College, without scholarship money, was out of the question. So, like millions of other high school graduates, he got a job.

He first worked in a liquor store as a stock boy and part-time cashier. Then he took a job at a tape warehouse, where he made $2.75 an hour driving a forklift. The work was demanding and tiring. But something else was sapping his strength as well, something over which he had no control: he grew from 5-10 to 6-3 in that short span.

His release came on the basketball court in summer league games at San Pedro. He'd hop on Bus No. 5 after work and be on the floor, playing for a team coached by his brother. Three other brothers were also on the team. Soon, his brother arranged a game against a local junior college and Dennis Johnson's life changed in one evening.

The opponent was Harbor Junior College in Wilmington. Johnson found the players on Harbor no different than any of the guys he was going against in the rec league. He was now jumping like a pogo stick, blocking shots, playing a complete game. The Harbor coach, Jim White, was intrigued by what he saw. He asked if Johnson might be interested in coming to Harbor and playing for him. Johnson didn't have to think twice.

At that time, to attend junior college, one simply had to be a resident of the area in which the college was located for one year. The education was free, and there was also financial aid for those who needed help with other college costs. Dennis Johnson would have qualified for financial aid, but he never applied for it.

"He was just another kid who came into the gym to play," Jim White recalled. "In the beginning, he didn't show a whole lot. But he could jump and rebound and was clever around the basket. Some of the things he does, you can't defend."

And some of the things he did could not be tolerated, either. Johnson and White developed a relationship that was reward-ing, contentious, and lasting. They are friends today. They were friends back then, too, when Johnson wasn't driving White crazy.

Johnson calls White "probably the one person who had the most impact on my life as far as basketball is concerned." White recalls Johnson as basically a wild stallion unwilling to be tamed but, eventually, coming to the realization that in order to succeed, he had to be tamed. The two survived each other and, in the space of two years, Johnson had grown enough personally and profes-sionally for White to recommend him to a Division I school.

"We struggled a lot," White said. "He was undisciplined on and off the court and I am just the opposite. I view basketball as a privilege. He was averse to doing what he was supposed to do. He was never defiant; he was just a little wild and undisciplined in his life and a very emotional kid. So when things didn't go his way, he would explode. And that's the way I am, too. Needless to say, there were a lot of explosions."

Johnson spent two years at Harbor. White said he kicked Johnson off the team three times, but Dennis only knew about two of them. "The last time, my assistant told me I wasn't being fair," White said. "Dennis had missed practice and had not called and, as far as I was concerned, it was over with him. But he had no money and he was living with his grandmother and her phone didn't work. I expected him to go next door to call, but maybe that was too much. From then on, one of our players made sure he was picked up every day."

There were problems with coaches throughout Johnson's NBA career as well. He feuded with Lenny Wilkens in Seattle and with John MacLeod in Phoenix, almost always over playing time and discipline. He even had one confrontation with the mild-mannered K.C. Jones in Boston. Now a coach himself, Johnson looks back on those years and says, "Yeah, I was a hand-ful. But all I wanted to do was win."

And despite his flare-ups with White, Johnson generally spent enough time on the basketball court to make Harbor a winner. In his second season at Harbor, the team won the state title, going 29-4. Johnson averaged 20.2 points and 13 rebounds a game and was the MVP of the state tournament in Fresno. "By the time he finished with us, not because of anything we did except provide discipline, Dennis was awfully good," White said. "He came so far."

But as good as Johnson had become, and as far as he had come, White had trouble selling him to Division I coaches he knew in California. "As a Division I coach, you don't have time to handle a guy like Dennis and all his emotional problems," White said. Southern Cal's Bob Boyd never called, and White didn't think Johnson was good enough to play for Cal State-Fullerton. But White had a friend who was an assistant at Pepperdine and that school's head coach, Gary Colson, had already seen Johnson play.

"I saw him jump center against this 7-2 guy who eventually went to Jacksonville, and Dennis got the tip," Colson said. "He finished with something like 30 points and 15 rebounds and I was just astounded."

Johnson had to get his grades up by going to summer school, and he almost didn't go at all because he was afraid of the workload. "He didn't read all that well, but he really worked at it. He really improved his reading ability by the time he left," White said.

White called Johnson into his office, told him he was going to Pepperdine and that was that. "Jim told me what I should do," Johnson said. "He got me into the summer league. He called the assistants. He sent me there, and they gave me a free ride."

Johnson was only there a year, and he almost didn't last that long. Around Christmas, his parents' house burned down. He thought about leaving and finding a job. "I never once thought about the NBA at that point," he said. "Then again, I didn't know what I could do to help out at home, either. So I stayed."

Pepperdine went 22-6 that season and advanced to the NCAA

tournament, where it lost a close game (70–61) to UCLA in the second round of the West Regionals at Tempe.

"At halftime, we were leading and pressing the devil out of them," Johnson said. "I think we really scared them. There were a lot of scouts at the game and I played well. I think I blocked three of Richard Washington's shots, a couple of Ralph Drollinger's, and maybe one of Marques Johnson's. After the game, we're going back to the hotel and these agents were coming up to me and asking me what I was going to do. I said I was going back to school to play another season."

But he didn't. Johnson, as a junior, was eligible for the 1976 draft because technically that would have been his fourth year of college had he gone directly from high school. (It was the same rule that applied to Larry Bird in 1978.) One of the spectators at the UCLA game was Bill Russell, then the coach and general manager of the SuperSonics. He came away very impressed, and with their second pick of the second round, twenty-ninth overall, Seattle drafted Dennis Johnson.

Johnson did not have to go pro. He talked it over with Colson and the coach's advice was, "Go for it if you get the money." Colson constantly uses the example of Johnson at his summer camps, starting with the 5-10 guy who couldn't play in high school and ending up as a potential Hall of Famer. "No one ever guesses who I'm talking about," Colson said.

Johnson decided to take the money, which wasn't great, but was more than he was accustomed to. He signed for $27,500.

"I was a naive young boy who didn't know any better," Johnson said, blaming his agent at the time. "Bill [Russell] told me, 'This is what we're giving you.' There was no haggling. Nothing. But it was a whole lot of money to me back then and I was able to buy my mom a car. Plus, I had paychecks for a whole year."

In his first year with Seattle, the Sonics went 40-42 and Russell turned over the coaching job to his cousin Bob Hopkins who had played with the Syracuse Nationals in the 1950s. The 1977–78 team, still being coached by Hopkins, started out 5-17 and Johnson was not happy with his role.

"I remember we had this meeting when Bob was still coaching and we were talking about playing together and all that kind of stuff, and DJ raised his hand," recalled Paul Silas, who had been traded to Seattle that year. "I thought he was going to add something to the discussion, but instead he said, 'Hoppy, what about me? How come I'm not playing more?' It was almost as if the losing didn't mean a thing to him.

"This was a young fellow," Silas went on, "who was really, really angry. And a fellow who didn't quite understand where he was in terms of the team and what he meant to the team and to the team's ability to win. That is a very difficult thing to teach a young guy."

Lenny Wilkens was summoned to right a sinking ship. One of the first moves he made was to put Dennis Johnson into the starting lineup. Seattle then recovered from its horrific start to make it all the way to the NBA Finals. But in Game 7 against the Bullets, Dennis Johnson established a record that still stands to this day: most misses without a basket in an NBA Finals game. He was 0-for-14 from the field. As the final seconds ticked away, Johnson could not pick up a loose ball, watching it roll through his legs as Mitch Kupchak scooped it up to secure the victory. Seattle lost, 105–99 and, to this day, that game ranks as one of Johnson's greatest personal disappointments.

"Sometimes people ask me if I can think of one great thing that happened to me and I tell them about this game," Johnson said. "And I tell them that I have never had that same feeling again. I completely let the team down and I vowed that would never happen again. That game continued to be a source of inspiration for me for years. I remember being so upset that night that no one could have talked to me. You tell yourself that things like this happen, but then you say, 'Why the hell did it have to happen to me?' Maybe God was telling me I was getting too big for my britches. He has a way of putting you in your place and making you humble. But if I had just hit three baskets that day, we would have won that game."

Determined, Johnson came back stronger the following year.

Seattle went on to meet Washington again in the NBA Finals, with the Sonics prevailing in five games. Johnson had a terrific series and was voted the Most Valuable Player of the Finals. He led both teams with 11 blocked shots, an astonishing feat for a guard. He averaged 23 points a game. And when the series was over, there was little doubt that Johnson was one of the dominant guards in the NBA—and he was only twenty-five.

"Before Magic Johnson came into the game and reinvented the guard position," Walton said, "Dennis Johnson had been the best guard in the league for a number of years. His teams *won* the damn game. He could move, defend, pass and he had leadership qualities. There was none better."

With the title, the Sonics seemed destined for success for years to come. They had a terrific backcourt in Johnson and Gus Williams, a fine young center in Jack Sikma, and an excellent supporting cast. But Johnson was feeling unappreciated and underpaid and that became a constant source of friction throughout the next season. The tension affected him, his relationship with Wilkens, and his relationship with his teammates, and the Sonics, although still a competitive team, were never the same.

The Sonics went 56-26 in 1979–80, but finished second to the Magic-led Lakers in the Pacific Division. By then, Johnson was making $400,000, but he knew that Gus Williams was headed for a bigger payday and there was always a sense of one-upmanship between the two. Johnson at first had liked Wilkens's approach, but by 1980 they were not always seeing eye-to-eye.

"Our relationship did deteriorate a little bit," Johnson said. "Like any player, I wanted more time, this and that, and I wanted to renegotiate my contract. They didn't want to do that. Lenny was trying to help me, but I didn't always see it that way. And we had our share of arguments."

Johnson had averaged 19 points a game that season, but Seattle had had enough. The Sonics lost to the Lakers in five games in the conference finals; following the playoffs, Johnson went to the Philippines in the summer of 1980 to visit his wife's family at a military base. Five weeks after the Sonics were eliminated, Johnson turned on the television and discovered he was no longer a SuperSonic. Seattle had traded him to Phoenix, even up, for Paul Westphal.

"My head just dropped," Johnson said. "I had never experienced the feeling of not being wanted mainly because you and the coach had had some difficulties. I got on the plane the next day and flew to Seattle and the people in the airport were great, telling me how sorry they were. And I said to myself then that I would never allow myself to be traded like this again. If I was traded again, it would be because someone really wanted me."

The Suns and Johnson proved to be a good fit at first. In his first year there, Phoenix won the Pacific Division title and had the best record (57-25) in the Western Conference. Johnson and Truck Robinson shared team scoring honors, each averaging 18 points a game. It was the best record in team history, but the Suns were upset in the playoffs by the Kansas City Kings, falling behind 3–1 and then rallying before losing Game 7 at home. The next two years, Johnson continued to play well for the Suns, but something was missing. The Suns were early playoff losers in 1982 and 1983, and Phoenix decided it was time to make a change.

During the 1982–83 season, Suns GM Jerry Colangelo had proposed a deal to Cleveland that would have sent Johnson there for Bill Laimbeer and Kenny Carr. The Cavaliers rejected it. The following year, Johnson and John MacLeod, the Suns' coach, were at odds and Phoenix felt it had no choice but to move Johnson.

"Me and John, well, we didn't always see eye-to-eye," Johnson said. "We didn't have real arguments, but I would speak up and he would do it his way. But they were lacking in big men and people thought we were feuding. We had no feuds. But I was more than happy to leave because we weren't going anywhere."

Johnson thought the Suns were going to renegotiate his contract, but instead they traded him to Boston for Rick Robey. Phoenix claimed they needed to break up the backcourt of

Johnson and Walter Davis since neither one was seen as a classic playmaker in the Suns' offensive scheme. The Celtics also got a first-round pick out of the deal, which they used to select Greg Kite. Johnson was talking to reporters at his house just after the deal was announced, and his wife interrupted, telling him K.C. Jones was on the phone.

"Tell him I'll call back and get his number," Johnson said.

Seconds later, he realized what he had done. He told the reporters the questions would have to wait and promptly called Jones, apologizing for the oversight.

The Celtics figured they were getting the defensive stopper they had so sorely lacked, someone who could defend anyone from the Sixers' Andrew Toney to Magic Johnson. They also knew they were getting a player who had a history of trouble with his coaches. And although Jones was easily one of the most mild-mannered men to ever coach Johnson, he too clashed with Johnson their first season together in Boston.

In an early-season game against Philadelphia, Jones thought Johnson looked upset and lethargic on the court. "He threw the ball to somebody and walked over to the side like he didn't want to be involved," Jones said. Afterward, in the dressing room, Jones brought up the matter. "Dennis went off the deep end," K.C. recalled. "Then I went off the deep end. Red and the owners were standing there and it was loud and raucous. I thought I had better back off and see what would happen the next day."

The next day, Johnson apologized. Jones said he never had another problem with Johnson.

"In those early years," Danny Ainge said, "DJ had a spat with everybody. We even got into it a couple times in five years. But there was always an apology the next day. That's the way he was."

The Celtics won easily in Seattle, 107–98. They then headed down Interstate 5 for a much anticipated rematch with Portland, the only team to have beaten them in Boston Garden. The game also marked Walton's return to the city where he began his NBA career for a team that he led to a championship in 1977.

The arrival of the Celtics in Portland meant the obligatory Walton story in the local paper and with it the pictures of his bearded, ponytailed days as a Blazer. Naturally, that led to an inordinate amount of ribbing. He had been back before as a member of the Clippers, but this was different: Larry Bird never played for the Clippers.

The Memorial Coliseum in Portland was one of Bird's favorite arenas. The previous year, he had scored 48 in the building, at the time his second highest output as a Celtic. In the Valentine's Day rematch, Bird scored 47 and the Celtics won, 120–119, in overtime. Bird not only added 14 rebounds and 11 assists to his haul, but he also made the basket to force overtime and the winning basket with three seconds remaining in overtime. It was his best game of the season and a sign that his back problems were finally over. He now had back-to-back triple-doubles and the Celtics were hot heading into Los Angeles for a nationally televised rematch with the Lakers on Sunday.

By now, the Celtics had vaulted past the defending champions in the overall standings. The Portland victory was the Celtics' fortieth in 49 games (and nineteenth in 21 since Christmas). The Lakers, meanwhile, had gone 15-9 since Christmas and were now 39-12. For them, this Celtics game seemed more like a bizarre scheduling quirk than an NBA game. They had just returned from playing in Atlanta and would immediately turn around and head back east for a five-game trip after this matchup.

The Celtics were still without McHale, sidelined with his inflamed Achilles. Although unable to play, McHale was still available to tease his teammates. His target this time was the unfortunate Danny Ainge, who had picked this road trip to go into one of the worst shooting slumps of his career.

Some of his teammates blamed it on the Austin Factor. Ainge had brought along his four-year-old son, Austin, and over the first three games of the trip he shot a horrible 3-for-17. At one

point, Ainge, his son, and broadcaster Gil Santos were walking
to a mall when Ainge said, disconsolately, "Austin, I wish I could
find my jump shot." Austin shot back, "Daddy, I didn't take it."
As the team waited in fog-shrouded Portland for its delayed
flight to Los Angeles, McHale noticed Ainge making a telephone call.

"Danny is calling all over the country to see if anyone knows
where his jump shot is," McHale cracked.

"That whole trip was wacky," Sichting recalled. "We saw Austin
at the airport with Danny and we figured he was going to a relative's house or something. He stayed with us the whole way. And
he would always have this backpack, so one day he gets on the
bus and Kevin called him over and said, 'Let me look in the
backpack, Austin. Is your daddy's jump shot in there?'"

Two of Walton's closest friends, Arthur Heartfelt and Mokie
Ruiz, decided to join the team for the trip, too. Heartfelt, since
deceased, was a social worker in San Diego. Ruiz ran a liquor
store in Santa Monica. They would show up for games, shoot-
arounds, practices, everything. They rode the team bus and
Ruiz ended up sitting next to K.C. Jones, cracking jokes. On an
off night in Los Angeles, Ruiz had a barbecue at his mother's
house that several players attended. So, too, did Walton's father,
who made the unfortunate decision to wear a Lakers jacket. The
players playfully tore it off his back.

"By the end of the trip, Arthur and Mokie would end up sleeping on the floor in Larry's hotel room," Sichting said. "The next
day, they'd get on the bus and Larry would go up to Bill and say,
'Hey Bill, have you met my friends yet?' It was something."

Sichting speculated that McHale was teasing Ainge to take attention away from his own injury. And even though Ainge continued to slump, the Celtics still prevailed over the Lakers,
105–99. The nation saw a deep Boston team continually make
the big play: whether it was Bird (22 points, 18 rebounds) or
Rick Carlisle, who had 10 points in 11 minutes—including one
memorable shot, a clock beater from just in front of the Lakers
bench—the Celtics rose to the occasion. That shot was not only

the signature hoop of Carlisle's season, it was the signature hoop of his career.

"After that game, I tried to act like it was no big deal," Carlisle said. "You know, I was saying things like, 'This is what basketball is all about' and 'You have to be ready when your time comes' and all that stuff. Then Dennis came over to me, looked me right in the eye, and said, 'Way to play.' From that moment on, things changed for me. It's not like I had arrived, but I had earned some respect from those guys."

There was also a beautiful backdoor feed from Walton to, of all people, David Thirdkill, who played 18 minutes that game. It was Thirdkill's only basket of the game but it was a sweet one. Scott Wedman also contributed with 11 points in 29 minutes. And then there was Walton.

Once again in comfortable surroundings, and playing against the team that would not even consider signing him, Walton ended up with 10 points, seven rebounds, and one block. But even more than his numbers show, he was a presence for each and every one of his 26 minutes on the court. In the final 3:05, he guarded the swifter James Worthy, pleading with K.C. Jones, "Let me have Worthy." Jones complied. And while Walton handcuffed Worthy, the other Lakers stars floundered as well. Kareem Abdul-Jabbar had only two points in the fourth quarter and Magic Johnson did not make a basket the entire game, only the fourth time that had happened in his career.

"The only word to describe the way Bill Walton played is maniacal," said Pat Riley, the Lakers' coach.

"I think Bill is the difference," Magic said. "You can pick up shooters anytime. There will be a hundred shooters in the draft tomorrow. But you can't get a big man who can do all the things that he does. Look at his enthusiasm. He wants to be out there. He wants to play. Last year, he got caught up with the losing and it was like, 'I'd rather be climbing a mountain or listening to the Grateful, what is it? Dead?'"

Afterward, the Celtics headed to Phoenix while the Lakers acknowledged the obvious: Boston was the superior team for now. "There's no reason for anyone to perceive us as a favorite now," Abdul-Jabbar said.

The Suns game was a bit of a letdown for the Celtics. Both Larry Bird and K.C. Jones were ejected by referee Mike Lauerman, and the Suns snapped the Celtics' winning streak at three with a 108–101 victory.

Lauerman had earned the reputation of being a bit of a hothead. Earlier in the month he had ejected Pat Riley from a game, a first for Riley as a coach or a player. Bird was ejected with 9:49 to play, but the Celtics had already started to unravel. Jones went on the floor to protest the call and he was summarily tossed as well. The Celtics were not playing well—they had only 13 assists—and Bird, who had been hit with a technical earlier in the season by Lauerman (one of Bird's seven), tailed off after a strong start.

"Larry got thrown out for yelling about a call," remembered Walton. "All game long they had been beating him and holding him and grabbing him and then he finally got a call. He said to Lauerman, 'So now you're going to start calling them?' That was it."

(Lauerman didn't last much longer in the NBA, but when the referees were locked out for the first month of the 1995–96 season, he returned to the NBA as a replacement referee.)

The Celtics' next stop on the West Coast swing was their third and final visit to California: a game against the Golden State Warriors. It would be reunion time for two members of the traveling party: K.C. Jones, who was to be inducted into the Bay Area Hall of Fame, and Robert Parish, who spent the first four years of his NBA career there before arriving in Boston in a deal that not only made him a certain Hall of Famer, but that ranks as one of the most one-sided trades in the history of sports.

CHAPTER EIGHT

Robert and the Egg Man

Robert Parish had to be beaten—literally—into playing basketball. As a sixth-grader growing up in segregated Shreveport, located in the northwest corner of Louisiana, Parish was shy, awkward, and tall. By the time he reached junior high, he had shown no interest in basketball. In fact, when he did participate in one workout, he ran with the ball as soon as he caught it. And he didn't always catch it, either.

Finally, Parish acceded to the pleadings of Coleman Kidd, the coach at Union Junior High School, to at least try out for the team. But on the first day of practice, Parish did not show up. He was a no-show the next day, too. Kidd had had enough. He brought Parish into a back room, took out an oak-handled wooden paddle, and gave it to the shy student on the backside, several times.

"I whipped him pretty good," remembered Kidd, who delights in telling the story not because of the corporal punishment inflicted, but because of the impact it made. Parish never skipped another practice and, after a year as a garbage-time, mop-up player with few skills and less coordination, he underwent a complete transformation. By the time he was in the eighth grade, Parish had developed into a truly formidable player, having honed his game on the Shreveport playgrounds.

Parish was one of four children of Robert and Ada Parish. The elder Parish worked various jobs at Beard Industries; one of his foremen was the father of football star Terry Bradshaw. The family home was small—five rooms—and a large piece of plywood covered a drainage ditch in the front yard. To get to the house, one had to tread lightly on the wood. There was no hoop in the driveway because there was no driveway. Basketball was not much of a factor in his life growing up. He preferred playing football, running track, or just hanging out.

"Everything there was very slow and laid-back," Parish said of his early days in Shreveport. "We were a lower-middle-class family, I guess, but we were never hurting for anything. We weren't poor, not by any means."

At Union, Parish was the star of the team and would have continued to be through high school had the city not integrated its public schools for the 1970–71 school year. Desegregation was a long and tedious process in Shreveport, and instead of remaining at Union, Parish ended up at Woodlawn High—the alma mater of two NFL quarterbacks, Bradshaw and Joe Ferguson. Union was closed and turned into a vocational center.

"We didn't like the fact that we were being bused and shipped all over town," Parish said. "Not all of us went to Woodlawn. Some went to other schools. And I didn't like that. I had a lot of friends and some of my teammates had to go to other schools. I didn't like being broken up and separated. I resented that."

Over the previous two years, the schools in Shreveport had been operating under the Freedom of Choice plan, but few blacks had bothered to attend previously all-white schools. The city then implemented a wholesale desegregation plan, uprooting many of the students, faculty, and administration. Coaching staffs were broken up as well. Parish ended up going to Woodlawn from seven A.M. to one P.M. because the new school, intended to accommodate the overflow from Union, had not been finished.

Parish didn't like the idea of starting new in the eleventh grade, but he did. Basketball made it easier; he was the starting center on a team that went 36-2, the best year in city prep history. Parish perfected his trademark rainbow jumper by shooting over raised broomsticks—the idea of his coach, Ken Ivy. Woodlawn lost in the state finals that year when Parish fouled out, but came back the following year to finish the season with a 35-2 record and a state title. Parish was named the Louisiana Player of the Year.

By then, of course, college coaches across the land were drooling over the athletic seven-footer. Bobby Knight had made a visit to Hughes Springs, Texas, to see Parish play; it was one of Woodlawn's two losses that year. But in choosing a college, Parish faced one giant hurdle: he could not qualify for a scholarship according to NCAA regulations because of poor test scores.

He heard that line from Indiana. He heard it from Florida State. Back then, to receive an athletic scholarship, an incoming freshman had to "project" to a 1.6 grade point average. Colleges took the student's high school grade point average, his high school rank, and his test scores and tossed them into an educational blender from which the projected GPA was produced. Parish had no chance at a scholarship because his test scores were so poor; he took the ACT twice, never scoring higher than an 8. The average score that year was close to 20. Florida State told him he needed to retake the ACT and score no worse than a 21.

But while the major schools were telling him that his scores made him ineligible for a scholarship, Centenary, the smallest Division I school in the country at that time, was telling him something else.

Located in Shreveport, Centenary had little basketball tradition to draw on, but it did offer scholarships. The year before, Centenary officials did what they had always done in determin-

ing whether entering freshmen could qualify for athletic scholarships. They converted test scores from the ACT to the SAT to
determine eligibility. The only problem was that the NCAA had
ruled almost two years earlier that it no longer allowed such
conversions.

At the time, Parish was unaware of any of this. The NCAA was
monitoring the situation because Parish was among the top
high school basketball prospects in the country. Well before
Parish was accepted to the school, Centenary was warned both
in word and writing that it would face severe penalties if it converted Parish's test scores. The school felt it was being singled
out, because it had done the same thing a year ago and the
NCAA had said nothing. The NCAA, however, had not been
watching Centenary in the summer of 1971 and was unaware of
the previous conversions. Things were different in Parish's year.

Ignoring the NCAA's repeated warnings, Centenary brought
Parish in as a scholarship freshman. In January 1973, halfway
through the basketball season, the NCAA took action against
the school.

Centenary would be placed on probation for two years if it
immediately ruled Parish and the others ineligible. If Parish
continued to play there, the probation period would last as long
as he played, plus an additional two years. The NCAA allowed
the Centenary players—there were four other freshmen besides
Parish—to transfer to another Division I school and be eligible
immediately. None did. Parish admired Centenary for supporting him and the other freshmen and had no intention of leaving. This was home.

The last time Parish's name appeared in any official NCAA
release was January 27, 1973. (The stats had already been com-
piled at that point, even though the probation was already in effect.) The report showed Parish averaging 23.3 points and 17.4
rebounds a game. In his four years at Centenary, he averaged
21.6 points and 16.9 rebounds a game, averages that earned
him a spot as a *Sporting News* All-America.

After the sanctions were imposed, Centenary tried to fight

back. A local booster club challenged the 1.6 GPA rule in court, but lost at both the federal and appeals court levels. Ironically, the NCAA voted in January 1973—the same month it imposed the sanctions on Centenary—to eliminate the 1.6 rule. But the change would not be implemented until 1974, by which time Parish was a junior.

Parish never regretted his decision to remain at Centenary. He was happy playing basketball, being close to home and, also, being close to his two children. He had fathered a daughter in high school and a second while a freshman at Centenary. Although he never married the girls' mother, he remains close to his children, one of whom made him a grandfather in 1994.

Considering his background and the financial obligation of supporting two kids, Parish was a prime candidate for the upstart ABA, which was then luring collegians with big money offers. In his junior year, Parish was offered a four-year deal by the Utah Stars. He turned it down to stay at Centenary and fulfill a promise to his parents that he would get his degree, which he did in four years. He figured the money would still be there when he turned pro. It was, but by the time he graduated from Centenary, the ABA had folded and a lot of the big money had disappeared.

Even though he averaged 22 points and 17 rebounds a game in his final two years at Centenary, Parish felt his game regressing. Larry Little, the coach at Centenary, was not a "big man's coach," according to Parish. He has never regretted his decision to stay in college, but he later decided that it cost him a little in terms of basketball development.

"I think after my first two years there I just didn't get any better," he said. "And it had nothing to do with the schedule. I played against some quality big men, but a lot of things I feel you should get from coaches on the college level, I didn't get."

Even though Centenary and Parish were personae non grata in the eyes of the NCAA, the coaches knew who they were. Parish landed a spot on the 1975 Pan American Team and the 1975 Intercontinental Cup team, coached by Dave Gavitt. He was also

pressured to try out for the 1976 U.S. Olympic Team, but ulti-
mately decided it was too risky because a few days of mediocre
play might hurt his draft status. He took some heat for the decision, but he was convinced it was the right one for him.

A year later, he was in the NBA, having been selected by the
Golden State Warriors with the No. 8 pick in the 1976 draft. On
the surface, it looked like an ideal situation. Golden State had
won the NBA championship in 1975 and had the best regular
season record in 1976. The Warriors had two experienced centers who could teach Parish the ropes.

Instead, his time at Golden State was anything but ideal, and
had he not been traded to the Celtics, Parish maintains that he
would have retired instead of stretching out his NBA career to
twenty-plus seasons. He was also shell-shocked by the attitude of
his teammates.

"I couldn't believe the behavior of some of these professionals," Parish said. Rick Barry, in particular, stunned Parish. "He
was the most arrogant person I ever met in my life."

The Warriors had won 59 games the year before Parish
joined them. They then dropped to 46 wins in 1976–77 and to
24 by 1979–80, Parish's final season with them. He put up respectable numbers but because so much was expected of him,
he became a convenient scapegoat for the team's demise.

"One of the biggest mistakes we made with him was that we
put a lot more pressure on him here than he ever had in
Boston," said Al Attles, the Golden State head coach at the time.
"In Boston, he just fit in and was a contributor. Here he was seen
as a high post guy who didn't get to the basket and took jump
shots. It just didn't turn out like we thought it would."

Golden State was also losing money at the time and Parish
had only had a year to go on his contract. There was concern in
the organization that, if another team made a rich offer to Parish,
the Warriors would be unable to match it. That had happened
to them recently with both Gus Williams and Keith Wilkes.

By virtue of their terrible season in 1979–80, the Warriors
had the No. 3 pick in the 1980 draft. They decided to trade it to

Boston along with Parish for the No. 1 pick (which the Celtics held thanks to their deal with Detroit) and the No. 13 pick. Golden State figured center Joe Barry Carroll from Purdue would be even better than Parish. He was also four years younger, and would come at a considerably lower price.

In addition, the Golden State doctors had told the team that, in their opinion, Parish's feet and ankles were so bad he would not last another three years in the NBA, if that. Parish was in the process of negotiating a new deal with the Warriors and was caught by surprise when informed of the deal.

"They had told me they were going to draft Kevin [McHale] and sign Truck Robinson and get some players around me," he said.

Instead, the Celtics took McHale with the No. 3 pick. (Utah, drafting second, took Louisville leaper Darrell Griffith.) Golden State used the two picks it received from Boston to take Carroll at No. 1 and Rickey Brown at No. 13. No one on either side had any idea at the time how lopsided this deal would turn out to be.

"There are very few Solomons out there," Attles said. "You do what you think is right at the time and you live with it. You don't run and hide."

The trade to Boston reinvigorated Parish. For the next fourteen years, he would virtually be a perennial All-Star. His first coach with the Celtics, Bill Fitch, made him run the floor, something he was unaccustomed to doing in Golden State. Eventually, Parish would run the floor as well as any big man in the league. Parish and Fitch never bonded as individuals, but the coach clearly saw something in Parish that few people, including the Warriors, saw: Hall of Fame potential. If Parish could put big numbers up occasionally, he could, with work, do it regularly.

"Once the Celtics accepted him for who he was, they didn't try to make him into something he wasn't," said Don Nelson, then the coach of the Bucks. "They let him play. They didn't complain about his effort, or say that he could give them more. They looked at him and said, 'Look at the numbers the guy puts up. Let's not try to ask for more, like they did at Golden State. Let's not accuse him of having to give more or being nonchalant or whatever his history had been because of his personality.'"

The first year Parish was with the Celtics, the team won the NBA championship; the following year he was named second-team all-NBA. The Celtics won another title in 1984, and by 1985–86, Parish was regarded as one of the elite centers in the game.

He was part of the greatest front line in the history of the game, and with the arrival of Bill Walton was able to get the much-needed rest to endure the long championship season. Parish had had his ups and downs in Boston before this—going AWOL in training camp in 1983 was the most noticeable—but with the arrival of K.C. Jones, whom he revered, and Walton, whom he admired, times were great for the Chief.

Parish was the playing personification of Jones the coach. He never sought acclaim, paid no attention to statistics, and never worried about playing time. He never begrudged the addition of another high-profile center. If Walton could help him and the Celtics, bring him on. In many respects, he was the ideal team player and teammate.

Parish usually played well whenever he returned to Golden State, just in case anyone needed a reminder of what the Warriors had given up. By 1985–86, Joe Barry Carroll was still underachieving with the Warriors and Rickey Brown was out of the NBA. For the Warriors game, the Celtics were still without McHale and were also missing Scott Wedman, who had come down with back spasms and was given permission to fly to Kansas City to see his personal trainer. K.C. Jones decided to start Greg Kite along with Bird and Parish and he got more than he might have reasonably hoped. The Celtics won the game easily and Kite played his best game of the season.

There was one member of the team who, as Clint Eastwood liked to say, knew his limitations. He worked hard every day in

practice, he never complained about playing time, and he embodied the role of the unselfish teammate as well as Red Auerbach could ever have preached it. That someone was Greg Kite.
Also known as Egg or, simply, Eggo, he knew who he was.

The game against the Warriors demonstrated exactly how
Kite fit into the scheme of the 1985–86 Celtics. He was summoned to put his large body on Larry Smith, one of the league's
premier offensive rebounders. There were many players who,
given the same assignment, were used as trampolines by Smith.
Kite played 34 minutes and Smith got one offensive rebound,
that coming when Kite wasn't in the game. Kite's moments of
public triumph were rare—his biggest was in Game 3 of the
1987 Finals where he had nine rebounds and one block in 22
minutes—but this was his Warholian stretch in 1985–86.

Kite served a very useful function on the Celtics, not unlike
Eric Fernsten and Hank Finkel had done before him. He practiced like a possessed man, constantly pushing Parish and
McHale to the maximum level of their ability. But he was also
smart enough to know that his skills, in all probability, would be
limited to the practice court unless special circumstances intervened.

Kite had an exceptional understanding of what the eleventh-
or twelfth-man concept is all about. He wanted to play more, as
any player would, but he also understood his role on the Celtics,
and he performed it to perfection.

"Everybody wants to play and I was no exception," he said.
"All I did was work hard at practice and try to stay ready. It was
always nice when I got a chance to contribute."

Kite was in his third year with Boston in 1985–86 and it was
the first time in his basketball life that he wasn't a regular contributor. He had no illusions about being an NBA star; he was a
role player who took his strong work ethic and translated it into
an NBA paycheck. Along with Parish and Danny Ainge, he was
still playing in the NBA a decade after the 1985–86 season.

"I always thought Greg would get a shot in the NBA," his high school coach, Paul Benton, said. "I just never thought he'd last as long as he did."

Greg Kite grew up in a Mormon family in Houston, the youngest of four children. His father worked for Exxon as a geologist while his mother, who could trace her ancestry back to the Utah pioneers, stayed home. Later, she took a job as a clerk in Madison High School, where her son graduated eighth in a class of 450. Kite got involved in basketball through church leagues and, in YMCA games, he would occasionally play against other Houstonians such as Larry Micheaux, Clyde Drexler, and Michael Young. He eagerly followed the University of Houston Cougars, idolizing Elvin Hayes, known as "the Big E." His father wrote the words "Little E" on the back of a yellow slicker when Greg was nine years old. At the age of eleven, Kite met Hayes at a basketball camp and actually got a chance to guard him during a demonstration drill.

With both parents being six feet tall, it was only a matter of time before Kite sprouted. He was 6-10 by the time he was fourteen; he is 6-11 today. He skipped a grade in elementary school so, physically, he wasn't as overwhelming as he had been earlier. He rejoined his class by repeating the seventh grade, taking extra language courses to avoid the repetitive coursework. He led Madison to a 39-1 record as a senior, with the team's only defeat coming in the semifinals of the state tournament, a 65–62 loss to Lufkin. It was a heartbreaker. Madison had steamrolled through the season, ranked No. 1, and Kite had been the star of the team, averaging 17 points and 15 rebounds a game and making the all-state team. Despite collecting 20 rebounds, he was disappointing in the Lufkin game, shooting only 2-for-12 from the field.

"Greg was never a dominant scorer," Benton said. "He could always see beyond the drills we were doing and he would work hard on having quick feet in every drill. He knew he had shortcomings in that area and he worked on them. He'd get a lot of points off rebounds, not a lot of offensive stuff. His biggest asset was that he worked his tail off and it stayed with him. I know a lot of guys with more talent who never made it as far. But he made it on sheer hard work."

At the time, Kite was one of the most intensely recruited high school players in Texas history. But he also made news in another court while still in high school—the one where lawyers argue and judges rule.

In the summer before his senior year, Kite was interested in attending a basketball camp. Today, such an interest would not turn heads; all the big-name high school players attend one camp or another. But Kite soon discovered that the regulations that governed high school athletics in Texas prohibited an individual from attending summer camps if the individual intended to return to school and play in that sport. In other words, Kite could not attend a basketball camp and maintain his basketball eligibility the following year.

The rule—pertaining only to three sports, basketball, football, and volleyball—was implemented in 1962 after a high school basketball team in Dallas spent an entire summer together in Colorado and then won the state title the following year. Kite found a lawyer who had just graduated from Brigham Young Law School and decided to challenge the regulation. He was joined in his efforts by Del Harris, then an assistant coach with the Rockets; Rudy Tomjanovich, then a player with the Rockets; and Dave Cowens, then a player for the Celtics. Harris got involved because he wanted his two sons to attend his camp and still maintain eligibility; Tomjanovich and Cowens got involved because they both ran summer camps.

Kite v. Marshall ended up in U.S. District Court in Houston, and among the witnesses were Guy Lewis, the coach at the University of Houston, and Tom Nissalke, then the Houston Rockets' coach. Kite won temporary relief and attended two summer camps, one in Georgia and another in California. A federal judge ruled in Kite's favor in 1980, but that decision was overturned by the 5th U.S. Circuit Court of Appeals in 1981. The regulation has since been amended.

"It was amazing," Benton recalled. "After Greg had been to

one of the camps, I got calls from Marquette, Notre Dame, all these colleges. All of a sudden, everyone is interested because no one had ever seen these Texas kids before."

By his senior year, he was on everyone's recruiting list and everyone's All-American team. He was named to play in the McDonald's all-star game with Isiah Thomas, Byron Scott, James Worthy, Dominique Wilkins, Ralph Sampson, and Sam Bowie. He was a recruiter's dream: he had size, grades, and ability. But he never got too caught up in all the hoopla. He used trips to three all-star games to pay back those who had helped him along the way, taking his junior high coach to one, his high school principal to a second, and Benton to a third.

By his senior year, Kite had already narrowed his list of choices to five: UCLA, BYU, Duke, Kentucky, and Texas. He visited all but Kentucky (which had dropped out by that time because they had recruited Bowie). Texas coach Abe Lemons came to the Kite house in a Lincoln Town Car that almost took up the entire driveway. Then his assistant coaches set him up so he could deliver the punch lines.

Houston's Guy Lewis convinced Kite to join him for pizza with a couple of other players and then told the group, "If we sign all of you, we go to the Final Four." Kite turned him down, but the next year Lewis signed Akeem Olajuwon and the Cougars went anyway.

Kite's parents wanted him to go to BYU and, coming back from the McDonald's game in March, Kite told Benton, "The Lord has spoken. He said to go to BYU." Ironically, Kite did not even play in the McDonald's game because he had broken a knuckle on his finger while playing in a pickup game with Danny Ainge during his recruiting visit, having hit Ainge on the head in the course of the game.

Kite chose Brigham Young because he thought it offered the best combination of what he was looking for: academics, athletics, and atmosphere. "It had the most complete package," he said. "If I had just been picking a nonbasketball place, I would have ended up there." He called the BYU coaches during the

1979 Final Four, the one where future teammate Larry Bird was playing against future adversary Magic Johnson, and gave them his commitment.

At BYU, Frank Arnold was laying the foundation for a team that, two years later, came within one victory of reaching the Final Four. He already had Ainge; Steve Craig, a lightning-quick guard from California; and Fred Roberts and Steve Trumbo, two sturdy forwards. Kite would be the centerpiece. Arnold knew Kite wasn't a scorer, but his height and work ethic made him an invaluable part of the team.

"He never played any offense in high school," Arnold said. "All he did was rebound. He never learned any low post skills. But he was tough, he could rebound. He could play defense. He knew his role. I mean, this was a kid who had a GPA of 4.2 on a 4.0 scale. And when I first met him, he was so flexible he could touch his elbows to the floor."

Kite was a sophomore when Brigham Young made its great postseason run before losing to Virginia in the Eastern Regional Finals. He averaged a college-best 8.3 points a game that season. Two years later, Kite's final year at BYU, the Cougars were only 15-14. Though they tied for the Western Athletic Conference title, they went to no postseason tournament, and Kite settled down to see where his next basketball stop would be. By that time, he was the third leading rebounder in BYU history and the No. 1 shot blocker. As a senior, he trailed only the backboard-eating Michael Cage of San Diego State in rebounding. He participated in the Aloha Classic, still uncertain as to where his future would be.

"In college, I didn't always play up to expectations, but I was still very confident that I would play pro ball at some level," he said. "I think I did well at the Aloha Classic and the Chicago pre-draft camp, especially on offense, and that may have upped my stock."

There is a general understanding in drafts regarding centers: anyone taken after the first ten picks is usually not worth the pick. Only a few (Jack Sikma, Mitch Kupchak) have disproved that notion. When a center goes No. 21, you're not getting the next David Robinson.

Boston was hoping to land Rutgers's Roy Hinson in the draft. But when the Cavaliers made him the twentieth pick, a disgusted Red Auerbach threw his pencil across the table and then announced that the team would take Kite. Many Celtics followers at least knew the name, if for no other reason than his association with Ainge.

Kite watched the draft from his in-laws' house in Orlando, Florida. He had had no contact with the Celtics and had no indication that the team was even considering him. But when Auerbach made his pick, Kite jumped out of his chair in delight.

Kite said he had trouble sleeping after his performance against the Warriors. Wedman was back for the next game, the trip finale in Denver, but Walton was unable to go due to a sore left ankle. Kite ended up playing a solid 24 minutes and collecting 10 rebounds. But Kite's performance wasn't enough to overcome a bad situation. Boston was on the last leg of a trip, playing without Walton and McHale, in the mile-high air of Denver against a good Nuggets team. Lafayette Lever hit a bomb to give Denver a 102–100 win. Bird, as he had in the trip opener against Sacramento, missed a big free throw—this time with 37 seconds left—that would have given the Celtics the lead.

The loss to the Nuggets made it a 4-3 trip, which, given the Celtics' high expectations, was not what the team had hoped for. Fortunately, they had surrendered nothing to the 76ers; the Celtics were eight games ahead when the trip began and were still eight ahead when they returned. Bird had started to turn it up, averaging 31 points, 14.9 rebounds, and seven assists per game during that seven-game stretch. Those numbers would eventually earn him the NBA's Player of the Month award for February.

While Bird was lighting it up, Danny Ainge was going through trash receptacles at the airport trying to find his jump shot. He

was 16-of-54 from the field during the seven-game trip. Jerry
Sichting, however, had more than covered for him, going 13-of-
17 in the final three games.

The final four games in February were all ridiculously easy
for the Celtics. Their first test back east came against Indiana at
the Hartford Civic Center. Bird had yet another triple-double,
his eighth of the season and his fourth in six games. Robert
Parish had 27 points and 15 rebounds and Wedman added 19 in
a convincing 113–98 victory over the Pacers. McHale was still
out of action, but was given clearance to return two nights later
in New York, and he did, playing seven minutes, scoring no
points, and committing five turnovers. Bird, however, was brilliant, registering 24 points, 18 rebounds, and 13 assists in a
91–74 Celtics victory.

The win in New York, however, was not the major basketball
news coming out of the Big Apple that day. Earlier in the day,
commissioner David Stern held a news conference to announce
that Micheal Ray Richardson, the Nets' talented guard, had
been banned from the league for life because he failed a drug
test. It was his third such failure and that meant the league had
no recourse. Richardson could apply for reinstatement in two
years.

Richardson already had been AWOL once in the season after
he failed to show up for practice following a Nets Christmas
party. But he came forward and was sent to a treatment facility.
It was his second drug infraction and he knew the next one
would be the last one. After spending two weeks in treatment,
he was activated on January 20 and had played another month
without incident. But he then was arrested on February 20 for
trying to break into his house, even though his wife had taken
out a restraining order. He then was checked again for drugs
and flunked the test. What made this all the more tragic was
that he had been the Comeback Player of the Year in 1984–85.

While Richardson's problems helped ruin an otherwise
promising season in New Jersey, the Nets still managed to make
the playoffs that year, despite a 39-43 record. They were swept in

the first round, as had been the case the year before, and, a decade later, were still looking for their first playoff series win since their startling upset of the defending champion 76ers in 1984.

"Michael was the heart and soul of that team," said Dave Wohl, the Nets' coach that season. "When we lost him, that just killed us. It just clouded the whole year for us because no one would let it go."

The penultimate game of the month for the Celtics, a 120–100 victory over the Spurs, was newsworthy in one respect: it meant that Boston had officially clinched a playoff berth. No one was surprised. It was obvious that the Celtics had bigger plans in store and, over the final seven weeks of the regular season, they played the game of basketball about as well as it could be played.

The Celtics closed out February with a 124–108 victory over the Clippers, as Larry Bird registered another triple-double and Kevin McHale showed he was back in form by making 10 of 11 shots. This game also marked a return by Cedric Maxwell to the Garden. Although the crowd gave him a rousing 45-second standing ovation, Red Auerbach was conspicuous in neither standing nor applauding.

March–April:
Almost Invincible

On the morning of March 1, the Celtics had a record of 46 wins and 11 losses, a four-game winning streak, and a nine-game lead over the Philadelphia 76ers. That day, John Havlicek attended practice and offered an assessment of the team: "The game comes so easy to these guys that sometimes they get into trouble with things like overpassing." The team was unfazed. It was like criticizing a Mercedes for its door handles or radio antenna. The Celtics then hosted Detroit, which had won 10 straight, and beat them like a drum, winning, 129–109. Ainge by now had recovered from his shooting slump, scoring 27 points and making 11 of 18 shots, including two three-pointers. The 27 would be his high for the season.

By now, of course, Ainge was a fixture in the Celtics' backcourt. But even though this was his second full year as an uncontested, undisputed starter, he was only beginning to enjoy the comfort level and the confidence of the position.

"That year was a fun year for me because all the practical jokes went to Bill instead of me," Ainge said. "But it was also fun because I felt I was starting to get some respect and I felt appreciated for the first time. People were beginning to think, 'Hey, this guy is a pretty good player.'"

Ainge knew people had been thinking other thoughts not too long before. His transition from baseball to basketball was a difficult one: he was joining a championship team, replacing a popular player (Terry Duerod), and coping with a devastating tragedy in his personal life.

In late September 1982, while Ainge was in training camp preparing for his first full season with Boston, his mother, Janet Kay, shot herself to death at the family's home in Santa Clara, California. She was found dead on a Sunday morning; the coroner's office had fixed the time of death at around five P.M. the previous Friday. The Ainges had been in California for only two years.

Janet Kay Ainge had been suffering from breast cancer and extremely painful migraine headaches for the past decade. She left behind a note telling her family she no longer wanted to put them through any more trouble and that she hated the person she had become because of the illness.

"She didn't want to go through it anymore," Ainge said. "My dad called me and he was crying and I started to cry. It was very traumatic. They had just moved there and my dad was starting a new business. That was a very difficult time in my life."

Ainge got no relief on the court. Coach Bill Fitch was merciless and demanding with Ainge, as he was with all his players. Fitch played few favorites.

"Bill didn't cut anyone any slack, except Larry, of course," Cedric Maxwell recalled. "It was like going to an amusement park with Bill. 'Let's see, which kewpie doll am I going to shoot today?' Danny just wanted to get along. But Bill was always testing his manhood, and Danny didn't want that. Danny just wanted to play.

"Also," Maxwell went on, "Danny was an outsider that first year. We had won a championship. Not only did he come to the team in the middle of the season, but we were a tight-knit group. It was like moving into a new neighborhood. That's the athlete mentality. When things are going well, you don't feel like you need anyone. And you don't feel like you want to lose anyone. You don't want to change a thing. We were upset about losing [Terry] Duerod. Danny kind of came in and at first he just stuck to himself. But we accepted him quickly when we found out he was a card-playing Mormon."

In his abbreviated first season in Boston, Ainge shot just 36 percent from the field in 53 games. He joined the team without the benefit of training camp and missed the first six weeks of the season because of the contract negotiations. He had struggled in baseball with Toronto, but this was the first time as a basketball player that things were not working out for Danny Ainge.

"They tried to make him a point guard and he wasn't a point guard," his father said. "Early on, he didn't fit in well at all and we had some long talks. Did he think it was going to be like that? No. But he liked the people on the team."

Ainge said, "At certain times, I don't think Bill Fitch thought I was that good a player, and I didn't play very well when he was in Boston. I felt guilty shooting the ball because I was surrounded by Hall of Famers. I eventually adjusted and used that to my advantage. I mean, with all those All-Stars, I could afford to take a few bad shots."

His first full year was hardly more satisfying, and the Celtics imploded as the season progressed, getting swept by the Milwaukee Bucks in the playoffs. Fitch then left, and K.C. Jones arrived. Although Ainge was not a starter in 1983–84 (he lost out to Gerald Henderson), he improved that season and played well in the playoffs. When Henderson held out during training camp in 1984, Ainge moved into the starting lineup and played well. It was enough to convince the Celtics to trade Henderson and give Ainge the starting nod. It was a decision Boston never regretted.

Another Celtics guard, however, was feeling a lot like Ainge had felt three years earlier. Things weren't working out the way

Sam Vincent had thought they would. Once seen as possibly a third guard, he was now simply a bench player, called on only in rare supporting roles.

K.C. Jones was not always sure what to make of Vincent. He saw Vincent's potential as a terrific NBA guard but only if Vincent could incorporate all his ability with a guard's knowledge of the pro game. As the season wore on, Jones was unhappy with Vincent's sense of commitment, and after seeing him leave early after practice one day, Jones apprised him of the situation. He told Vincent that rookies have to earn minutes. Vincent said that that was exactly what he was attempting to do. It was a classic argument that affected all Boston rookies (including the coach in 1958) unless they were named Bird or McHale.

Until that point, only two rookie guards for the Celtics had ever averaged as many as 12 minutes a game, Jo Jo White (22.1 in 1969–70) and K.C. Jones (12.4 in 1958–59.) Bob Cousy played more than 12 minutes a game as a rookie, but minutes played were not kept in his first season. But players like Sam Jones, Don Chaney, and, much later, Reggie Lewis (8.3 minutes in 1987–88) all had to wait their turn.

By March 1, Vincent had become a player who watched and watched and watched from the bench. He played 17 minutes over the seven games in the February road trip. Over the final 34 games, he didn't get off the bench in 13 of them and played more than 10 minutes in only four.

"It was difficult to adjust to not playing," he said. "I understand now the value of having a veteran in there as opposed to an inexperienced rookie. But at that time, you're trying to shape your game and make things happen and it's hard. I'll never forget K.C. telling me, 'You're a rookie' and just not grasping what he was saying at the time. I have all the respect for him. Now that I'm older, I see the vision he had. But when you're twenty-one, you can't see it. You think you're a world-beater."

As was the case with most first-round picks, Vincent had been a world-beater before joining the Celtics. He had never not played because he wasn't good enough or wise enough or old enough. It seemed like a case of reverse age discrimination.

His season high game of 12 points came in an April blowout against Cleveland in Hartford. Twelve points; Vincent would have that many before halftime in many a Michigan State game. A 10-pointer against the Knicks, also in April, represented the only other time that season he reached double figures. If you had suggested the aforementioned numbers to Vincent in the summer of 1985, he would have looked at you in total disbelief.

"My game was geared to create tempo," he said. "I had just come off a season where the game was to get it up the floor fast, create opportunities, and drop it off. We were entering a time that year when it was definitely not speed it up. It was like we don't care when we get the ball up the court as long as we get Larry a shot. Or Robert. Or Kevin. So forget getting it off the glass and flying out and looking for guys because there is going to be no one out there with you and if you're down there too soon, you're going to piss everybody off. That was real confusing to me, because that wasn't my game. I was not effective just walking it down, getting it inside, and then waiting for the pass out to knock down the jumper."

What Vincent said had some validity. The Celtics were a running team in the early 1980s but, by the mid-1980s, they ran selectively. The 1985–86 team was as accomplished a halfcourt team as the Celtics had had since the Bill Russell days. They had the inside covered with three great post-up players, Bird, McHale, and Parish, and they had perhaps the greatest passing center ever in Bill Walton, who loved to work the pick-and-roll with Bird. With the arrival of Sichting and the ongoing improvement of Ainge, the Celtics also had a solid backcourt to step up when the big men were double-teamed underneath. As years went on, the Celtics would rely more and more on the halfcourt game. But that year, their choices were so many and their options all lethal that it hardly mattered whether they ran or not. They were successful either way.

"In the last two minutes of a game against them," said Bill

Fitch, then the Houston coach, "you don't feel you will ever get the ball back unless you take it out of the net."

McHale returned to the starting lineup on March 4 after going 20-for-21 from the field in the previous two games. With the team healthy again and steamrolling opponents, especially at home, questions started to surface over whether this might be the best Celtics team in the franchise's storied history.

The Celtics had put fifteen championship banners in the Boston Garden rafters and yet their best team, record-wise, had not won the title. The 1972–73 team finished 68-14 in the regular season, but, thanks to an injury to Havlicek, lost in the conference finals in seven games to the New York Knicks. Red Auerbach, who coached nine Celtics champions in the 1950s and 1960s, thought the 1985–86 team was as good as he had seen. Ditto for Don Nelson, who played on the 1972–73 team and was on a handful of other Celtics championship teams.

"This is the best Celtics team, period," he said. "It certainly is better than any I played on."

Added K.C. Jones, "This is the most talented Celtics team ever."

Statistically, the 1985–86 team compared quite favorably to the 1972–73 team, which had as its stars Havlicek, Dave Cowens, Paul Silas, and Jo Jo White. Both teams made significant off-season acquisitions: the 1972–73 team acquired Silas and drafted Paul Westphal, while the 1985–86 team added Bill Walton and Jerry Sichting. The 1985–86 team was superior at home; the 1972–73 team went 32-8 on the road (there were three neutral site games that year). The 1985–86 team lost only 5 games all year to teams with winning records; the 1972–73 team lost 11. But the earlier team lost only three games to sub-.500 teams while the 1985–86 team lost 10.

The 1972–73 team never won more than 10 games in a row, while the 1985–86 team had streaks of 13 and 14. The 1985–86 team scored more points, allowed the same as the 1972–73 team, but was not as good a rebounding team and allowed opponents to shoot better from the field. The big difference between the two was in the attendance: the 1985–86 Celtics sold out every game (14,890) while the 1972–73 Celtics averaged 10,827.

Both teams had the league MVP on their roster. Dave Cowens won it in 1973; Bird was, by then, en route to a third consecutive Most Valuable Player award, something that had, to that point, been done by only two other players: Bill Russell and Wilt Chamberlain. Not only was Bird's back feeling better, but he was about to begin a stretch of phenomenal long-distance shooting, going 25-for-34 from three-point territory over one 10-game stretch.

Against the Knicks on March 7, Bird showcased another side to his shooting: the banked three-pointer. He did it for a reason—to win a bet. Larry Bird was tough enough without any added incentive; throw money into the mix and he was unstoppable.

Bird and Danny Ainge were warming up before the game and were banking in three-pointers. Knicks trainer Mike Saunders came out and told Bird, "Bet you ten bucks you don't make one of those in a game." That was all Bird had to hear, and after a brief reminder late in the game, Saunders found out the hard way: never bet against Larry Bird.

The Celtics built a 20-point lead after three quarters and Jones pulled his starters in the fourth. Saunders then got Bird's attention and held up his ten fingers. "Oh no," Bird said to Ainge. "I forgot all about the bet."

But the Knicks started to make a comeback and Jones had to put Bird back into the game. On the first possession, Bird got the ball on the wing and banked in a three-pointer. The Knicks called time and as Bird passed by the New York bench, he proclaimed proudly, "Ten bucks, Mike. Ten bucks."

In the eyes of Bird, that may have represented his biggest

three-pointer in a twenty-four-hour span, but to his teammates, it was merely the second-biggest. The day before, he had made a three-pointer that emptied the practice gym at Hellenic College.

Ten minutes after practice began, K.C. Jones gathered his troops at halfcourt for the regular preworkout spiel. But on this day, he offered the boys a bone: if anyone could make a shot from midcourt, he would call off practice. Bird, of course, drained the shot.

"I can still see it," Walton said, a decade later. "K.C. knew the guys were going to stay anyway. I mean, do you think Kevin [McHale] wanted to go home to all those kids? So Larry took two deep-knee bends, two dribbles, and hit nothing but net."

The same thing happened a couple of months later with a most improbable hero: trainer Ray Melchiorre. He was the last hope and he was called out of his seat, where he was contentedly drinking coffee. Melchiorre got up, emptied his pockets, and banked it in from halfcourt. Then everyone went out to lunch.

"That's the kind of year it was: crazy," Walton said.

In the win over New York, Bird wasn't the only one smiling. Walton came up big once again, this time registering 15 points, 12 rebounds, and three blocked shots; and as the team headed off for a five-game trip, they had stretched the winning streak to eight games.

The first stop was in Washington and the trip got off to a rotten start when the Bullets took a 110–108 overtime decision. Once again, a late three-pointer (this one by Gus Williams) burned the Celtics. The loss was highlighted by a 10-for-30 shooting performance by Bird and by a broken nose for Walton, the thirteenth time that had happened to him. Parish had 25 rebounds in the game, but the team was not sharp. They were rattled by Manute Bol and deserved to lose.

Dallas was next. The Mavericks had been in the league since 1980 and were still looking for their first win over Boston. On this occasion, their chances did not look particularly good. This Celtics team had lost two in a row only once so far that season and had been playing as if they would never lose two in a row again. They were 29-5 since Christmas, and Dallas hardly seemed a threat.

Dallas had just arrived home, following an all-night flight from Sacramento, using the private jet of team owner Donald Carter. Then, just before game time, the Mavericks found out that their leading scorer, Mark Aguirre, would be unavailable to play because of a stomach virus. Midway through the fourth quarter, the Celtics were firmly in control, leading by 13 with five and one-half minutes to play. Then they stopped playing.

Dallas rallied, got the Reunion Arena crowd into the game, and overtook the Celtics, getting critical three-pointers late in the game from Brad Davis and Dale Ellis. Larry Bird wasted a 50-point effort, including 31 in the second half, a performance that had the Dallas columnists drooling but had at least one of his teammates shaking his head.

"You may have scored 50, but you were the worst player on the court," Walton told him. Bird agreed. He knew, as Walton knew, that he had been going for points at the expense of the team—a move that was so atypical of Bird.

The final score was 116–115 Dallas and, as the buzzer sounded, coach Dick Motta, the only coach the team had ever had, raised his fist and said one word: "Finally." Reunion Arena erupted in a Texas-size celebration and the game was deemed so historic that the team made a videotape of it and put it up for sale. Thousands of copies were sold. At the time, it was considered the most significant regular season victory in the history of the franchise.

"I remember that game real well," Dallas guard Rolando Blackman said years later. "I remember just trying to get over the nervousness of being so close to beating a great team with a great legacy and never getting it done. Anytime you played the Celtics back then and you got close, it was almost like, 'This isn't supposed to be happening.' You got that feeling because you read about it all the time, heard about it all the time, and it was always there in the back of your mind. You would always think,

McHale is going to do this or Bird will make a three-pointer. You always had that feeling until you actually did it.

"In our huddles, all we talked about was going at them, going at them, attack, attack, attack. And basically, not slowing the game down because you didn't want to do that. It was a great feeling for all of us in that we beat them when he [Bird] was at his best. It was tremendous for us. You never get over that feeling, that you're getting close and that it's actually going to happen."

Motta was so pleased he gave his team the next day off. And two nights after their memorable triumph, Dallas lost at home, to Sacramento, in overtime.

On any other night, a Mavericks loss to the Kings, then 29-36, would have been seen as a mild upset. But beating the Celtics took a lot out of a team. Those fortunate enough to win generally got to enjoy it for one game; on only four occasions out of a possible fifteen did the team that beat the 1985–86 Celtics go on to win its next game. The 76ers, one of just two teams to beat Boston twice (the Nets were the other) won both of their post-Celtics-victory games. Denver and the Knicks were the two others.

The loss to Dallas represented Boston's thirteenth of the season and guaranteed that the Celtics would not post the best record in NBA history; the 1971–72 Lakers were 69-13, while the 1966–67 Philadelphia 76ers were 68-13. (Both of those records were eclipsed a decade later by the Chicago Bulls, who went 72-10.) The Celtics were now 50-13 thanks to the back-to-back losses.

The next game on the road trip was against Houston, a team they had yet to play this season. The Rockets were without their vibrant young center, Akeem Olajuwon, who was sidelined with a knee injury, and exploiting the Rockets' weakness inside, the Celtics emerged with a 116–104 victory.

The Rockets were leading the Midwest Division at the time, but after the game, their point guard, John Lucas, went on a drug binge, putting an end to his season and seemingly ending any serious postseason hopes the Rockets may have had that year.

Lucas had had a history of drug abuse and, at that time in his career, was a risk for any head coach. When he was on, Lucas was a terrific point guard with great court vision and keen floor smarts. But that season, he was still using cocaine. He hadn't missed any games but he missed an occasional practice, prompting several drug tests. Unbeknownst to the Rockets, Lucas avoided detection by changing urine specimens with a cooperative teammate. There was no definitive proof so there was no action—until the night after the Celtics game.

The game had been close much of the way and Lucas, after arguing a call, got a technical by referee Billy Oakes. Bill Fitch, the Rockets' coach, pulled Lucas out of the game. Afterward, still seething from both the technical and Fitch's quick hook, Lucas went to a party before going home. Lucas's wife, knowing full well her husband was a drug abuser, would lock the door from the inside and hide the key so he couldn't get back out. But Lucas found the keys this time, unlocked the deadbolt, and headed back out into the night wearing a suit and tie but no shoes.

The following morning, Lucas awoke in downtown Houston, remembering nothing from the night before. His pants were soaked with urine and he missed that day's practice. The next day he reported, and Fitch made him take a drug test. This time, the coach watched the procedure and took the specimen bottle himself. The inevitable results soon came back and Lucas was done for the season.

So, it appeared, was Houston. Lucas was deemed essential to any Houston hopes; without him, the team would have to rely on the likes of Lewis Lloyd, Robert Reid, and Mitch Wiggins, none of whom could play the point as well as Lucas could. (The following season both Lloyd and Wiggins would get nailed for drug use, too.)

The victory over the Rockets stopped the skid at two and the Celtics finished off their Texas swing by beating the Spurs, 135–119. Bird was 11-for-11 from the field in the first half. The Celtics then headed to Atlanta for another meeting with the Hawks, who had won seven in a row and were feeling it again. But Boston made it a 6-0 season sweep against Atlanta with a 121–114 victory even though Walton broke his nose again. But Walton did something worse that night, although during the season it was never revealed: he broke the navicular bone in his right wrist blocking a shot by Tree Rollins.

He can talk about it now, but back then it was listed as a bruise or simply as a sore wrist. In fact, he had done the same thing to his wrist ten years earlier. He ended up having an operation, and having it placed in a cast for almost five months. "It never got any better," Walton said.

"So when I broke it this time," he said, "I just said, well, I'm going to go with it. And even though it was bad, it was still a lot better than if they tried to operate on it. I remember the next game, I was so sore I could hardly play. I had to pass left-handed and I couldn't do anything right-handed. I couldn't bend the wrist at all. I was very cautious after that and I learned to fall on my body, not on my hand. Ray [Melchiorre, the trainer] asked if I wanted X-rays. I said, 'No, let this one be.' I had an ice pack on my wrist, an ice pack on my nose, and there was blood everywhere. Kevin came up to me and said, 'We're going to win the championship this year, but you're paying one helluva price.'"

Eight days later, after routine dispatchings of the Sixers, Pacers, and Cavaliers, the latter thanks to a Bird three-point barrage, the Celtics hosted the Chicago Bulls. For Walton, it was a significant game because it would be No. 68, and that represented a personal high for him. He would miss only two regular season games that year, something that a few years earlier seemed unimaginable.

The Chicago game also marked the first Garden visit that season for Michael Jordan, who had missed 64 games with a broken foot. He had come back a week earlier with his playing time carefully monitored, taking 16 shots in 20 minutes. Bird, meanwhile, was in his best moneymaking form, taking five dollars from a writer who bet Bird that he couldn't make a left-handed three-pointer. The writer was willing to give Bird five tries. Bird made it on his second and gleefully collected the money.

After the Bulls game, which the Celtics won, 126–105, it was announced that McHale, whose contract was up at the end of the 1986–87 season, had agreed to a new four-year deal. The team had approached him earlier in the season about an extension, but McHale declined to talk until his Achilles problem disappeared. Once it had, the negotiations went smoothly. GM Jan Volk and McHale's agent, John Sandquist, had a two-hour dinner at Grille 23 in Boston, discussing McHale's future with the team. They discussed everything but money. The following day, Sandquist called Volk with his figures. Volk came back with his. After chatting with McHale, Sandquist called Volk back and the deal was done. It took less than twenty-four hours.

The last time McHale's contract had been up for renewal, things went a little differently.

In the summer of 1983, Kevin McHale was a free agent. The Celtics never let Larry Bird get into that situation or, for that matter, Robert Parish either (at least not until he was well into his late thirties). The Celtics were never seriously concerned about losing McHale because they had the right to match any offer without having to worry about the salary cap. There was concern, however, about losing McHale if coach Bill Fitch decided to stick around. McHale had started to tire of Fitch's heavy-handed style. "It's like I learned when I had my first kid," McHale said. "If you keep yelling at them, they stop listening."

There was undeniable interest in McHale from the Knicks. New York publicly lusted after the 6-11 forward and spent much time trying to think of constructive and creative ways to make

McHale an offer that the Celtics might not match. McHale truly
wanted to remain in Boston and said he would take less money
to do so; nonetheless, he was perceived to be a greedy ingrate in
Boston and Auerbach called him a traitor for even talking to the
hated Knicks.

"I was only doing what the Players Association had told me to
do," McHale said. "You play out your contract. You don't bitch.
And then you see what's out there."

New York talked money with McHale, but never presented an
official offer sheet, despite all the internal machinations and ex-
ternal speculation. The Celtics decided to call their bluff by pre-
senting offer sheets to three Knicks who, like McHale, were free
agents. The players were Sly Williams, Rory Sparrow, and Marvin Webster.

The Celtics figured that New York could not afford to sign
McHale to an offer sheet and still match the offers to keep its
own players. Once the Knicks matched the offers on their own
players, they would have no money left to entice McHale. In retrospect, of course, the Knicks probably should have called
Boston's bluff and let the players go, but they could not afford
to lose all three players and not get McHale, which is what
would have happened. So the Knicks matched the offers and
McHale re-signed with Boston for $1 million a year for four
years. It represented a raise of almost 400 percent, but McHale
claimed he could have made more money by simply signing
with New York.

"I left a ton of money on the table in New York," he said. "But
I still got paid more money in that one year [$1 million] than I
ever thought I would make in my whole life."

McHale also had to consider an intangible, that one thing
that money could not give him: a chance to win a title in Boston.
This line was vintage Red Auerbach, who time and again used
the Celtics' greatness, sense of family, and potential for success
as a valuable weapon in contract negotiations.

McHale had been so eager to stay with Boston that he had

kept calling Auerbach during his talks with New York. "I'd get on the phone and I'd say, 'Red, they're talking about this much.' And Red would say, 'Fine, fine,' and that would be that."

There had been times in the past, however, when Auerbach misjudged the situation. When Paul Silas, a truly valuable member of the 1974 and 1976 world champions, came looking for a new deal after the 1976 championship season, Auerbach wouldn't pay him what he wanted and traded him to Denver in a three-way deal that brought Curtis Rowe to Boston. Silas was already in salary arbitration and might have won his case, thereby making him a free agent. Auerbach also refused to re-sign the valued Don Chaney and, the year before, had traded a young Paul Westphal to Phoenix for Charlie Scott.

He had not wanted Bob Cousy, either, but had to settle for him when he drew his name out of a hat when the Chicago Stags, who had Cousy's rights, folded and a dispersal draft was conducted. He had, however, seen the future greatness of Bill Russell and traded a popular Celtic (Ed Macauley) and the draft rights to a promising rookie (Cliff Hagan) for the draft rights to Russell in 1956.

The current team was a tableau of Auerbach's master strokes. McHale and Parish were there via the infamous trade, although that deal was first proposed by then-coach Bill Fitch. Still, Auerbach had swindled the Pistons into taking Bob McAdoo for two first-round picks, and it was those two picks that brokered the Parish-McHale deal. He needed luck, and he got it, but he also was unafraid to take a shot when no one else even bothered to load their gun. Agent Ron Grinker has always liked to say that "Red was playing chess while everyone else was playing check-ers." Back then, much of that was true.

Bird was there because Auerbach gambled a year ahead of time when no one else wanted to take the risk. Ainge was there because Auerbach took a chance when no one else would and sensed that Ainge really wanted to play basketball. And Johnson was there because Auerbach saw an All-Star who was unhappy.

He always reasoned that a change of scenery might be all someone like that really needed.

"You look at that starting lineup," Walton said, "and Red stole
them all. All five of them. He out-thought everyone else."

The Rockets made their only regular season visit to Boston
shortly after the Celtics had defeated them in Houston. With
the 114–107 victory, the Celtics clinched a tie for the Eastern
Conference title. Scott Wedman (9-for-10) played a big part in
this one, but he may be the only one who remembers his contribution. To everyone else, the game was memorable for one
extremely scary sequence in the first half in which Ralph Sampson, then playing a terrific game (17 points, five rebounds), got
undercut going for a rebound and hit the Garden floor hard.
He had to be taken off in a stretcher and was unable to move his
legs. The usual festive atmosphere in the building wasn't the
same after that. This was a town that had seen Darryl Stingley,
the New England Patriots' wide receiver, paralyzed during an
exhibition game with the Oakland Raiders eight years earlier.
Sampson's thud shook foundations as far away as Albany.

"The last time I saw anything fall that hard," Fitch said, "was
when they blew up the [Madison] hotel next to here." Sampson
was taken to Massachusetts General Hospital, had X-rays and
other tests, and gradually got the feeling back in his legs. He left
the hospital the next day, having only a sore back, but missed
their next game against Indiana, the first absence of his career.
Houston won anyway.

Bird, meanwhile, nailed two more three-pointers in the
Houston game and was now on a remarkable long-distance tear.
Two nights later, in a conference-clinching victory against Milwaukee, he was 2-for-2 from behind the arc, concluding a 10-
game stretch where he was 25-for-34. In the Cleveland game a
week earlier he had drained five consecutive three-pointers as
part of a 34-point first half.

At this torrid pace, Bird was on his way to another Player of the Month award. In one four-game stretch at home, he scored 36, 35, 27, and 40 points. There was the 43-point performance in Hartford against Cleveland (accomplished in only 29 minutes) and the perfect first half in San Antonio. But the threes came in waves in that wondrous 10-game streak, even as Bird continued to trash the whole concept of the three-point basket.

"If they did away with it, I could live without it. But as long as they have it, I'm going to shoot," Bird said.

And he kept shooting it. Bird tailed off after that remarkable 10-game run, but by season's end, he was the all-time leader in three-point field goals with 267.

Two nights after the conference clincher against Milwaukee, Robert Parish sat out a game against the Bullets with a sore back. With nine games left to play in the season, Bill Walton was getting his first start as a Celtic.

With the prospect of starting, Walton was even more crazed than usual on this game day. Bird went up to him during warmups and reminded him what he was supposed to do. "I know what you're thinking," Bird said. "Forget about it. Those [Parish's] shots are my shots. You just get on the weak side and rebound."

More than any other teammate, Bird reminded Walton of a coach. Coaches wrack their brains and deny themselves sleep for the sole purpose of getting more from their players. Bird did that, too, as a teammate. This was the coach in Bird reminding the player in Walton what was expected.

Bird should have known better. Walton had no interest in scoring. That never was, nor would be, his driving motivation.

"I just wanted to have the ball, touch the ball," he said. "I just wanted to have something to do with the play. My shot was not pretty-looking, but that's the way it came out. As Coach Wooden told me and Jamaal Wilkes, 'I'm not going to say a thing about your shot until you start missing.' And he never said anything. But my shot changed significantly for me over the years because of my wrist injuries. I didn't have the snap there anymore. I have dead bones in there now."

Despite Bird's stern admonition and Walton's protestations, the big redhead squeezed off 10 shots in 26 minutes. He made eight of them and finished with 20 points. He also had 12 rebounds and the Celtics, by now ripping through opponents at home, won comfortably, 116–97. Twelve days later, Walton got his second start of the season when K.C. Jones allowed the Green Team to begin the game. Walton had a season high 22 points and 12 rebounds in that game, all in 28 minutes.

As March ended, all eyes in the basketball world focused on the NCAA Final Four in Dallas. A poll revealed that John Wooden rated Gail Goodrich's 42-point performance against Michigan in 1965 as the best individual effort ever in the Final Four. Wooden didn't have much company in his decision; twenty-six out of thirty voters contacted by the *Dallas Morning News* rated Walton's 21-for-22 game against Memphis State in the 1973 Final Four as the best. Wooden thought that that not only wasn't Walton's best game, but that Walton should have gone 22-for-22 given the way Larry Kenon was playing defense that evening.

"I did have better all-around games," Walton said. "And I would never question anything Coach Wooden said."

Walton, a junior at UCLA in 1973, had to face some interesting off-the-court distractions during that Final Four weekend in St. Louis. He had already been approached by representatives of the American Basketball Association, who laid out the parameters of an offer that basically gave him veto power over everything but the weather. He was also having trouble sleeping, so the school's athletic director, J.D. Morgan, graciously offered Walton his suite, which had a king-size bed. Walton gratefully accepted.

At three A.M. the following morning, a petrified Walton awoke to the sound of someone trying to enter the room. Then his phone rang, but there was no one on the other end. As Walton frantically assessed the situation, he heard voices at the door saying, "Police, open up!" Walton did so and was taken downstairs in a case of mistaken identity. A call was made to his original hotel, where Morgan was staying, and the matter was settled: the hotel, seeing Morgan leave, had given the room to someone else.

By four A.M., Walton was back on the elevator, looking forward to several hours of uninterrupted sleep. He wasn't headed back to Morgan's room, however; after the mixup, the sheepish hotel boss gave Walton the penthouse suite for the rest of the night. It was a room befitting a king. There were several televisions, a food spread, the works. A thought crossed Walton's mind as he climbed into bed: wouldn't this be just the perfect setting for an NCAA title party celebration? He then went out the next night and delivered his historic game against Memphis State, leading UCLA to an 87–66 victory. Maybe it wasn't his best game, as Wooden had suggested. Even Walton thought the team had played better on several occasions, but one thing was definitely clear: he would never have another room like that on any road trip, for any team, in any league.

On April 2, the Celtics beat the Pistons, 122–106, in Boston Garden. It was another routine beating of a decent opponent, but this game established the Celtics as the new record holder for consecutive home wins in a single season, a record broken by both Orlando and Chicago in 1995–96. It was their twenty-eighth straight home win since the blowout loss to Portland back on December 6. The victory over the Pistons also stretched the Celtics' winning streak to 13 games (their last loss had been the giveaway at Dallas) and only one other team, the 1970–71 Milwaukee Bucks, had won as many as 13 straight on two different occasions in the same season. Other than their still astounding 33-game streak, the next best the 1971–72 Lakers could put together was a pair of eight-gamers.

Bird was named Player of the Month for March, just as he had been for February. K.C. Jones was honored as Coach of the Month as the team went 15-2. An April 4 victory over the Knicks gave the Celtics 38 home wins, at that time the most ever by a team in one season. They were now 43-6 since Christmas, and the home games were not even close, despite the fact that there was little incentive and Jones at times used his bench as if it were the exhibition season.

The Celtics' winning streak ended at 14 on a Sunday afternoon in Philadelphia in a most unusual fashion. The Celtics led by 11 with 4:37 left, and by six with 77 seconds left. They led 94–92 with seven seconds left and then Larry Bird missed two free throws. (If you gave the Celtics the games they lost because Bird missed key free throws at critical times, the Celtics would have won 70 games that year. And it's not as if Bird usually wasn't up to the task; he led the league in free throw shooting that season.)

After Bird's second miss, the Sixers called a timeout. After the break, McHale tied up Charles Barkley for a jump, but no one controlled the tip and the ball squirted free. Julius Erving retrieved it and tossed in a long, banked three-pointer to beat the clock and the Celtics, 95–94. The Doc wasn't exactly a three-point threat; he made just nine that season in only 32 attempts.

More than a decade later, Walton still has trouble with that one loss. He always remembers the losses, at least the ones that season in Boston and the four at UCLA; he doesn't have enough memory space for all the losses he suffered while playing for the Clippers.

"I mean, can you believe Larry would miss two? And then Kevin couldn't outjump Charles? And the Doc hits a three? How much else had to go wrong? But that's the only way that team ever lost, except the Portland game. Strange things had to happen," he said.

The Celtics learned in the last week of the regular season that their first-round playoff opponent would be the Chicago Bulls. It was a team that would be the first since the league went to sixteen playoff teams in 1969 to make the postseason with 50 defeats. The Bulls had edged out the Cavaliers for the eighth and last playoff spot, a spot that usually meant an early exit.

Knowing who they would play meant little to the Celtics. They were so convinced of their own superiority that the identity of the opponent meant absolutely nothing to them. On April 8, in the seventy-ninth game of the season, the team arrived in Milwaukee, one of the toughest gyms in the league, and Jones surprised everyone by using a starting lineup of Bill Walton, Scott Wedman, Greg Kite, Rick Carlisle, and Jerry Sichting. Dennis Johnson took the night off, Danny Ainge played only eight minutes, Robert Parish just 16, Bird played 31 off the bench—and the Celtics won by 12.

"I thought it was a chance to rest the starters," Jones said. "We've got nothing left to play for."

Rick Carlisle remembered being told at the morning shoot to get some rest that day.

"I said, hmm, okay. I didn't know what was going on, but that was typical. I had basically been an abuse receptacle my first two years there, so I wasn't sure what was going to happen," he said. "Then, at game time, their guys were all jacked up to play against Larry and Kevin and it took the wind right out of their sails. They all exhaled. What is this? That was the only NBA game I ever started."

The game, however, is remembered for more than simply a radical shift in the starting lineup. It saw the spectacular ejection of the normally mild-mannered Kite, who got so upset at referee Lee Jones (Kite has plenty of company in that department) that he threw a basketball at him.

"It was a Nolan Ryan fastball," Kite recalled. "I was really excited about the chance to play, and then Lee Jones called a second foul on me 10 minutes into the game. I went up with Sidney Moncrief and he pulled me to the ground with his right hand. And Lee called the foul on me. I was so mad, I reacted and fired it at him. It knocked the whistle out of his mouth and the whistle flew under our bench. No one moved. He had to reach down under guys' legs to get the whistle back. It was a dumb reaction."

When the team woke up the next morning, Scott Wedman was on crutches; he would miss the next two games with an Achilles problem. The crutches made it look a lot worse than it was. They also awoke to discover that they would have a lottery pick in the 1986 draft, because Seattle, which had traded their pick to Boston in 1984 for Gerald Henderson, was officially eliminated from the playoffs.

The Celtics concluded the 1985–86 regular season hosting the New Jersey Nets. It had been more than five months since New Jersey had rallied to beat the Celtics in the season opener. Four days before the finale, the Celtics again had journeyed to New Jersey only to come away with a loss, this one punctuated by a 41-point, 22-rebound performance by Mike Gminski. Dennis Johnson and Robert Parish didn't help the cause, each missing two big free throws down the stretch.

Larry Bird started the finale, completing an 82-game season, the last time he would ever do it. He had survived the early injury scare with the back and recovered to carry the Celtics over the second half of the season, when, during one punishing stretch, they won 43 of 49 games.

But on this particular afternoon, Bird again had money on his mind. He and Chris Mullin were neck and neck in the battle for the free throw shooting title. Bird was already ensured of being in the top ten in five different categories: scoring, rebounding, free throw percentage, steals, and three-point percentage. No one had had such a well-rounded season since Cliff Hagan in 1960.

But while Bird was assured of finishing among the top ten free throw shooters, he had $30,000 coming to him as a bonus if he won the title. (The Celtics historically have shied away from giving bonuses to players for individual achievement. Bird's particular bonus came from a sporting goods company.) But Danny Ainge, playing the prankster, had a plan in mind to get some of Bird's bonus money—or to deny it outright to the Celtics' forward.

Ainge might have been the best free throw shooter on the team—statistically he was—but he never qualified for the title because he could never muster the minimum number of conversions in a season (125). Heading into the finale, Ainge was shooting 90.3 percent, having made 112 of 124 free throws—to Bird's 89.5 percent.

As game time approached, Ainge realized that if he went 13-for-13 from the line, or even 13-for-15, he would win the title and Bird would be out $30,000. Bird needed to make at least five free throws without a miss to pass Mullin, whose season had ended the night before.

Bird went about his business, making free throws as usual. Ainge, however, startled everyone by uncharacteristically driving to the basket and getting fouled. Soon, Bird and the rest of the Celtics caught on, and K.C. Jones told Jerry Sichting to go into the game for Ainge. But Sichting couldn't get in because Ainge was the one who kept getting fouled. Early in the fourth quarter, Ainge was 11-for-12 from the line. With 8:58 to play, Jones pulled him out of the game and he never got a chance to make the two more he needed. Bird, meanwhile, went 7-for-7 to clinch the title.

"Larry screwed me out of the title," Ainge said. "Larry told me I'd never get to the line enough anyway and even if I did, I'd miss three or four so it wouldn't matter. And I told him I knew how he could miss; I'd just step over the line while he was shooting so it wouldn't count."

After Ainge was yanked, he went back to Jones and asked to be put back into the game. Jones said no. The coach had been getting heavy lobbying from the bench to keep Ainge out of the game. "I couldn't believe what Danny was doing," McHale said. "I was ready to ask K.C. to go back in so I could step over the line while Danny was shooting."

"What I told K.C. was that I wanted to go in, get fouled, and make the first one," Ainge explained. "Then I was going to call timeout and tell Larry that if he promised me $5,000 [of the $30,000], I'd miss the second on purpose. It was a good plan. But I guess it was my fault for bringing it up because I never got the chance."

Almost as an afterthought, the Celtics won the game, 135–107. The victory gave them a 40-1 home record that season and a 67-15 record overall, the fourth best winning percentage in NBA history (.817). It was only the second best in team history, but the 1972–73 team (with a 68-14 record) did not win the championship. For the Celtics, that was the only measure of team greatness.

Despite their impressive record, the Celtics were still 15 wins shy of their ultimate goal. Their first obstacle would be a Chicago Bulls team that had won only 30 games, but had a second-year star by the name of Michael Jordan who, by the time the Boston-Chicago series was over, would establish himself as the next great star of the league. But his time for a championship would have to wait. If you wanted to celebrate in June, this was not the year to be a Bulls fan, or a fan of any other team, except the Boston Celtics.

CHAPTER TEN

Chicago:
Michael Comes of Age

In April 1985, Michael Jordan was merely a terrific basketball player, not yet a one-man conglomerate. He had lived up to much of the advance billing the year before, winning Rookie of the Year honors and making second-team all-NBA. The Bulls made the playoffs for the first time in four years, but were eliminated in the first round.

Better things were expected in 1985–86. The team hired Stan Albeck as its new head coach, replacing the easygoing Kevin Loughery. The front office, too, was changed, as general manager Rod Thorn, the man responsible for drafting Jordan in 1984, was replaced by Jerry Krause.

Chicago started off with three victories before an injury to Jordan brought their season to an end before it ever really got going. Jordan broke a bone in his left foot, and ended up missing 64 games as Chicago's early-season promise went unfulfilled.

The Jordan foot story dominated much of the season in Chicago as the basketball team started to lose time and again. Krause had already started to turn things around before the season by arranging a draft day deal with Cleveland that brought bruiser Charles Oakley to Chicago. But he still had inherited a team that, as he put it, "was a total menagerie."

"When I got the job, there were three guys on the team that I liked," Krause said. "Michael, Dave Corzine, and Rod Higgins. The other nine guys I didn't want around and it took me four years to get rid of them all. They weren't bad basketball players; it was just bad chemistry, people who couldn't play together, people I didn't want representing us as I was attempting to rebuild the franchise."

Krause started making deals at every opportunity, going through seventeen players that season. He acquired Kyle Macy from the Phoenix Suns for two second-round picks. He stole John Paxson from San Antonio for $100,000, money already owed to him by San Antonio from a previous deal.

"I told Angelo [Drossos], the Spurs owner, that he owed us $100,000 for the Dave Corzine deal," Krause recalled. "I said to him, you keep that and give us Paxson. And he said, 'Done.' I then went to our owner and told him I thought I had just spent the best $100,000 I had ever spent. We had checked Paxson out with a friend at Notre Dame and we were told that, in this guy's opinion, he was the finest human being he had dealt with in thirty years. That was good enough for me."

But the Bulls were then, as they would be later, dependent on Michael Jordan. He had no Scottie Pippen, Horace Grant, or even B.J. Armstrong to help him. He had yet to moan about his supporting cast. He still had hair on his head. And he had a bad foot.

As the season progressed, Jordan got more and more frustrated with his inability to play. He had never before missed a game due to injury, going all the way back to his days at Laney High in Wilmington, N.C. Originally, after the break was diagnosed, Jordan was told he might be able to play again in two months. Unable to watch the Bulls, he went back to North Carolina.

"At first," he said, "I couldn't deal with it. I just wanted to get away because I wanted to play so badly and I couldn't. So I stayed away. Finally, I got into a situation where I could watch the games. But it was hard."

Shortly after Christmas, he was placed in a walking cast. The Bulls had gone 12-28 since his injury. Jordan decided he'd do some shooting around with the boys at Chapel Hill. Nothing too strenuous, he figured, just some light shooting. These were the guys he played with during the summer, and, unable to limit himself to a single shootaround, Jordan was soon going five-on-five with no supervision. Krause knows about it now; he did not know about it then.

"We would have had a bigger problem had I known," Krause said. "But I did not know until after all of it had happened. If I had known, I would have gone crazy. If he had reinjured himself, it would have been scary. Doctors tell me the navicular bone is the hardest bone to heal because there's no blood supply."

In March, Jordan met with the Bulls' management as well as a trio of doctors familiar with his case. Wearing nonprescription eyeglasses to make himself appear serious, Jordan said he was ready to return.

"I wanted to test it then," he said, "because if something was wrong, I'd have the summer to correct it. I didn't want to wait until next season, because if there was still a problem, I might miss some of that season, too."

That sounded logical. Tests had revealed that the bone was healing properly but that there was still a 10 to 20 percent chance he would reinjure himself if he returned at this point. Jordan focused on the 80 to 90 percent probability he would not hurt himself again. Krause focused on the small but devastating possibility of reinjury.

"I simply did not want to take the chance," Krause said. "In a meeting, Jerry [Reinsdorf, the owner] asked Michael, 'If I gave you a ten-chamber gun and it had only one bullet in it, would you spin that around and put it next to your head and pull the trigger?' Michael said he would not. Reinsdorf asked him if he would take any Tylenol if he knew the bottle was 10 percent cyanide. Michael said he didn't have a headache. It was wild. I did not want to go down in history as the guy who ruined his career. I mean, I'm thinking of my career, too. I'm a young general manager. But he talked us into it."

Jordan said, "No one understood my point of view. It was my body. I was the one taking the risk. Why didn't anyone back me up?"

He was activated March 14 and returned under a strict schedule. His minutes were limited and the limits were enforced. On two occasions, the Bulls lost games they might very well have won because Albeck pulled Jordan once his time allotment was reached. That led to the inevitable speculation that the Bulls were not interested in making the playoffs and would take their chances in the lottery.

But then Chicago won six of its last 10 games to sneak into the playoffs with an appalling record of 30-52. Jordan averaged 22.7 points a game in the 18 games he did play, with a high of 33. He averaged only 25 minutes in those 18 games.

But when the playoffs arrived, Jordan was off the leash. He would be able to play as long as he needed to play. No one, not even Krause, gave the Bulls any chance, even though Chicago had beaten Boston once and had played them tough on a couple of other occasions, all without Jordan.

"I thought it would be a great learning experience for us," Krause said of the series. "We didn't have much of a chance to beat them. Maybe we could steal one at home and learn something. But that was a great, great team. We knew that."

The Bulls were, as Krause said, a collection of characters. Their non-Jordan scoring threat came from Orlando Woolridge, who played a flashy, hotdog, irritating game, but who also had a knack for the hole. He, however, had gone AWOL briefly in midseason. By playoff time he was back causing Bird a myriad of problems.

Dave Corzine, who could have passed for a defensive lineman, was the center, and Oakley, who was playing as well or better than any rookie that year in April, was the other forward. Oakley started the last 30 games and averaged 15.4 points, 12.8 rebounds, and 2.7 assists in that stretch, much of which he spent at center. An unrelenting bull on the boards, he had the NBA's top rebound game of the season (26) and was one of many Krause finds from obscure colleges (Virginia Union). Earl Monroe (Winston-Salem) and Scottie Pippen (Central Arkansas) were others.

Kyle Macy, a true coach's son, started with Jordan in the backcourt and while he never turned into the pro many thought he would be, he was a suitable point guard and a certifiable three-point threat. John Paxson, Sidney Green, and Gene Banks were the primary reserves for Albeck, who in the previous six years had coached at Cleveland, San Antonio, and New Jersey.

The Celtics, meanwhile, had a minor concern as they prepared for the Bulls. Before the regular season finale, Bird had had a corn removed from his right foot. He took off the following day, but said he would be ready for the opener three days hence.

Jerry Sichting also had a little trouble before the series, but his was mental, not physical. He told everyone that he was excited about participating in the playoffs after so many down years in Indianapolis. He openly wondered what it would be like. Were the playoffs really as different as everyone said they were?

Sichting's comment took everyone by surprise. Although he told everyone differently back then, and although he swears to this day he has no recollection of ever appearing in a playoff game for Indiana, he did. Sichting not only played 73 seconds in an April 2, 1981, playoff game against Philadelphia, but he also created a turnover, stealing the ball from Steve Mix.

"I still don't remember it," Sichting said, even when given the updated information. "All I remember was maybe going to the scorer's table to check into the game. But I can't remember playing in it."

Sichting would have no such problem in Boston.

Game 1 was on a Thursday night with Game 2 scheduled the following Sunday for national television. Back then, Boston, not Jordan, was the darling of the network. The fact that Jordan—even then the most electrifying player in the game—happened to be on the other team was an added enticement. The network execs wanted the Celtics because they drove the ratings then as Jordan would in the late 1980s and 1990s.

It did not take long for everyone to understand two things: the playoffs were different and Jordan was going to make this an interesting series. He came flying out of the box in Game 1, scoring 30 in the first half, as the Bulls took a two-point lead into the locker room. The man whose task it was to defend Jordan was Dennis Johnson, still regarded as one of the top defensive guards in the game. He was having no luck. His offense wasn't much better; he missed his first seven shots.

The second half was another story. Jordan continued to score but the rest of the Bulls were no match for the Celtics. Jordan finished with 49 points, and only three others—Elgin Baylor, Bob Pettit, and Wilt Chamberlain—had ever scored more points in a playoff game against the Celtics. Jordan took 36 of the Bulls' 86 shots and scored almost one-half of their points. It wasn't enough.

Johnson had a complete turnaround in the second half, scoring 24 of his 26 points. Boston's big men dominated underneath and the Celtics won going away, 123–104, as Bird, McHale, and Parish scored 30, 27 and 23 points respectively. Boston's front-line dominance was no surprise. In a 123–105 victory over Chicago in early April, the Big Three had outscored the Chicago front line 83–26 and outrebounded them 37–13.

There was no way the Bulls could compete in the trenches, so they waged war on the perimeter with the spectacular Jordan. "That was their only chance," McHale recalled. If they were going to go down, they would go down with their best man shooting.

The aftermath of Game 1 was filled with Jordan tributes from both locker rooms, but no one was prepared for what would happen seventy-two hours later. This game, as much as any, probably served as Michael Jordan's coming-out party in the NBA. In front of a national television audience, Jordan came very close to single-handedly beating the best team on the planet.

A decade later, Jordan could still marvel at that day. He scored 63 points, making 22 of 41 shots, ranging from perimeter jumpers to a baseline dunk. On this day, there was no doubt in anyone's mind who the greatest individual talent in the game was. The Celtics, however, were the better team, defeating the Bulls, 135–131, in double overtime.

"The points," he said, "didn't mean a thing to me. I would have rather gotten a victory. But that was one of my better games in that building."

The NBA was now officially on Jordan Alert. At some point in the not-too-distant future—five years to be exact—the game, the ball, the gym would all be his. This game told Bird, Magic Johnson, and the other stars of the day that they were all playing on borrowed time. Jordan had arrived.

Jordan was fouled 10 times in the act of shooting—by five different Celtics. Bill Walton, who had the misfortune of matching up with Jordan on switches, fouled him four times. Dennis Johnson fouled him three times, and Danny Ainge, Kevin McHale, and Robert Parish each fouled him once. Of Jordan's 22 baskets, only one was a dunk. But that one was a thing of beauty: a quicksilver baseline drive and dunk, right over the helpless McHale.

"That day," Krause remembered, "he was as good as anyone I've ever seen. I saw Elgin Baylor dominate like that once, but Michael, on that day, was as good as anyone I've ever seen. And what made it even more amazing was that he did it within the context of our offense. He made plays in addition to scoring."

Jordan had six assists and three steals in his 53-minute virtuoso performance. He made 19 of 21 free throws. He made 13 jump shots, seven drives, one follow-up and got one basket on a goaltending call. The 63 points broke the NBA record for most points in a playoff game, the previous best being 61 by Elgin Baylor in 1962. A decade later, Jordan's record remains. Baylor's is still second.

The game's biggest basket, however, came not from Jordan, or from Larry Bird, but from Jerry Sichting. And the Celtic who bailed out his teammates in the second half was neither Bird nor Kevin McHale nor Dennis Johnson but Danny Ainge, who midway through the third quarter had yet to score a point. The Celtics may have had their share of superstars, but first and foremost they were a team, with different men stepping up at different points in the year.

After struggling for two and a half quarters, Ainge finally got hot in the third, scoring 13 points in the quarter, 11 in the final 2:36, to cut a 10-point Chicago lead to one after three quarters of play. The Celtics had the Bulls exactly where they wanted them when the fourth quarter began, but Jordan would not go quietly. He scored 18 points in the fourth, nailing two key free throws with six seconds left to send the game into overtime. At the end of regulation, Jordan had 54.

In overtime, however, Jordan missed an uncontested 15-footer with two seconds left that likely would have won the game. He had made much harder ones all afternoon, but this one spun out, sending the game into a second overtime. With the game tied at 131, Sichting made his huge basket from the perimeter on an inside-out feed from McHale. Jordan then missed from the left baseline, and Bird and Parish sealed the victory by working a picturesque pick-and-roll, with Parish swishing a 12-footer to finally kill the beast.

Everything else that happened that afternoon was lost in the glare of Michael Jordan's performance. McHale actually made a basket while sitting on Dave Corzine. Bird played the final three quarters with a hyperextended right pinkie finger and had only one basket in the final 16:32. Chicago had eight three-point plays, but no three-point baskets. Bill Walton had 13 rebounds in the first half, in 13 minutes.

It was an amazing game all around, but when the final buzzer sounded, the only words that anyone could utter were Michael Jordan. Everyone knew he was good, but this was extraordinary. "It was God disguised as Michael Jordan," Bird commented. From that point on, Michael Jordan would be regarded in a different light altogether.

But after the accolades had been handed out—and everyone had them after this game—Jordan still faced the unpleasant truth that his Bulls were now down 0-2 in a best-of-five series against the best team in the NBA.

The series shifted to Chicago Stadium, at the time one of the loudest buildings in the NBA. This was back before expansion when basketball was a game to watch and enjoy, not an event complete with laser light shows, fireworks, numbing public address announcers, and other assaults on the senses. Back then, the noise wasn't contrived or staged; it was genuine and spontaneous.

Everyone expected Chicago Stadium to be wild. What would Jordan have in store in his own building for a team he had nearly beaten on the road single-handedly? The Celtics were expecting the worst, but arrived optimistic. They only had to win once in Chicago to end the series. McHale announced that he had brought only his toothbrush because he didn't anticipate spending more than one night in town.

The third game could not possibly live up to the standards set in the first two, and it didn't. The Celtics put on their road faces and smothered Jordan in a human sandwich whenever possible. The same player who had averaged 56 points against them in the first two games was held to a mortal 19, and just five in the last three quarters.

The Celtics survived a 14-point Jordan first quarter and never trailed during the game. They led by 14 at the half and then ran what Ainge rightfully called "a clinic" in the third quarter, building the lead to 28. At one point, Chicago's Sidney Green turned to Ainge and said, "You guys are an amazing team to watch. It must be fun to play like that."

Jordan added 10 rebounds and nine assists, but those were

not the numbers the Celtics cared about. They were determined to stop his scoring assault and they succeeded. Every time he turned, he saw two, sometimes three, green jerseys blocking his way. He had no choice but to pass the ball. Frustrated, Jordan was hit with a technical and later fouled out with 5:24 to play. In Game 3, Jordan finally seemed human.

With a final score of 122–104, the Celtics' sweep was complete. The series had signaled Jordan's arrival as a major player, but it had also showcased Ainge as a crucial member of this Celtics team. He played a big role in Game 2, and then outscored Jordan in Game 3, scoring 20. Time and again he would hit from the perimeter when the big men were double-teamed underneath. Other times, he would take his man off the dribble before the Bulls front-liners could react. Ainge's defense was also superb throughout the series.

What the rest of the league did not need was another threat on the Celtics, but that was exactly what Ainge had been against the Bulls. With Jordan gone from the picture, the Celtics prepared for the next round. They found out two days later they would be playing the Atlanta Hawks, who eliminated the Pistons in four games.

"That's great," Bird said. "I'm tired of playing the same teams every year. This will be a little different."

CHAPTER ELEVEN

Atlanta:
The Perfect Quarter

As much as the emerging greatness of Michael Jordan came to personify the Chicago Bulls, the ongoing excellence of Dominique Wilkins defined the Atlanta Hawks in the mid-1980s.

Unlike Jordan, however, Wilkins was never able to elevate the play of his teammates or to make a serious run at an NBA title. There was always a missing dimension to Wilkins's game, a sense that he was interested more in personal statistics than in winning percentages. At times, Wilkins was the best player on the floor, other times he was a player out of control—unable to channel his intense, competitive energy into a successful post-season run.

Wilkins was one of the greatest players ever to wear an Atlanta Hawks uniform, but in his thirteen-plus years there, the team never once won a seven-game series. With Jordan out for most of 1985–86, Wilkins was, if only temporarily, the most exciting player in the game.

He was also one of the most offensive-minded players in basketball. The season before, he had the dubious distinction of

being the first player in NBA history to miss 1,000 shots in a season. He again missed more than 1,000 shots in 1985–86, but the
Hawks improved from 34 victories to 50.

"One player carried us that season," said Hawks coach Mike
Fratello, "and that player was Dominique."

Wilkins won the league scoring title, averaging 30.3 points a
game. He also averaged a career high 7.9 rebounds, 2.6 assists,
and 1.8 steals a game; he also shot 81.8 percent from the free
throw line. He played an average of 39.1 minutes a game, and
finished runner-up to Larry Bird in the balloting for Most Valuable Player.

That year, the Hawks, the second youngest team in the NBA,
finished second in the Central Division, seven games behind
Milwaukee. Just one year before, they had failed to make the
playoffs. Fratello, in his third season, was named the league's
Coach of the Year. General manager Stan Kasten was named the
Executive of the Year. And Spud Webb, a 5-7 rookie, won the
Slam Dunk contest during All-Star weekend; he was ten inches
shorter than the next-smallest contestant.

Wilkins enjoyed playing against the Celtics. He averaged 35
points a game against Boston during the regular season in six
close games. Nicknamed the Human Highlight Film, Dominique's sheer athleticism was at times stunning. The Hawks
were a collection of young players who loved to run the floor
and crash the boards, trying to win on sheer energy and ability.
For most of the season, especially over the final 55 games when
they were 37-18, that strategy worked. When Fratello had his
starting lineup intact, which he did for this series—Atlanta had
a 23-5 record. Fratello had to use seventeen different starting
lineups during the regular season because of injuries (primarily
to Doc Rivers), and it wasn't difficult to imagine how good Atlanta would have been had they played healthy throughout the
year. But they were healthy for this series, and they were ready
for the Celtics.

The Celtics, meanwhile, spent their three days off preparing
for their next opponent and twenty-four hours focusing solely

on Atlanta. The Hawks had clinched the Detroit series with a double-overtime win on a Friday night. Game 1 against the Celtics was Sunday afternoon.

The opener of the Boston-Atlanta series was held on the first day of Daylight Savings Time. The Hawks may have moved their clocks ahead physically, but mentally they were still an hour or two behind.

"That was the first time for a lot of our guys and we were still young, without a clear understanding of what it takes to win in the playoffs," coach Mike Fratello recalled. "Yeah, we had won 50 games that season and we had just beaten Detroit, but at the playoff level, we didn't have [what veteran teams like Boston did]. But going into that series we were excited, it was new, and we came up against this roster of All-Stars and future Hall of Famers. They put you to sleep quickly."

That was the case in the opener, as the Celtics, still nowhere near as efficient as they had been in the Chicago clincher, won, 103–91.

The 12-point margin is misleading. Atlanta was never really in the game. Wilkins was a stone-cold 4-of-15 (thanks in part to some excellent defense by Kevin McHale), and Boston led by 26 with 10½ minutes left before garbage time ensued. The Celtics had put together a 37–17 run in the second half that effectively finished off Atlanta.

The highlight of the run was a beautifully executed Bird-McHale play where Bird pump-faked five times before dishing it off to McHale, who finished the play with a rolling scoop. McHale explained his shooting theory simply: "When you have three men on you, shoot. When you have four men on you, pass."

Neither team figured Game 2 would be as lopsided as the first, and it wasn't. The Celtics were working on a 144-day home winning streak that seemed in jeopardy when Atlanta rallied from an 18-point deficit to trail 109–108 with four minutes left to play. By that time, everyone had forgotten about a confrontation between Mike Fratello and a former Celtics scoring official, who had to be ejected for taunting the Hawks' head coach. And everyone had forgotten about an altercation between Danny Ainge and Scott Hastings that led to Ainge's ejection. Referee Earl Strom had mistakenly booted Ainge for kicking Hastings; Ainge, as the game tapes would later confirm, had indeed kicked Hastings, but only to free himself after Hastings had pulled him to the floor.

But those events were long gone and the Celtics, holding a perilous one-point lead against a young, rampaging team, had to turn to Bird to bail them out. For the first time in these play-offs, Bird truly delivered. The Celtics closed the game by running the table, scoring 10 unanswered points, with Bird getting eight of them. He converted off a Robert Parish miss and then drained three straight shots, including a banner-scraping moon shot. He assisted on the other basket, a Parish layup, and he finished the game with 36 points. The Celtics won, 119–108, and took their 2–0 lead to Atlanta.

It was critical for the Celtics to win the first two games at home. Only a handful of teams have ever rallied from 0–2 deficits, and in order for the Hawks to win the series, they would have to win at least one game at the Garden. That wasn't their only concern.

The Hawks also had to worry about a now-hot Larry Bird, who was feeling like a young pup. The year before, he was dragging during the playoffs with his sore elbow. Earlier in this season, he had the back problem. But now he felt as good as he ever had at this stage of the season, and when Bird felt good, no one could stop him.

"When the playoffs started that year," he said, "I was feeling terrific. Earlier that year, I didn't have an inside game because I couldn't bump, and I didn't have an outside game. I was a different Larry Bird than what people were used to seeing. But, in about a month and a half, I went from the bottom to the top. And once the playoffs started, I felt so good it was almost like I had taken the first two months off. I never felt that good at the end of a season again."

The team generally mirrored Bird's performance, so they, too, were feeling good for this series. One of the real talents of the 1985–86 Celtics was their passing ability. They moved the ball as well as any team, always found the open man, and made the extra pass that drove opponents crazy. Any team with Bird, Bill Walton (there has never been a better passing center), Dennis Johnson, and Danny Ainge was going to have its dazzling moments. Parish was adept at finding an open man every now and then, and even McHale, who amassed 22 assists in the three Chicago wins and the first two Atlanta victories, started to get into the act.

In their first two wins over the Hawks, the Celtics registered assists on two of every three baskets, an outstanding ratio. They may not have been the quickest or most athletic team, but Mother Nature has yet to invent a human who can outrun a crisply passed basketball. The Celtics' ball movement made up for whatever lack of quickness they had.

As the series shifted to Atlanta, the Celtics received some bad news: Bill Walton would miss Game 3. In Game 2, he bruised his left knee in a collision with Tree Rollins (the same guy who broke Walton's wrist in March), and despite rigorous therapy he could not play. (He also would miss Game 4.) The Celtics remained undaunted. They were heading into a building where they had not lost in more than five years, a streak of 12 straight wins. And, after their two wins in Boston, they had won 27 of the last 30 games against the Hawks, including all eight this season.

Atlanta needed Game 3 to have any hope. The Celtics made sure the Hawks didn't get it. K.C. Jones played his starters an average of 42 minutes each and the Celtics won, 111–107. They now had a 3–0 lead, and the only remaining question was whether Atlanta would die fighting at home or at the Garden.

Thanks to an inspiring performance by Spud Webb, the

Hawks opted for the latter. Webb was an intriguing player, a 67-inch rookie who was viewed by most as being too small to play in the NBA. The Pistons had selected him in the fourth round of the draft and released him at the end of training camp. The Hawks picked him up on the recommendation of Brendan Suhr, a trusted Fratello lieutenant. He made the team and played some serious minutes when Glenn (Doc) Rivers was injured. He added a certain panache to the team, becoming an overnight sensation by winning the Slam Dunk title.

By April, he was tired of talking about dunking. He felt he was a legitimate NBA player who could contribute quality minutes to any team. He was right; he was still playing a decade later with the Minnesota Timberwolves after a four-year stop in Sacramento and a brief return to Atlanta. (Incidentally, so were five other members of that Atlanta team: Kevin Willis, Jon Koncak, Glenn Rivers, John Battle, and Antoine Carr. Wilkins was playing in Greece and Tree Rollins was only a year into retirement.) In Game 4, Webb was the bolt of electricity the Hawks needed to revive themselves.

Webb had 21 points and 12 assists in 24 minutes and was equal parts breathtaking and energizing. Dominique Wilkins fed off Webb's intensity, scoring 37, but it was Webb who took control of the game. He keyed a 12–1 run at the end of the third quarter, erasing a 61–58 Boston lead. The Hawks almost panicked at the end, as they had in Games 2 and 3, but an 8–2 run late in the fourth preserved a 106–94 victory. The Celtics were not at their best and did not deserve to win, shooting 34 percent and making only 29 field goals (just seven more than Michael Jordan had made all by himself two weeks earlier). The Celtics were overdue for a poor outing—their six straight postseason wins had established a franchise record—but they were going back home and had absolutely no intention of returning to Atlanta.

Those fortunate enough to witness the third quarter of Game 5 saw one of the game's finest moments of basketball—by any team in any decade. Danny Ainge has a videotape of this game at home and, when he wants to reflect on the golden moments in Boston, he pops it into his VCR and fast forwards to the first twelve minutes of the second half.

"I call it 'The Way Basketball Is Supposed to Be Played,'" Ainge says with the air of a proud papa. "That was maybe the most impressive quarter of basketball ever played. Atlanta just had no sniff."

Ainge was right. The Celtics delivered the coup de grâce to the Hawks that day in the third quarter, outscoring Atlanta by the still astounding total of 36–6. It made the final 12 minutes and the result of the series utterly superfluous. The Celtics were advancing. The Hawks were heading home.

There was nothing to indicate the Celtics were about to hit hoop heaven that day. They had constructed a 66–55 lead at halftime, nothing insurmountable, and appeared on their way to mercifully ending the series in five games. Bill Walton returned to the lineup, but played just seven inconsequential minutes. On this day, though, Walton's return did not matter.

In the first six-plus minutes of the third, Boston put the hammer down, expanding their 11-point lead to 17. In that stretch, they outscored the Hawks 12–6. With 5:17 left, Larry Bird stepped to the line to make a technical after Atlanta was called for an illegal defense violation. Bird's shot started a truly historic run of 24 points over the remaining 317 seconds.

The Celtics could do nothing wrong. On defense, Ainge and Dennis Johnson either stopped their man, forced a turnover, or directed him into the interior, where Parish, Bird, and McHale stood waiting. Atlanta committed five turnovers, had two shots blocked, and looked as though they had just witnessed their own public flogging. "All you can do is call timeout and make substitutions," Fratello observed. "The league doesn't let you make trades during games."

The Celtics threw everything at them: Danny Ainge drained a three-pointer that prompted the normally stoic Dennis Johnson to do a little dance; Parish executed a beautiful backdoor layup; and McHale wowed the crowd by jamming home a fast-break dunk that completely blew the lid off the building.

"Who wants to remember those things?" Mike Fratello said years later. "It seemed like it was raining baskets from everywhere. It seemed like they made every shot. They were all on fire at the same time and it didn't matter what you did."

Atlanta tried timeouts, substitutions, anything. Nothing worked. Tree Rollins got so upset he threw the ball at Ainge on an inbounds pass. Ainge caught the ball, made the layup and promptly returned the ball to the frustrated Rollins, who was still standing out of bounds.

"That was the kind of day it was for us," Rivers said. "The game was close and, just like that, it was over. That was a tremendous team."

The onslaught continued, unabated, until McHale made two free throws at the end of the quarter. The score was now 102–61. By the time the game ended, the Celtics had delivered the ultimate haymaker, a 132–99 win, ending the season for the Hawks.

"I don't think you'll ever see a quarter of basketball like that ever again," McHale said. "I mean, the look on the faces of those Atlanta players leaving the floor after the game; it was like they had just been in a war. It was shell-shock. I think they couldn't wait to get out of there. It was as close to perfection as you're ever going to see."

Once again, the Celtics found themselves waiting for their next opponent. It would either be Philadelphia or Milwaukee, who at that time were engaged in a seven-game battle that would be decided by a single point. The final play of the season dictated who went where: Julius Erving missed a shot at the buzzer and the Bucks, the Central Division champions who had the second-best record in the East, advanced to the next round. They were ecstatic then. It would soon become apparent that there was no cause for celebration. The Bucks were headed to Boston.

Milwaukee:
Six Days in May

Unlike most teams, the Milwaukee Bucks' public persona was defined not by one of their players, although they had some good ones, but by their coach. In the mid-1980s, Don Nelson *was* the Milwaukee Bucks.

By 1986, he had been in Milwaukee for a decade, earning respect around the league as an innovative coach for whom any player would like to play. Fans adored him. He raised money for Wisconsin farmers with Nellie's Farm Fund and launched a business selling fish ties. He was arguably as popular as anyone in the state and had total control over the team, thanks to a terrific relationship with his boss, owner Jim Fitzgerald.

He had just coached Milwaukee to its seventh consecutive division title, winning 57 games. He was now in the conference finals for the third time in four years, one series away from the NBA Finals. But if there was ever a fitting epitaph for Nelson's Milwaukee teams, it would be "One Series Away." Despite a string of 50-win seasons, there was always someone better in his path, usually Boston or Philadelphia, and he never made it out of the Eastern Conference.

The problem, generally, was that he never had a legitimate
NBA center. (He did have Bob Lanier for a few seasons, but
Lanier was on the downside of his career.) In the summer of
1985, the same time the Celtics were romancing Bill Walton,
Nelson was putting together an offer sheet for Joe Barry Carroll,
who had played a season in Europe but was still the property of
the Golden State Warriors. But Golden State matched it and
Carroll returned to play for the Warriors. Nelson got nothing.

In the 1985–86 season, Nelson went to war with three centers—Randy Breuer, Paul Mokeski, and Alton Lister—which
meant, in reality, he went to war with none. The following year,
he acquired Jack Sikma from Seattle, but he, like Lanier, had his
better years behind him. Eventually, Nelson left Milwaukee in a
dispute with new owner Herb Kohl, retaining his popularity but
still without that elusive trip to the championship. That would
continue to dog him through the next decade. "Yeah, he might
be a great coach, but what exactly has he ever won?" was a com-
monly heard retort after he left Milwaukee and then reestab-
lished himself in Oakland and, briefly, in New York.

Nelson would prefer that his epitaph read that he was a ver-
satile coach, able to work the chalkboard and to get along with
his players. No one ever knocked Don Nelson in those days. He
maintained that reputation until his famous contretemps with
Chris Webber in 1994 forced him out of his job as the coach and
general manager of Golden State. The idea that Nelson could
not communicate with any player seemed preposterous, until
others surfaced in the wake of the Webber rebellion to report
that they, too, were not exactly living an Ozzie & Harriet life under Nellie. Mario Elie, who won two rings with Houston, played
for Nelson at Golden State and said, "He treated us like dogs."

But there was no dissent in 1986 when the Bucks and Celtics
met in the conference finals. Nelson was undeniably successful
and was just coming off an emotional victory over the 76ers. To
make things more interesting, he was, of course, a former Celtic
who tried to incorporate the notion of Celtic pride into his
coaching philosophy. He had been a valuable role player on five

Boston championship teams and was hired in Milwaukee by Wayne Embry, a former Celtic teammate, to be an assistant to Larry Costello in 1976. Eighteen games into the first season, Costello was gone and Nelson, who hardly knew how to call a play or ask for a timeout, was suddenly an NBA head coach. He was thirty-six years old.

His first playoff meeting against the Celtics (in 1983) resulted in a 4–0 Milwaukee sweep. Nelson had some choice words to say that year about Danny Ainge, whom he labeled a "cheap shot artist." In the Celtics' previous series against the Atlanta Hawks, the ultra-competitive Ainge had a fight with Tree Rollins, who ended up biting Ainge's finger. As the years went on, the story got so twisted that some people actually thought that Ainge did the biting. Ainge played well in the first two games of that Milwaukee-Boston series, scoring 25 points in Game 2; but when the teams played Games 3 and 4 in Milwaukee, he was booed every time he touched the ball. Nellie's words were gospel in Milwaukee.

Nelson's shot at Ainge temporarily enraged his former boss and mentor, Red Auerbach (although Auerbach also recognized gamesmanship when he saw it). The following year, in the 1983–84 Eastern Conference Finals, Boston dusted off Milwaukee in five games on the way to an NBA championship. This year, few gave the Bucks a chance to win more than one game; they had lost all five to the Celtics during the regular season and their key player, Sidney Moncrief, was ailing.

Moncrief was a special player, an exceptional defender who was one of the most respected individuals in the game. He was so popular in his home state of Arkansas that the governor at the time, a young Democrat named Bill Clinton, remarked, "The only comfort I can take from having the smallest governor's salary in the country is that it might stop Sidney Moncrief from running against me."

Moncrief had grown up in the projects of Little Rock, developed into a terrific player at the University of Arkansas under Eddie Sutton, and then went on to Milwaukee as the No. 5 pick

overall in the 1979 draft. He had been a first-team all-NBA selection in 1982–83 and the Bucks needed him healthy if they
harbored any hopes of defeating the Celtics in this series. But
Moncrief was hobbled by an incredibly painful torn plantar fas-
cia ligament in his left foot and was questionable for the first
game.

The Bucks still had some good players around him. They had
Terry Cummings, whom Nelson had stolen from the Clippers
along with Craig Hodges and Ricky Pierce for a declining Marques Johnson and Junior Bridgeman. They had Paul Pressey, a
defensive-minded player whom Nelson called his "point forward" and through whom much of the Bucks' offense ran. He
also guarded Larry Bird, surrendering four inches and thirty-
five pounds.

But Milwaukee's Achilles' heel was at center. With Robert
Parish and Bill Walton on the agenda, not to mention Bird,
McHale, and the continually brilliant Boston backcourt, Nelson
felt overmatched, undermanned, and a bit out of sorts.

"It was like that show, *The Man of La Mancha,*" he said. In
other words, beating the Celtics was an impossible dream. He
knew better. So did everyone else.

The first game provided a clue of just how lopsided this series
would be. Yes, the Bucks were still on an emotional high from
their grueling seven-game series with the 76ers. And yes, the
Celtics were home and had had several days to rest. But does
that explain a 32-point Boston win during which the Celtics
trailed for exactly 12 seconds?

The Celtics led 29–12 after one quarter and led by as many as
29 in the first half. The final score was 128–96. Boston had now
won their last two playoff games by a total of 65 points. It was the
first time in the Celtics' playoff history that they had won consecutive games by 30 or more points.

The Celtics, as always, behaved like professionals afterward,
but, inside, they knew the outcome of this series was a foregone
conclusion. They had felt the same way against Chicago and At-

lanta, too. Why would Milwaukee, a team that had yet to beat them this year, be any different?

Even the fans realized that this series was merely the last prelude to what everyone figured would be a third straight Boston–Los Angeles final. The crowd was silent in Boston Garden during much of Game 2—which the Celtics won, 122–111—as all five starters scored 20 points or more. The fans were already taking Boston's dominance over the Bucks for granted.

Boston never trailed in Game 2. Over the first 96 minutes of the series, the Bucks led for only 12 seconds. The Celtics were running the show. But Milwaukee didn't fall down in this one and was actually within four points midway through the fourth before the Celtics finally put it away. The Celtics didn't do anything flashy or spectacular; they just played good, solid basketball to defeat a less-talented team. Moncrief returned after missing the opener and was ineffective, scoring only two points in 37 minutes. Milwaukee's play was best summed up by the fact that Randy Breuer, their mediocre center, was their leading scorer after two games.

There was, however, an event that night that spoke volumes about what the philosophy of the 1985–86 Celtics was all about: Bill Walton was named the winner of the NBA's Sixth Man Award. Considering that it was Auerbach who first popularized the sixth-man concept with Frank Ramsey and John Havlicek, and considering that Kevin McHale was a two-time winner, the achievement by Walton was especially noteworthy. He had appeared in 80 games and was the difference in more than a few. He was seen as the man who upset the delicate balance among the league's elite teams.

Walton wanted this award. He repeatedly had voiced displeasure and even disgust at the prospect of being named Comeback Player of the Year, although he would have qualified for that, too. But the Sixth Man was special. It meant contributing to a team. It wasn't based on any other statistic but winning. It was what the Celtics stood for and, even though he played only one meaningful season in Boston, Walton, like so many others who had brief stints in Boston, to this day still considers himself a Celtic.

How had the season gone? "On a scale of one to ten," he said, "it has been about a twenty-five." There couldn't have been a more content individual on the planet that night. The Celtics and Walton had been a perfect fit and this award honored that.

There was, of course, the obligatory Walton ribbing, mainly from McHale, who was now a full-time starter and ineligible for the award.

"Geez, it just shows you how far the league has gone downhill," McHale said. "This one probably means more to him than the MVP award because he was playing against all those 6-5 centers back then."

But McHale, as much as anyone, knew and appreciated what Bill Walton brought to the Celtics, both as a player and as a source of fun and excitement.

"Bill was my idol growing up. I had one picture in my dorm room and it was of Bill. He was unique. I mean, how many guys can say they had Patty Hearst living in their basement?" McHale said jokingly.

Games 3 and 4 in Milwaukee were held on a weekend. If the Celtics played their cards right, they could be home Sunday night to await the winner of the Western Conference finals. Already the matchup everyone anticipated was in jeopardy. The upstart Houston Rockets had split the first two games of their conference final with the mighty Lakers. In Game 3 of that series, with the Celtics' coaches rooting them on from a Milwaukee bar, the Rockets defeated the Lakers, 117–109.

Chris Ford, the Celtics' assistant coach, was cheering for Houston on every possession. Didn't he want to take on the Lakers? Didn't he prefer Los Angeles to Houston? Ford showed his hand and said, simply, "Another ring. I want another ring." If that piece of jewelry would be easier to obtain at the expense of the Rockets, so be it.

There was still work to do in Milwaukee, however. The Bucks pulled out all the stops for Game 3: the governor of the state proclaimed it "Nellie Day" in honor of the Bucks' coach. In addition, Nellie, who had just become a first-time grandfather, was asking for donations to help the state's farmers; he would later ride a tractor across the state, soliciting donations and talking hoops with the people.

His team needed something, too, something that went beyond money or sympathy. The Bucks gave it all they had, but it still wasn't enough. The Celtics prevailed, 111–107, rallying from a 13-point deficit in the third quarter, keyed by a play in which Bird dove for a loose ball, tore it away from Paul Mokeski, and, while sitting on the floor, two-handed a pass to McHale for a layup.

Boston trailed by five after three but then outscored the Bucks 29–20 in the fourth. Their frontcourt accounted for 76 points and 39 rebounds. Afterward, Nelson admitted the Bucks had taken their best shot and he told his players that they were now in a big, big hole. How big? "I believe the Grand Canyon is what I told them," Nellie said.

The Celtics, however, suffered their first serious injury of the playoffs when Scott Wedman was hurt in a freak collision in the third quarter. He sustained broken ribs when Terry Cummings's left knee nailed his chest. The team said Wedman might be out as long as two weeks. Given that the NBA Finals were going to start in a week or so, Wedman's availability for the rest of the season was iffy at best.

Boston now led 3–0 and the players did not need to be reminded that two years earlier they had been in a similar situation in Milwaukee and lost Game 4, necessitating a fifth game in Boston to officially bury the Bucks. Bird did not want that to happen. "We come to sweep," he said. "We don't come to split."

However, before Game 4, a controversy erupted. A Bucks season ticket holder sitting behind the Celtics bench saw some discarded capsules under the bench and took them to the police. It was, the man said, evidence that the players were using drugs. After the Boston victory in Game 3, some Milwaukee policemen came into the locker room with the capsules and asked what was going on. An infuriated Bird offered right then and there to be tested. "Get me a cup," he said defiantly. "I'll go right now."

The capsules had been full of ammonia, although the police would not discover that until Monday because their crime lab was closed for the weekend.

"A lot of guys then, but especially Larry, sniffed ammonia capsules before every game to wake them up and clear their heads," Jerry Sichting said. "You would break the capsules into a towel and then put your head in the towel. It was something we did every game."

NBA publicity man Terry Lyons called NBA commissioner David Stern, who quickly issued a statement denouncing the publicity hound. Bird firmly stated, "I've never been involved in anything like that. All I do is drink beer and that gets me in enough trouble."

Bird got his revenge the next day. He went out and tormented the poor Bucks, destroying them with a memorable fourth-quarter shooting exhibition that led to a 111–98 Boston victory and a 4–0 sweep. Ainge played a brilliant game (going all 48 minutes for the first time in his career) but Bird was the man who received all the attention after this game. He had 13 assists, 16 rebounds, and outscored the entire Milwaukee team in the fourth, 17–16. Bird rained five three-pointers on the Bucks, four in the final four minutes while playing guard after Dennis Johnson had fouled out.

The final two three-pointers were absolutely demoralizing. With Boston leading 103–94, Bird basically dared the Bucks to come out and guard him. He waited until the 24-second clock was about to expire and then launched a rocket that hit nothing but net. He concluded his one-man show with another ceremonial three to beat the final buzzer. Before that one had even gone through the net, he raised his index finger in triumph as he walked off the floor.

"Larry Bird! Oh my God!" Walton said as he settled into his seat in the Boston locker room.

As the Celtics flew home, they landed knowing that the Rockets had gone up 3–1 on the Lakers. Game 5 was back in Los Angeles, but not until Wednesday. That meant the NBA Finals could not begin until May 26, Memorial Day, at the earliest. Boston had at least a week off, and the prospect of playing Houston was now looking more and more like a reality. Never mind that it wouldn't be quite the same without the Lakers.

"I know the fans would like us to play L.A.," McHale said. "And we probably would, too. If the Lakers are the better team, well, they'll be able to come back. If they don't, well, all I know is that it's a lot easier to shoot over Kurt Rambis than it is to shoot over Ralph or Akeem."

No one could quite fathom what was going on in the Western Conference. The Lakers had been the class of the conference all season, amassing 62 wins. Earlier that season, they had been so good that *Sports Illustrated* was already calling them the greatest team in NBA history. They led the league in scoring and in field goal percentage.

They also had had no problems with the Rockets during the regular season, winning four of five. Kareem Abdul-Jabbar had been particularly dominant in those five games.

There was, however, the notion that these Lakers were a little complacent and self-absorbed. They had been to the NBA Finals four straight years and felt it was almost a birthright. They had made some personnel changes, the most notable being the addition of Maurice Lucas and the deletions of Jamaal Wilkes and Bob McAdoo. But they were still the Lakers, and no one figured they would have a serious challenge until the Finals.

Los Angeles began with a first-round annihilation of the San Antonio Spurs, winning the three games by margins of 47, 28, and 20 points. They then eliminated the pesky Dallas Mavericks in six games and prepared for the Rockets, who had won the Midwest Division title and had the second-best record in the conference.

The Lakers won the first game easily, 119–107, and Pat Riley canceled practice the next day and told his guys to go to the beach instead. The following day's practice was horrible and Riley realized then that he had made a mistake. The Rockets won Game 2 in the Forum and won both games in the Summit. Abdul-Jabbar was getting outplayed by the exuberant Olajuwon and was so ineffective on the boards that Wilt Chamberlain came out and ripped him in the paper.

"He's even ducking away sometimes," Chamberlain sniffed. "He's like an old batter at the plate, bailing out, afraid of inside fastballs. I tell you, he's not trying to get rebounds."

The Lakers were in a state of crisis. Magic Johnson's mother came out to visit, but he was so intent on concentrating on basketball that he put her up in a hotel, despite having ample room at his house. The Lakers then came out and played hard in Game 5, carrying the action, outrebounding the Rockets 51–31 (Abdul-Jabbar had 13), and never trailing over the first 47 minutes and 59 seconds. Olajuwon and Mitch Kupchak had been ejected with 5:14 to play, but the Rockets would not die.

With the Lakers leading 112–109 late in the game, the Rockets missed a three-point field goal, but Robert Reid got a second-chance trey and connected. The Lakers then worked the clock to the end—or so they thought—but Byron Scott missed a jumper and Allen Leavell grabbed the ball and called timeout. There was one second left in the game.

Since Houston called time, they got the ball at halfcourt, and an unpressured Rodney McCray threw a lob pass in to the 7-4 Ralph Sampson. Afraid to foul, the Lakers allowed Sampson to retrieve the pass. In one motion, Sampson caught the ball and, with a twisting motion, redirected it to the basket. Incredibly, the ball went in and the Rockets registered a seismic 114–112 victory to win the series in five games.

Michael Cooper staggered to the floor in disbelief. Watching at home on television, ex-Laker Bob McAdoo started to cry. Had this shot signaled the end of the Lakers' domination of the West? Some thought so at the time. Houston was young, strong, bullish, and seemingly the team of the future. With Kareem Abdul-Jabbar nearing the end of the line, how could the Lakers expect to combat Sampson and Olajuwon throughout the rest of the decade?

That summer, the Lakers almost pulled the trigger on a blockbuster deal with Dallas, involving James Worthy for Mark Aguirre and the draft rights to Roy Tarpley. General manager Jerry West decided against it.

Later, Riley would write about how the Sampson shot was not the perceived death knell, but a wake-up call that jolted the Lakers from their state of smugness. L.A. won the next two NBA titles. But on that day, the only reaction in Lakerland was one of shock. How could this have happened? How could there be an NBA Finals without them? Without Dancing Barry, Jack Nicholson, and the Rambis Youth?

"I think everyone wanted to play the Lakers," Jerry Sichting said. "It was kind of a downer that Houston won, even though they were a good team. But everyone on our team wanted to play the Lakers."

The jubilant Rockets celebrated and returned home to a hero's welcome. The NBA announced that the 1986 Finals would start Memorial Day in Boston. It would be a rematch of the 1981 Finals, which the Celtics won in six games. Both teams were vastly different now. The result would not be.

CHAPTER THIRTEEN

Houston:
Too Close to New Orleans

When the Celtics and Rockets first met in the NBA Finals, Houston was an improbable entry, having won only 40 games that season and surviving an upset-marred playoffs in the West. Two years later, Moses Malone, the backbone of that 1981 team, was gone and the Rockets were struggling. They won only 14 games that year and earned the first overall draft pick.

They chose Ralph Sampson and more than doubled their number of wins, but 29 wins still represented the worst in the West and the Rockets again won the rights to the No. 1 pick. They selected Akeem Olajuwon (ahead of a 6-5 prodigy named Michael Jordan) and won 48 games. In 1985–86, they increased the total to 51 as Sampson averaged 18.9 points and 11.1 rebounds, and Olajuwon averaged 23.5 points and 11.5 rebounds. They were the latest of the Twin Towers, presumed to be a match for Robert Parish and Kevin McHale, and also presumed to be the team of the future. Sampson was twenty-six, Olajuwon only twenty-three.

"We had a young, up-and-coming team," said Carroll Dawson, the longtime Houston assistant. "The surprise was that we beat the Lakers four straight [after losing the first game]. We were a good team. I don't think it's a fluke when you beat a team like the Lakers four games in a row. At that time, I thought we were one of the top teams in the league."

Ironically, this series would never have happened had the Celtics and Red Auerbach been able to do what they wanted to do in the spring of 1980: convince Ralph Sampson to leave the University of Virginia and turn pro. Had he done that, Robert Parish and Kevin McHale likely would have wound up together, but in Golden State, and Larry Bird might have ended up playing his entire career in Boston without winning an NBA title.

Even though the Celtics had the best record in the NBA in 1979–80, they also had maneuvered through a series of trades to obtain the No. 1 pick in the 1980 draft. The pick belonged to the Pistons, who finished with a 16-66 record that year. But prior to that year, Auerbach had convinced Detroit to take Bob McAdoo as compensation for the Celtics' signing of free agent M.L. Carr. Incredibly, Auerbach also convinced the Pistons to part with the two No. 1 choices Detroit held for the 1980 draft, their own and the Bullets'. Considering the Celtics had no use for McAdoo, that deal ranks as one of the league's all-time swindles.

After winning the coin flip to get the No. 1 overall pick, Auerbach set his sights on Sampson. At the time, Sampson had just completed his freshman season and had said, even before enrolling, that he was unlikely to remain at Virginia beyond his sophomore year. Auerbach assumed that one more year in college was not a serious obstacle, given that Sampson was going to be an NBA player anyway and that he had stated his desire to leave school before his class graduated.

But a funny thing happened to Auerbach when he flew to Virginia to try and talk Sampson into leaving immediately to join Larry Bird in Boston: Sampson said no. He was having too much fun in college. He wasn't interested in turning pro. Auerbach, who wasn't accustomed to having anyone tell him what he didn't want to hear, was furious.

The legendary Celtics executive doesn't try to put a revisionist spin on this pursuit. He wanted Sampson then, convinced, as many were, that this was going to be the next great NBA center.

"You couldn't tell that his career wouldn't pan out," Auerbach said. "At the time, he looked like a helluva prospect. We would have taken him if he had come out."

But he didn't. And he didn't the following year or the year after that. Sampson instead stayed four years at Virginia and got his degree. That he couldn't deliver an NCAA title to Charlottesville did nothing to tarnish his image among NBA personnel. He was the consensus No. 1 pick in 1983, just as he would have been in 1980, 1981, or 1982. In 1983, it was the Rockets who ended up with Sampson. The Celtics, rebuffed, recovered quite nicely and worked the deal with Golden State that brought them Robert Parish and Kevin McHale.

In addition to Sampson and Olajuwon, the Rockets had a terrific small forward in Rodney McCray, who had come in the same draft as Sampson. They also had Jim Petersen, a poor man's McHale, a native Minnesotan and a University of Minnesota alum. Those four represented the front line and were a challenge for anyone. The Houston backcourt was another story.

Once the Rockets lost John Lucas in March, they were forced to go with a three-man rotation of Robert Reid, Lewis Lloyd, and Mitchell Wiggins. None was a point guard, though Reid took over the duties by default. Lloyd and Wiggins were classic shooting guards, with Lloyd being one of the top finishers in the game. But with no one to run the offense, there was nothing to finish.

"Lucas was the point guard who could get it to anyone. He made it all happen," Carroll Dawson said. "It was a nice team. It was a shame it couldn't stay together."

Despite their impressive win over the Lakers, the Rockets were heavy underdogs for the Finals. They had lost both regular season games to Boston, although the defeat in Houston had been without Olajuwon and the one in Boston had been marred by Sampson's scary fall. Even so, the Rockets would have their hands full with the Celtics, who were rested, were 11-1 in the postseason, and, again, had the luxury of opening a series at home.

Memorial Day finally arrived, and with it came a special feeling among Celtics fans. A year earlier they had opened the NBA Finals against the Lakers on Memorial Day and destroyed them, 148–114. The 148 points is the most scored by any team in an NBA Finals game. Scott Wedman was 11-for-11 from the floor, the best shooting day in the history of the NBA Finals. Four of his shots were three-pointers. The Celtics led by 30 at halftime (also a record), scored 79 points in the first half (a record), and made 62 field goals (another record).

But they lost four of the next five games as the Lakers used the humiliating defeat to regenerate their team. Thus, whatever happened in the opener, the Celtics fans would be careful not to get carried away.

Robert Parish's wife, Nancy Saad, was chosen to sing the National Anthem before the opener. In light of what she said happened a year later, it was an interesting choice. The two had a tempestuous marriage that, Saad alleged, was punctuated by both mental and physical abuse. Saad charged that the following year, before the Celtics opened the NBA Finals in Los Angeles against the Lakers, Parish beat her in a hallway outside his hotel room. Parish denied the charges and Saad's complaint was subsequently wrapped into the couple's divorce settlement, the results of which are sealed.

The anthem apparently stirred Parish, who went out and scored 23 points. Unfortunately, on defense he had to deal with the slippery Olajuwon. The young Rockets center was devastating, scoring 25 in the first half. He had 30 when he was forced to the bench with 4:49 left in the third quarter after collecting his fifth foul. At that time, the Celtics led by five. Two minutes later, their lead was 11. At the end of three, the Celtics led 91–76 and the damage was done. Olajuwon returned for the fourth, but it was too late; he managed only three points the rest of the way and the Celtics again held serve, winning, 112–100.

Houston could look back at the game and, despite the defeat, take some consolation from it. Someone had arrived at the game looking a lot like Ralph Sampson, but had gone out and missed 12 of 13 shots. This same individual was never in the game after picking up three fouls in the first five minutes. Sampson was an easy target for Boston fans, given his height, his reputation, and his spurning of Auerbach in 1980.

But more critical to the outcome of this game was the spectacular play of the Boston backcourt. Danny Ainge continued his brilliant postseason with 18 points, seven assists, and three steals. And Dennis Johnson, always regarded as the consummate big-game player, had 19 points, a team-high 11 rebounds, and four steals.

It was Ainge and Johnson who led the third-quarter charge, combining for 22 points and six steals. They sent a not-so-subtle reminder to the Rockets that the Celtics had someone other than Bird (21 points), McHale (21), and Parish (23) capable of inflicting damage.

Bill Fitch, watching this time from the opposing bench, could only shake his head and marvel. He had coached the 1981 NBA champion Celtics when they beat the Rockets. He knew this beast was something bigger, better, stronger, and frighteningly efficient.

"More important than the talent, they were totally devoid of any players who thought personal statistics meant anything," Fitch said. "You knew what they were going to do. You knew they were good enough to do it. That wasn't always the case when I was there."

Or, as Olajuwon noted later, "It was men against boys."

There were two days between Games 1 and 2 and that was more than enough time for the Celtics to focus on the value of leaving Boston with yet another 2–0 stranglehold. They had done it against the Bulls, Hawks, and Bucks, but this was the Finals and the format was different.

After the memorable 1984 Final, the NBA and its television confederate, CBS, decided to make the finals a 2-3-2 affair as opposed to the standard 2-2-1-1-1 format. The league figured it would result in less travel, and it noted that with less travel, each team would be more rested, and the games more competitive. That wasn't necessarily true; there is nothing more flat than a visiting team for Game 5, having had to spend a week on the road.

The real reason for the 2-3-2 was television, because it increased the likelihood of a six-game series. And for the network that was when the profits really started to roll in, as casual fans got interested in the developing series. Never mind that the league didn't see the format as necessary for any other seven-game series; the network didn't enter into the picture on a full-time basis until the Finals.

The 2-3-2 format made it almost imperative for the home team to win the first two, lest it risk the possibility of never returning home for Game 6. The format was introduced in 1985 and the Celtics split the first two and barely made it back to Boston, where they succumbed in the sixth game. This year the Celtics had no intention of losing at home. The 2-3-2 format made it possible for the home team to trail 3–2 and still not have lost at home. It also made it harder to close out a series in five, as winning two of three on the road was hard.

The Boston Garden was steamy for Game 2, and Larry Bird turned it into his own playground. Frequently using the under-sized Rodney McCray as a prop, Bird had 31 points as the Celtics again broke it open in the third quarter, winning easily, 117–95.

"It was one of those special nights," saluted Bill Walton. "Larry had his hands everywhere. You felt great to be a part of it all."

Ralph Sampson showed up and scored a respectable 18 points, but he paid dearly for his effort: an accidental Robert Parish elbow opened a five-stitch cut over his left eye and forced him out of action for four minutes. The relentless Olajuwon continued to impress by scoring 21. On many nights, that effort would have been enough, but on this one it wasn't even close. McHale continued to dominate Sampson, scoring 25, and the Boston backcourt outscored their Houston counterparts 43–22. The Celtics led by 10 at the break and then outscored Houston 34–19 to lead by 25 after three. Houston shot 41.3 percent and no one was happy with the team's lackluster performance.

"It was our worst game of the year," Olajuwon said.

"We lost and played bad," agreed Robert Reid.

The Celtics were again up 2–0, having won the first two games by a total of 34 points. They now faced at least five days in Houston and, unless they swept, a week there. Did someone say sweep?

"Ha! That's a big joke," said the ever-discerning Olajuwon. "I can't believe anyone is serious about that. I don't see any way they can beat us in Houston."

Olajuwon was still a young pup, although he played well enough to earn second-team all-NBA honors. He was only twenty-three and still learning the game, the life, and the country. Soccer had been his game in Nigeria. He was cultured and educated—the only wild animals he had seen were in a zoo in Lagos, and he spoke five languages. He was polite, interested in what you had to say, and had a distinguished air about him. He drove a black Mercedes with the license plate DREEM and wasn't afraid to speak his mind.

"I know nothing about this tradition," he said upon entering Boston Garden and seeing the fifteen championship banners. "I am not from here."

Countered Larry Bird, "We'd like to give him a two-week history lesson."

Olajuwon had been in the United States only five years and still recalled the time when he got into a taxi to go to the University of Houston, and the driver misunderstood him and thought he was saying "Austin." He was amazed to discover that most everyone drove cars, even the guys who played down at Fonde, the famed Houston rec center. He was amazed you could speak into a box and order lunch at a restaurant and never get out of your car.

And he was amazed that anyone thought the Rockets would not prevail at home. "We feel comfortable in our building and in front of our fans," Olajuwon said. "No way."

Still, the Rockets had yet to show they were capable of beating the Celtics. They already had lost more games to Boston than they had to the Lakers.

"Nobody expected us to be here," Petersen said. "We beat the Lakers and showed we are a great team. But the Celtics are treating us like a bunch of kids."

The Rockets had lost only five times at home all season, and only once since the Celtics had beaten them in March. That one loss was a meaningless season finale setback to a horrible Phoenix team. They were 7-0 at home in the playoffs, winning by an average of almost 15 points a game. The city was juiced for the week. The Rockets weren't used to such fan support; the last time they were in the Finals (in 1981), their games were on tape delay because of poor ratings and the Rockets players sported T-shirts saying, "Not Ready for Prime Time Players."

The Celtics treated their final road trip of the season the same way they treated all the others, as an opportunity to disappoint a lot of people. They were 27-14 on the road in the regular season and 4-1 in the postseason.

"What's there to worry about playing on the road?" McHale said. "I've never seen a fan come out of the stands and block a shot or make a basket. Maybe when you play a team like Golden State there's an advantage to being at home. But I don't think it makes much of a difference if it's the Boston Celtics. Sometimes the officiating may be a little different, but that's all. But it's just a call here or there, that's all."

Never were McHale's words more prophetic than in the closing moments of Game 3. After two unimpressive games, Sampson awoke and so did his teammates. They had the Celtics to thank, however, as Boston uncharacteristically froze in the final three minutes with victory and a 3–0 lead seemingly in hand.

The Celtics had survived the expected Houston opening rush led by the rejuvenated Sampson, who would finish with 24 points and 22 rebounds. (This was the Sampson Auerbach had wanted to bring to Boston.) But Boston hung tough and, in the third quarter, pulled ahead by 11. Bird was on his way to a triple-double (25 points, 15 rebounds, and 11 assists) and McHale was doing his customary dirty work inside (28 points, 11 rebounds). Houston shaved it to four at the end of the quarter, but Boston was still in control, leading 102–94 with 3:14 remaining.

Houston then scored the next nine points before a Danny Ainge basket gave the Celtics a 104–103 lead. Mitchell Wiggins, left unchecked under the basket, squeezed inside and tipped in an Olajuwon miss with 31 seconds left, giving Houston a 105–104 lead. The Summit went wild.

Then came one of the more bizarre sequences of the series. The Celtics, with the 24-second clock about to expire, got the ball to Robert Parish, who had missed 12 of 15 shots. He moved for his customary turnaround but missed the shot. As Parish executed the play, however, a whistle blew and the Summit grew quiet.

Everyone in the arena fixed their eyes on veteran referee Jake O'Donnell, who had blown the whistle. A foul on Houston? A three-seconds violation on the Celtics? What was it? O'Donnell conferred with fellow referee Joey Crawford and decided to call for a jump ball at center court. It was, O'Donnell said, an "inadvertent whistle." That was a new one to the Celtics.

"Maybe," suggested Parish, "he was hyperventilating. He made the call but when he got to the [press] table, he got amnesia."

So not only was there no foul, the Celtics, still trailing by one point, now had to go back to halfcourt and jump against the 7-4 Sampson with seven seconds left.

In the Houston huddle, Fitch called for Sampson to direct

the tap to Olajuwon, which he did. K.C. Jones, expecting that, told his players to foul immediately. Bird hacked Olajuwon, who made only one of two free throws. The Celtics had five seconds left and called timeout, but their inbounds play resulted in a hurried pass from Dennis Johnson to Parish, who stepped on the baseline. Houston ball. Houston victory.

A call here or there, that's all. McHale's words resonated through the locker room.

Yes, there had been a couple of tough calls at the end, but the Celtics knew they were responsible for this loss. "We gave this one away and they should feel lucky," Bird said. "But I still think we're the best team and the best team usually wins."

Bird had not played well at the end of Game 3, scoring just four points in the final 18 minutes and missing 15 of his last 21 shots. He had been hounded relentlessly by Robert Reid, the Rockets' 6-7 point guard. Reid had also guarded Bird in the 1981 NBA Finals and had done a creditable job. Now he was back in the picture again, doing this year what Michael Cooper had done the last two.

Reid's was an interesting story: three years earlier, the year the Rockets won only 14 games, Robert Reid retired from professional basketball. He was a Pentecostal minister and he returned home to Miami to devote himself full-time to his faith. When he wasn't preaching, he worked in a department store, and had no thoughts of returning to the game.

The following year, Fitch took over the Rockets and remembered what Reid had done against the Celtics in the 1981 Finals. Fitch called and inquired if Reid wanted to return. Reid decided he still had the bug and returned as an elder statesman, not the flashy, dashy, Afro-to-the-rafters player he was prior to his sabbatical.

Now he was back in the Finals again, guarding Larry Bird and getting credit for doing what no one else could do: contain the soon-to-be MVP. Even Bird, who loathed all the attention showered on his so-called stoppers, promised things would be different the next time. "It's a good thing that everyone is giving Robert all the publicity now, because most guys never have that chance before I go out and score 40 on them."

•

Bird did not score 40 in Game 4. He scored 21, and collected 10 rebounds and nine assists. But his last three points broke the game's final tie and the Celtics took firm control of the series, winning, 106–103. Basically, they did what they had failed to do in Game 3: they converted down the stretch.

The Celtics were mentally ready for Game 4, but were still the same easygoing pranksters they were all season. K.C. Jones called the team to his hotel suite to go over game films and assignments for Game 4. Forty-five minutes into the session, David Thirdkill snuck into the room and crawled on the floor to avoid detection. Bird and McHale both saw him, however, and jumped up and welcomed him to the session.

"Third, how are you," they said. "Here, Third, we saved you a seat. Thanks so much for coming. What time is it anyway?"

Jones just shook his head, not saying a word. If nothing else, Bird and McHale were still loose and that always was a good sign.

Game 4 was the best game of the series. The largest lead by either team was only eight. The game was tied after one, and saw one-point margins at halftime (Houston, 64–63) and at the end of the third quarter (Boston, 86–85). In the fourth quarter, the largest margin by either team was three.

Dennis Johnson tied the game for the twelfth and last time at 101–101 with 3:07 remaining. At that point, K.C. Jones did something he almost never did during the regular season: he removed a winded Robert Parish for a rested and eager Bill Walton. These were the moments Walton wanted when he called Auerbach the previous year. That was when championships were determined, and Bill Walton wanted nothing more than a championship.

The night before, he had been outside in the Texas evening, by then hot and summerlike. He found a pond near the Celtics' hotel and quietly lay on the grass, scanning the heavens. A jogger stopped by and recognized him, saying, "Bill, what are you doing here?" He responded, "I'm meditating. Focusing. We're going to win."

Walton made the most of his minutes, as he usually did. His first significant contribution came on an inside-out feed to Bird, who at that point had taken only five shots in the second half. Bird didn't hesitate to pull the trigger and swished a three-pointer, giving Boston a 104–101 lead with 2:25 left. After a Rodney McCray hoop, Walton arguably made what was his biggest play as a member of the Celtics. After a Dennis Johnson drive bounced off the rim, Walton swooped in from the right, maneuvered by Olajuwon, grabbed the rebound and then, incredibly, put it up backhanded for a layup.

"I got it, came down, and then went right back up," he said. "You can't pump-fake at that point because then you'll start getting pushed and you don't have a chance. That was a big basket, but I really had played very poorly up until that point."

There were 99 seconds left, but neither side would score another point. McHale made two steals in the final 46 seconds, the second one coming on the Rockets' final possession when a befuddled Sampson found himself far from the basket unable to get rid of the ball. The Celtics dribbled out the clock and, in the locker room, engaged in serious self-congratulations. They knew then that the title was theirs. The only question would be how long the Rockets would hold out.

Had this series been in 1984, it would have shifted back to Boston and the Celtics would have put the Rockets out of their misery in five. Instead, it remained in Houston, giving the Celtics a chance to clinch in the Summit where they had clinched five years earlier. The team was divided: they wanted to win quickly but they also wanted to clinch on the Garden floor. They knew deep down that if the series shifted back to Boston there was no possibility the Rockets would win two in a row.

Unlike the hotly contested and hard-played Game 4, Game 5 was more of a free-for-all. Houston, which had feasted on the backboards in Game 4, did so again but this time the Celtics paid for it. The Rockets won going away, 111–96, the second-worst beating of the year for the Celtics.

Houston chose to flex their collective muscles at a most surprising time: early in the second quarter, Ralph Sampson started a fight with Jerry Sichting. From that point on, chaos reigned on the court and the young and inspired Rockets thrived under the wild conditions.

While the Rockets dominated the boards and Olajuwon was again routinely terrific (he blocked a record eight shots), the fight overshadowed the game. It occurred just 2:20 into the second quarter with the Rockets leading 34–33. Sampson, irked by an early Sichting elbow, came down and elbowed him in a pick. He then unloaded a roundhouse right and all hell broke loose.

Sichting had been unable to sleep during the Finals. "I was so keyed up by then. I had been playing my whole life to get there. He had given me an elbow and a shove and I asked him what he was trying to prove. From out of nowhere he threw a punch. And as soon as it hit, nothing happened. It didn't hurt. Aside from being stunned for a split second because he had swung, I was fine. Then I wanted to get one in myself."

Soon Dennis Johnson, Bill Walton, Olajuwon, and Mitch Wiggins were in it. Greg Kite tried to play peacemaker and Allen Leavell jumped onto his back. Johnson emerged with a cut over his eye.

"Kevin and Larry were probably shooting free throws," Sichting cracked. Neither, especially McHale, had a predilection for fighting.

Across the court, Celtics broadcaster Johnny Most, one of the legendary figures in the team's colorful history and an unabashed homer, ripped into the 7-4 Sampson.

"He started the whole damn thing," Most shrieked. "And big Ralph Sampson is a foot and three inches taller than Sichting . . . he's the last guy who has a right to complain. The big, brave bull. I'm Ralph Sampson. I have the right to hit you. I have a right to bite your head off. Ralph Sampson is a gutless big guy who picks on little people and he showed me a gutless streak. That was a gutless, yellow thing to do."

That was language usually reserved for the likes of Bill Laimbeer. But apparently the refs felt the same way: Sampson—and no one else—was ejected from the game. The Rockets could have done one of two things at that point: pack it in or fight like a cornered animal. They did the latter and totally outplayed the Celtics over the final 33 minutes. The Houston crowd, who had given Sampson a farewell worthy of Charles Lindbergh, went wild and even started to taunt Red Auerbach in the stands.

"The fans were rude, obnoxious, outrageous," said team owner Alan Cohen, sitting with Auerbach. "The fans had started to threaten Red, and I had to go to the NBA to complain about the lack of security. I spoke directly to David [Stern]. That was an absolute disgrace. I thought someone was coming after him."

Afterward, there was no love lost for Sampson or Houston in the Celtics' locker room. Bird warned that Sampson had better wear a hard hat to Game 6. "I can't believe he picked a fight with Jerry. Heck, my girlfriend could beat him up." Dennis Johnson suggested there could be more fisticuffs in the next game.

"We were so angry coming home. So mad," McHale recalled. "It should have been 4–1 and everyone was really disappointed."

Added Danny Ainge, "We just fell apart that night. That was a tendency that we had and were always criticized for: the lack of a killer instinct. It just got boring. As I played longer, I've come to realize that that, as much as anything, used to frustrate me.

"But the plane ride home the next day was complete silence. There was no one joking around or anyone talking about anything. It was dead silence, and that was unusual for that team. When we got to practice, it was the most awesome display of basketball I've ever seen. The starters were playing the Green Team and the Green Team had no chance. They couldn't even get the ball over halfcourt. DJ was beating people up. Larry and Kevin were beating people up. K.C. finally had to call it off. And there was no doubt in my mind, none at all, when I left practice that day, that the series was over."

The Celtics fans were just as ready. The day before Game 6, Sampson said he had never heard of Johnny Most and referred to the fight as "an unfortunate incident." He was now an official member of the Celtics' Hall of Villains, joining Laimbeer and Wilt Chamberlain, among others.

Sampson seemed undeterred. "I'm going to play to win," he said. "I came here to win."

Larry Bird made sure that did not happen. Heading into the sixth game, Bird was one of a few who merited serious consideration for the series Most Valuable Player. After Game 6, he made sure there was only one choice. Bird turned that game into his own showcase, dominating the Rockets and leading the Celtics to a 114–97, series-clinching victory. He was, he said years later, as pumped as he had ever been for a basketball game.

"I never quite had a feeling like that before in my life," Bird said. "I was so pumped up for that game, that I think I hit my max. I was never fired up for a game like that again. I didn't play that well. [He had a triple-double.] But I know one thing: I came to play that day. And I'll never forget walking off that court with my heart pounding so hard I thought I was going to have a heart attack. I never reached that milestone again. I loved it. I never got there again. That's why I wanted to win another championship, to see if I could. Because there's not a greater feeling than winning a championship in your own building and walking off the court at the end."

The Celtics had anticipated the best even before the game started. After all, they were now 46-1 at Boston Garden, so the Rockets would have to do in three days what the rest of the NBA couldn't do in an entire season. Management told the players to drive to the Hellenic College practice site, and from there they would be transported to Boston Garden via bus.

Once they got to the Garden, they made sure the return trip would be a celebratory one. They never trailed and the game was never tied. The closest Houston came over the final two and a half quarters was 11. At one point, the Celtics led by 30. Bird, who had 29 points, 11 rebounds, and 12 assists, added insult to injury when, after getting a behind-the-back pass from Bill Walton, dribbled away from the basket to the Houston bench, turned and swished a three-pointer. His trey made it 87–61 and the noise in the building was deafening.

Dennis Johnson, given the assignment of blanketing Robert Reid, responded with a classic, big-game performance typical of his career, holding Reid to 12 points before leaving the game in the final two minutes.

"That's the way our team was," said Ainge, who had 19. "If DJ came out and wanted us to win, we'd win. He was that kind of a leader with his defense. He could shut guys down and he could post up and no one could stop him. His personality was how the team was. He just played with so much confidence."

The Rockets were never in the game after the first quarter. Three straight steals by Olajuwon (all from Walton) had given them brief hope, but they were never a serious threat. Sampson, booed every time he touched the ball, missed his first seven shots from the field and scored only eight points. When he took a seat on the bench, the Boston fans taunted him, chanting, "We Want Ralph."

Sadly, Sampson would never again be the same player, as injuries limited him to 91 games over the next two years. He was eventually traded to Golden State. The 1985–86 season marked Sampson's high point as a pro. It also marked a high point for the Rockets. It would be another eight years before Houston returned to the Finals, with Olajuwon as the only remaining member of that 1986 team. With Michael Jordan playing minor-league baseball, Olajuwon was by then the best player in the NBA, and he led the Rockets to back-to-back titles in 1994 and 1995.

"We never felt the urgency in '86," said Carroll Dawson. "That's because we were so young and we all felt we would be around and together for a long time. Then Ralph got hurt and the team went in different ways and it just didn't happen. It was a shame. But the feeling then was, 'This was a start. We are going to be here for a while.' Then, it was all torn apart. But another problem that year was that we were playing what may have been the greatest team of all time."

Olajuwon, so consistent, managed only 19 points in Game 6. Unlike Sampson, he would finally get his just reward, though it would take almost a decade for most people to realize what some felt then: that he was the best center on the planet. But on this day, he was just another guy in red. The Rockets shot 43 percent and were outrebounded by the Celtics. This was basically a pistol whipping, with Larry Bird holding the gun.

"That sixth game was really a clinic," McHale said. "Bill tried to keep them in the game with those turnovers, probably for TV ratings. But I thought the game was over in the first part of the first quarter. They sensed the urgency we had. They knew. They were trying to play out the clock and make it look respectable."

The starters all left the floor before the game ended. K.C. Jones played all twelve players, including Scott Wedman, who played two minutes after missing the previous six games with fractured ribs. Houston's Craig Ehlo, then a twelfth man, scored the final basket on a dunk.

Inside the Celtics' locker room, Danny Ainge gave everyone high-fives punctuated by the phrase "Forty-five grand, babe." That was to be their playoff share. Someone asked Walton what he thought about Houston.

"Houston?" he said. "Too close to New Orleans."

It was a line from the Grateful Dead song "Truckin."

Later, Walton sat in front of his locker with his two oldest sons, then ten and seven, and savored the moment. This is why he had come to Boston. Several years ago, he had been told he'd be lucky to walk with a limp; now, he was celebrating his second NBA championship and it was a lot different than his first one in 1977.

"That championship," he said later, "was different from the first for two reasons. First, things had gone so badly for me in my career, and then to finally get traded and you're instantly on a championship team. You forget what that's like. And once you've been on a great team, like I had been at UCLA, nothing else matters. The other reason is that I had so little to do with it. I was able to be a part of it when everyone else was doing all the work. There's nothing like being the guy who's out there all the time. You go back and look at those games and you see the effort. Today, guys don't even sweat. Those guys on that team left a lot on the court that year. When you put that much into something, and it works, there's nothing really like it."

Being a part of it all was what Walton had wanted twelve months earlier: being able to make his contribution, at whatever level, as long as there was a chance for a championship. He figured that out the previous June. What stunned him was how much he came to enjoy Boston, the team, the city, the whole package. For one, brief, shining moment it was, well, almost as good as Southern California.

"It was unbelievable," he said. "I knew the basketball would be great, but you never know how special Larry Bird is until you see him every day. It turned out to be even better. And I had no idea life would be so special there, either. In Southern California, there is no tradition, no loyalty. The people are transients and everything is oriented toward football and baseball. There truly is nothing like being a Celtic in Boston. It was just such a joy. I had gotten to the point where I never, ever thought it would happen again for me, and then it did, overnight."

Also in a reflective mood was Sichting. He recalled an incident in January, when Joe Barry Carroll of the Warriors had come up to him and Walton and said, "Don't you guys ever, ever forget how lucky you are." Now, with his high school coach, Sam Alford, in town and at the game, Sichting was finally enjoying the big win that had escaped him at Martinsville High and at Purdue. He wanted a memento from the game, so he decided he'd take his sneakers, but he couldn't find them.

"I didn't know what had happened to them," he said. "I really wanted to save them. This was a big thing for me. Well, I called up Bill a few weeks later and he was already answering his phone saying, 'Boston Celtics, World Champions, West Coast Head-quarters.' But he's not there so his housekeeper, Picasso, picks up the phone. And the next thing I hear is, 'Thanks for the sneakers, Jerry. Bill gave them to me. I'm wearing them right now.'"

EPILOGUE
TEN YEARS AFTER

In the fall of 1986, Bill Walton was preparing for his second season with the Celtics. He was hoping it would be as rewarding and as injury-free as the first. It wasn't.

Walton and Robert Parish met at Hellenic College for some one-on-one work a week before training camp opened. Parish went up for one of his patented turnaround jump shots and Walton went up to block it. His right hand hit Parish's elbow and he felt an instant pain. He went to the hospital and his worst fears were confirmed: he had broken the pinkie finger on his right hand.

The injury prevented Walton from participating in camp, so he took out his frustrations on an exercise bike, pedaling furiously, sometimes as much as eight hours a day. The pain in his finger gradually subsided, but something else started to hurt, something quite familiar: his foot. All the hard work on the bike led to a stress fracture, and Walton's basketball career was basically finished.

He underwent surgery with hopes of returning later in the year for the playoffs: he did, but was never able to play the way he had the previous year. He limped through the postseason and had another operation in the summer of 1987, determined to play for the Celtics again. The Celtics had guaranteed the third year of his contract, but Walton never played. In the summer of 1988, while the Celtics were on a team cruise, they discovered that Walton, then an unrestricted free agent, had investigated playing in Italy, as was his right, and that he had stopped by the New York Knicks' office on his way back from that trip. As a free agent, his actions were legal, but the Celtics thought they were disloyal. If Walton owed playing time to anyone, they felt, it was to them. Over the past two years, they had paid him close to $1 million, and he had played in just 10 games. The point proved moot; Walton would never play again—not in Boston, New York, or Italy. His foot was still a mess. He opted for fusion surgery in March 1990 and set about conquering his stuttering problem for a career in television instead. His brutal candor and his love for the game made him a natural. With the help of legendary broadcaster Marty Glickman, Walton was able to communicate his views and passion almost seamlessly on television.

Ten years after his last title, his only title with Boston, Bill Walton was one of the top pro basketball analysts for NBC-TV. He still attends Celtics functions when possible, and he considers himself part of Boston's extended family. He remains close to several players on the team, particularly Bird and McHale. In the summer of 1988, Bird and his wife came out to visit him. Walton suggested a little game of one-on-one down at the Muni Gym, with the winner buying beers. Walton quickly jumped to a 10–1 lead, needing only one point to finish off Bird. On his last possession, going for the game winner, Walton chose to give Bird the ball instead. He felt sorry for him. Insulted, Bird made 10 straight baskets and won the game. Walton has been buying the beer ever since.

Walton's wasn't the only career that basically ended with the Game 6 victory over the Rockets. Scott Wedman's did, too. Although his ribs had healed, two weeks after winning the title, he felt pain in his heel that required surgery. His heel was never the same, and Wedman lasted only six games the following season. He played a little in the exhibition season, then decided to rest. Nothing happened. A second operation in January ended his season, but he was back with the Celtics for training camp in September 1987.

Boston's first exhibition game that year was in Houston. At halftime, Wedman and Sam Vincent were ready to go out, hoping to get some playing time. Neither had played in the first half and they soon discovered why: they had both been traded to Seattle for a second-round draft pick.

"We were both speechless," Wedman said. "It was pretty strange."

With the additions of Reggie Lewis and Brad Lohaus, the Celtics felt Wedman simply was not going to make the team. In Seattle, he found himself on the bubble and was waived when the Sonics decided to keep Russ Schoene instead. Two weeks later, while negotiating with the Clippers, Wedman hurt his back working out. That was it; he stopped playing basketball and settled in Kansas City, where he now works in real estate and runs a basketball camp.

Sam Vincent was traded because he never lived up to the expectations the organization had for him. K.C. Jones didn't feel Vincent was going to develop within the context of the team, so a decision was made to let him go. Wedman was a veteran who had been traded before, so he knew the procedure; Vincent, of course, was not and he remembers that trade as a total shock.

"K.C. was telling me that Seattle was a good situation and that he knew Bernie [Bickerstaff, the coach] and that Bernie was fair," Vincent said. "But I wasn't hearing him. I didn't understand what he was saying. Here he was, telling me I wasn't going to be a part of one situation anymore, but, at the same time, telling me how great this other situation was going to be. I took a cab back to the hotel. It's a bad feeling when you're traded."

Vincent at first fit in well with the Sonics, although there were questions about his toughness. Vincent said he also ran into trouble for ripping K.C. Jones in the newspaper, although he said the quotes were taken out of context. He said his relationship with Bickerstaff was never the same after that and, in February, he was traded to Chicago for Sedale Threatt.

Doug Collins was the Bulls' head coach and he had seen Vincent play reasonably well while doing some television work during the 1987 Eastern Conference finals. The Bulls needed a point guard, so Vincent became one of four players to ever play with both Michael Jordan and Larry Bird (the others were Darren Daye, Artis Gilmore, and recently, Robert Parish).

Once again, Vincent had an encouraging start with his new team. And once again, things went downhill after that. After a year and a half with the Bulls, Chicago left him exposed in the expansion draft of 1988. The Orlando Magic took him and he spent three years there; he was traded to Milwaukee in 1992 so the Magic could have some money to sign a rookie they had just drafted: Shaquille O'Neal.

"Ever since Boston, I've been a step behind all along," Vincent said. "After I left Chicago, they won three championships. That was really a burner. Then, just as I leave Orlando, they get Shaq."

He never played another NBA game. He tore an Achilles tendon during an exhibition game with Milwaukee and sat out the 1992–93 season. The following year, he played in Greece, where he was well known before he even got off the plane.

"My first day in Greece, they had this big picture of me, Greg Kite, and David Thirdkill sitting on the bench with our fists up," he said. "They were very aware of who I was and that I had played on the Celtics. I enjoy being identified with that team. I'm very proud to have been on that team. I wear the [championship] ring every day and I'm proud of that, too."

Vincent has settled in the Orlando area, where he is in private business.

Vincent wasn't the only member of the 1985–86 Celtics to try his hand overseas. Over the last several years, David Thirdkill has made it a yearly thing.

He was, however, back with the Celtics in the fall of 1986, preparing for another year in Boston. This time, the situation was reversed from the year before: he made the team, but was released two months into the season. He played 17 games before getting the ax; he never played another NBA game.

He finished out the 1986–87 season in the Continental Basketball Association in Rochester, Minnesota. With no feelers coming from the NBA, Thirdkill decided to try the European leagues. He has never regretted the move.

"Over the past several years, I've learned to speak a couple of different languages. The whole thing can be very educational if you want it to be," he said from Israel, his basketball home for the last five years. "And what I can say for sure is that for the last eight years, I've had fun playing the game. I think that's important. It's great to be able to display my talents. But it's just as important to have fun."

He started out in Italy, then played for three years in France. In 1991 he moved his game to Israel, where he has played for two different teams, both near Tel Aviv. The slower pace and less grueling schedule appeal to him.

"I'm not Robert Parish," he said of the center, still playing in the NBA in his forties. "It's good for my age." He turned thirty-six in April 1996.

Thirdkill still remembers his big game against the Warriors, the one in which he scored 20 points and had eight rebounds in 22 minutes. But he is prouder that his reputation as a defensive player, a role player, never suffered in his year with Boston. He may not have been an integral part of the team, but he was a part of it. That's important to him.

"I did very well for a short period of time," he said.

What does he remember from the championship team? Mostly the fun, the same thing he has found overseas.

"You wanted to come to practice every day," he said. "Everybody enjoyed everybody else. You could say anything and it was still fun. But that goes with winning; the atmosphere is always great when you're winning. We would go into other arenas and we knew we were going to win. It was a magical year for me, being on a championship team. A remarkable year, really. To see the things that happened to me, it was just unbelievable."

Rick Carlisle managed to make it through the 1986–87 season, but no further. He became expendable when the Celtics drafted Reggie Lewis. Carlisle was still with the team after Vincent and Wedman were traded to Seattle. Boston planned to make Antoine Carr an offer sheet with Wedman's money; Carr at that point was a free agent whose rights were owned by Atlanta. Carlisle was not affected by the Carr signing—they played different positions. He was more concerned about simply staying on the club any way he could.

Once the offer sheet was made, the Hawks had fifteen days to match it. During that fortnight, Carlisle had his girlfriend call general manager Jan Volk, telling her to say she was calling from Stan Kasten's office. Kasten was the Hawks' general manager and Carlisle knew Volk would take the call because of the Carr signing.

Volk did take the call and the two had a pleasant chat, but Carlisle's girlfriend could not convince him to keep her boyfriend on the team. He was waived. He spent a couple of weeks in the CBA before the Knicks picked him up; New York's coach, Rick Pitino, remembered Carlisle from the days when Pitino was coaching at Boston University and Carlisle was playing for the University of Maine.

Injuries started to surface, however, and New York let him go.

He tried out for the Nets and lasted a month. "I was falling apart physically," he said. "So Bill [Fitch, the Nets coach in 1989–90] waived me and hired me as an assistant all in the same phone call. I had always played well against his teams, so I think he saw the best of me."

Carlisle stayed in New Jersey with Fitch and Chuck Daly and then went to Portland to work with P.J. Carlesimo. He does, however, have a lasting memory of Boston: he scored his final points in the building, playing against the Celtics for the Nets in 1989. It was his only basket of the season.

Greg Kite spent four full seasons with the Celtics. In each of those four years, Boston went to the NBA Finals. When he was released in February 1988, the Celtics' good luck ended and Boston hasn't been back since.

Kite was the ideal eleventh or twelfth man on the 1985–86 team, but three years later his game had not progressed and the team was not good enough to warrant keeping him around. His work ethic, however, especially in practice, made him eminently employable. There were only three members of the 1985–86 team still on active NBA rosters a decade later and Greg Kite was one of them. (Danny Ainge and Robert Parish were the others.)

It may be hard to find someone who scored so rarely but lasted as long as Kite did. He scored 1,717 points in 10,080 minutes over 680 games. That worked out to a career average of 2.5 points a game. But scoring was never what Kite was about, not in college, not in the NBA.

Once Kite was waived by Boston, he was out of work for all of forty-eight hours. The L.A. Clippers picked him up and he finished the year there. He also started the following year with Los Angeles, but was waived in late March. Again, his unemployment lasted just two days; the Charlotte Hornets signed him for the remainder of the season.

In the summer of 1989, Kite was an unrestricted free agent.

He signed with Sacramento and spent a year with the Kings, re-uniting with Danny Ainge. The following summer he was a free agent again, and the Orlando Magic signed him; the Magic were then in their second season.

Something good finally happened to Kite there: he became a starter. He played in all 82 games, averaging almost 30 minutes a game. He averaged 4.8 points and 7.2 rebounds a game, both career highs. He even upped his notoriously poor free-throw shooting from 48.6 to 51.2 percent.

After that season, the Magic gave him a four-year deal worth $1 million per season. For Kite, that was substantially more than he made at any time in his career. He played three more seasons in Orlando behind Shaquille O'Neal. In his final season there, 1993–94, he played in only 29 games.

The Magic released Kite in November of 1994, even though they still owed him one more year. Kite stayed in Orlando, where he had started a construction business, and waited for the phone to ring. It did, and Pat Riley was on the line; he wanted Kite in New York. But Kite lasted only six weeks with the Knicks before he was released.

But his career wasn't over. He had one more call coming, this one from Indiana coach Larry Brown. The Pacers needed a big body late in the season, so they signed him. They even kept him on their playoff roster and Kite appeared in eight postseason games as Indiana advanced to the conference finals, losing to Orlando in seven games.

"It was pretty neat," Kite said of that series. "I was getting paid by both teams."

His career ended in 1995. He still thought about playing and got some calls in the fall of 1995, including one from his old teammate Kevin McHale, who by then was running the Minnesota Timberwolves. But Kite didn't want to return unless there was guaranteed money involved; there wasn't, so he stayed home. He did play briefly in the CBA to try to generate some interest, but none came.

Kite has fond memories of the 1985–86 team. He was as

much a part of the intense daily practices as anyone. Parish claims he might have lasted even longer had he not played against Kite every day in practice for five and one half years.

"Practices were fun and so competitive," Kite said. "We were always winning until Larry, Kevin, and Danny started to cheat. Everybody joked around and got on each other's case, but we were deadly serious about winning the championship. Even after practice, guys would stick around to shoot and play one-on-one. It was such a great team. We mowed everyone down that season."

Jerry Sichting joined Kite in the 1988 exodus. Well before that, the Celtics had set their sights on Jim Paxson, the Portland Trail Blazers' guard. Just before the trading deadline in February 1988, a deal was struck.

The Blazers had come to the conclusion that Paxson and Clyde Drexler were incompatible. Originally they asked the Celtics for Fred Roberts. The Celtics countered with Sichting instead. The deal, however, would not work under the salary cap rules. Paxson agreed to redo his contract in exchange for an extension and the deal went through.

Sichting was, at the time, recovering from knee surgery. He had felt a pop in his knee while chasing John Stockton that was diagnosed as a cartilage tear. The Celtics put him on the injured list, signed Dirk Minniefield, and proceeded full speed ahead on the Paxson deal.

"As I was rehabbing, I figured something was up because they weren't in any hurry to activate me," Sichting said. "No one wanted to even talk to me."

On the night of February 23, 1988, Michael McHale turned three years old. His dad, Kevin, took him to Chuck E Cheese for a party. Sichting came along with his kids. When Sichting got home, he got a phone call from Danny Ainge, who told him about the trade. Sichting was one of the last to know.

"I guess they had been trying to reach me, but I was out," he said. "Still, it left a bad taste in my mouth."

Sichting finished out the season in Portland and also played for the Trail Blazers the following year. He then signed as a free agent with Charlotte in November of 1989, but was waived the following February. He appeared in 34 games, starting eight.

"It was weird the way I left Charlotte," he said. "I was banged up all the time and had a stress fracture in my foot that they didn't diagnose. I didn't want to go on the injured list and they didn't want to bring me back. So I told them to waive me and they did."

The Milwaukee Bucks signed Sichting, but after one game the pain in his foot was so severe he couldn't continue. The Bucks did a bone scan and discovered the stress fracture. He filed a grievance against the Hornets, but nothing ever happened. That, too, left a bad taste in his mouth.

"I was a player rep for four years," he said, "but I guess I wasn't important enough for Charlie Grantham [the players union head]."

Sichting never played again. He worked for a year as a radio analyst for the Pacers and for four years as an analyst for the Celtics. In 1995, he accepted the position as the director of scouting and player development for the Minnesota Timberwolves. His boss was Kevin McHale.

Dennis Johnson finished his career with the Celtics, but the ending wasn't exactly the way he envisioned it. The deal he had signed in the fall of 1985 expired in 1989, so he re-signed for one more year. In the fall of 1990, he and his wife were in Los Angeles watching a taping of the television show *Full House*. When they returned to their hotel after dining with cast members in Santa Monica, there was a message to call his agent, Fred Slaughter.

"They want to know," Slaughter said of the Celtics, "if you can handle coming off the bench."

Johnson thought the question preposterous. He was thirty-five. He played with younger, quicker teammates. Of course he could come off the bench. Slaughter told him to fly back to Boston. He thought that if the bench issue could be resolved— Johnson saw no problem there—then the Celtics would bring him back for another year.

When he got to the Celtics' offices, he met with general manager Jan Volk, Chris Ford, the new head coach, and Dave Gavitt, the new director of basketball operations. As soon as he heard them say "Hello, Dennis," Johnson knew he was not going to get one more year.

"I said to myself, 'Something's wrong here,'" he said. "They told me they were going to let me go and I told them they were doing the wrong thing. I left the office not mad, but feeling a little let down. I had been expecting something else."

The Celtics told Johnson there would be a job for him in the organization when he was ready. Johnson wasn't ready; he continued to work out daily and nearly took an offer from the Pistons. The Bucks and the Magic also expressed interest.

"Finally, one day I said to myself, 'This is it.' My pride wouldn't let me end my career like that. If I leave now, I've still got all my credits. I didn't want to sign a ten-day contract, so that was it."

Johnson ended up spending seven seasons with the Celtics and his uniform, No. 3, was retired. He eventually took a job scouting for the team and in 1993 was elevated to the job of assistant coach under Ford. He remained in that capacity when M.L. Carr took over as head coach in 1995.

Over his fourteen-year career, Johnson averaged 14.1 points a game. He was all-NBA in 1981, second-team all-NBA in 1980, and from 1979 to 1987 was either first- or second-team on the All-Defensive team. He helped the Celtics win the 1984 title over the Lakers, scoring 20 or more points in each of the last four games of that series while guarding Magic Johnson. In the seventh game, he was 12-for-12 from the line.

Johnson was eligible for election to the Hall of Fame in 1995, but was not selected by the voters. Walton was furious. "It's a black eye on the sport of basketball," he fumed. "The fact that Dennis Johnson did not make it to the Hall of Fame is a disgrace to the sport of basketball and I am embarrassed." He still should get in.

Johnson's value to his team always transcended numbers. He was simply a great clutch player, much like the baseball hitter who goes 0-for-3 but then comes up in the bottom of the eighth with men on second and third and knocks them in. He never feared taking the big shot—he wanted the big shot—and, when the spirit moved him, he was as authoritative as any guard in taking the ball to the basket. The only statistic that reflects his true value as a player was his number of championship rings. He retired with three.

And what does he recall of the 1985–86 team?

"It was an untouchable year," he said. "All I think about is that if we had the private plane then that we have now, we would have won 70 games that year, easily. I believe that. I really believe that. It was just a good, fun, great time and, even to this day, guys ask about this team."

Danny Ainge feels the same way. "You think about all the games we blew," he said. "We could have won 70. Maybe more."

Ainge would have liked to have finished his career as a Celtic. But by the end of the decade, he was not happy about his new role on the team, having been replaced in the starting lineup by rookie Brian Shaw. He suggested to management that a trade might help him and the team. After all, he was still young and marketable.

"If Danny had not expressed to me, as he did, his displeasure and that he would not have been unhappy if he was moved, I don't think we would have traded him," general manager Jan Volk said.

Exactly one year after Ainge had broken the news to Jerry Sichting of his trade to Portland, his own turn came. Bill Russell, the general manager of the Sacramento Kings, called Volk at 4:30 A.M. California time on the day the trading deadline expired, to reopen talks on a previously discussed deal involving Ainge. Volk thought the deal had died at the All-Star Game, ten days earlier.

Russell proposed sending Joe Kleine and Ed Pinckney to Boston for Ainge and Brad Lohaus. The Celtics needed big bodies because Larry Bird was out for the year following foot surgery. Ainge had been briefed on the possibility of going to Sacramento when the talks were on in early February. He told the Celtics and Russell he did not want to go there.

But, the night before the deal, Ainge played well in Sacramento and the Celtics beat the Kings. The following morning, Russell was on the phone and the deal was made.

Ainge wasn't happy with the move. He finished out the season in Sacramento and played one more year there. Then the Kings acceded to his request to be moved to a contender and traded him to Portland, where he joined a team that had been to the NBA Finals the year before. The 1990–91 Trail Blazers won more games than anyone else in the NBA, but were upset in the conference finals by the Lakers. The following year, Portland made it back to the Finals, but lost to the Chicago Bulls in six games.

There was one more stop on the Ainge career train. Following the 1991–92 season, he signed as a free agent with the Phoenix Suns. That team also posted the league's best record, but lost in the Finals to the Bulls. Ainge played two more years in Phoenix, and the Suns were eliminated in the playoffs both times by the eventual champion Houston Rockets. Following the 1994–95 season, the Suns offered Ainge a position on the bench as an assistant coach. He still thought he could play another year, but eventually decided to do neither. He also rejected coaching overtures from Minnesota, the Los Angeles Clippers, and even his alma mater, Brigham Young. Instead, he retired from the NBA at the age of thirty-six and accepted a job as an NBA analyst for Turner Network Television. A year later, he became an assistant coach for the Phoenix Suns, taking the job with the assurance he would become the head coach within two years.

Larry Bird lasted six more seasons in the NBA. Statistically, Bird's three best scoring years were 1984–85, 1986–87, and 1987–88, reflecting the lack of balance that was not there in 1985–86. Bird and Kevin McHale were an unstoppable one-two punch in the late 1980s until injuries cut them both down to size and hastened their demise.

For Bird, the beginning of the end came in the fall of 1988. Bone spurs in each of his Achilles tendons became so severe that, six games into the season, he elected to have surgery. Everything was cleaned out at once, but Bird could not make it back for the playoffs.

He played in 75 games the following year, but had trouble coming to grips with the lack of strength in his legs. In addition, coach Jimmy Rodgers wanted to diversify the offense, which meant fewer shots for Larry Bird, and Larry Bird didn't like that. Rodgers was fired in 1990 and replaced by Chris Ford. The following season, back trouble limited Bird to 60 games and the pain was so bad he needed off-season surgery. He walked out of the hospital the following day and seemed healthy in the fall of 1991.

But that would be his final year. The back problems resurfaced and he was basically day-to-day the rest of the year. The team even went on a late-season winning streak without him, a streak that continued in the playoffs. He finally returned midway through the conference semifinal against Cleveland, delivered one last vintage game in Boston, and played his final game in the Richfield Coliseum on May 17, 1992.

He did not officially retire until the following August. By then, he had joined the Dream Team and won an Olympic gold medal at Barcelona. He then accepted a front-office job with the Celtics that allowed him to do whatever he wanted. He adopted two children, moved his family to Naples, Florida, and played a lot of golf in between endorsements and speaking engagements.

Bird is still involved with the Celtics and many feel the urge to get more involved could land him either on the Boston bench one day as the head coach or in the front office in a more active role. He has denied any interest in coaching and turned down an offer to coach the Pacers before the team turned to Larry Brown.

Undoubtedly, Bird was one of the game's greatest players and, perhaps, the greatest forward in NBA history. He is the only noncenter to win the MVP three straight years, with 1985–86 as the last. His number was retired in Boston in an elaborate ceremony at the Garden.

On the day he announced his retirement, Bird again said he thought the 1985–86 team was the best he played on or saw in his years in the league. That was at least partially due to his performance that year. He still had some good years left, but that one year might have been his best all-around season.

"I believe that when the definitive history of basketball is written, whenever that is, today, tomorrow, or fifty years from now, that this man [Bird] will occupy a special place among the top five players ever to play this game," Dave Gavitt said. "God may not have granted him an all-world body. But from the shoulders to the top of his head, and from his wrists to his fingertips, he played the game better than anyone who has ever played it. And he played it with a heart five times bigger than anyone I ever saw."

Red Auerbach agreed: "Nobody has been more self-motivated, and nobody I've had or seen in the last forty-two years here played hurt the way this guy did. It was for the love of the game."

Nine months after Bird officially retired, so did his frontcourt soulmate, Kevin McHale. The venue was quite different. Instead of a hastily called news conference that was aired live on local television, McHale announced his retirement on the floor of a rollicking Charlotte Coliseum, where the Celtics had lost a play-off series to the Hornets.

McHale had hoped that the first post–Larry Bird season would be time for him and his teammates to show that life can, indeed, go on. The Celtics didn't play poorly, but injuries reduced McHale to a bit player over the second half of the season. The injuries, all to his feet, stemmed back to 1986–87. In fact, 1985–86 was the last time McHale went through a season without some major discomfort or through a summer without some kind of surgery.

Until March of 1987, when Larry Nance stepped on his foot, creating a small fracture, McHale may have been the best player in the NBA that season. He was on his way to a remarkable year in which he would make first-team all-NBA and first-team All-Defense. He would shoot better than 60 percent from the field and better than 80 percent from the line.

Had he simply stopped that night and had his foot taken care of, he might still be playing today. But he kept playing on it, the injury got worse, and in the first round of the playoffs the bone split like a piece of wood. He limped through the Finals against the Lakers, still averaging more than 20 points a game, then had extensive off-season surgery.

Foot and ankle problems never left him after that. He severely sprained an ankle in 1991, an injury, he said, that "basically ended my career." His final year was one of frustration over not playing, and he twice had to be talked out of retirement during the season. He saved one memorable game for the Boston fans, scoring 30 points in a Game 2 loss to Charlotte. He led the team in scoring in the playoffs after averaging a career low 10.7 points a game that season.

McHale is unequivocal about the 1985–86 team. He speaks often about the ravages of expansion and player attitudes, and thinks no team today could even come close to beating the last Celtics NBA champion.

"Not even close," he said.

After retiring, McHale moved back to his native Minnesota

and worked in broadcasting for the Timberwolves. The next year he was hired as an assistant general manager and, in 1994, he was given control of the team's basketball operations.

Robert Parish kept right on playing. In 1995–96 he passed Kareem Abdul-Jabbar to become the all-time leader in games played. He also moved into sixth place on the all-time rebounding list as he completed his twentieth NBA season.

He wanted to retire as a Celtic, even though he knew he was trade bait in the summer of 1990, when the team almost dealt him to Seattle. (When asked about such a prospect, Parish said at the time, "Lovely.") But after the 1993–94 season, the team felt it could not re-sign Parish, thinking the money should go elsewhere as it tried to rebuild. (It did, but to an over-the-hill Dominique Wilkins, who lasted a year in Boston.) Parish, then a free agent, chose to sign with the Charlotte Hornets, with whom he expected to end his career. He signed there for personal and basketball reasons and never regretted the move. In the summer of 1996, at the age of forty-three, Parish said he was leaning heavily toward retirement but then decided to accept a contract with the Chicago Bulls.

Parish is not one to compare teams, but he does feel the 1985–86 squad was the best team he ever played on. He had better statistical seasons with Boston, best seen in 1988–89, the year Larry Bird missed 76 games. Called on to be more of an offensive force, Parish responded in a huge way, raising his scoring average from 14.3 points to 18.6. He also had more rebounds that year (996) than at any time in his career.

In the late stages of Parish's career, off-the-court incidents started to haunt him. In February 1993, he was arrested for possession of marijuana. The police came to his house after a package of marijuana was sent there from California. He pleaded guilty and was given six months' probation. Then, in August 1995, a national magazine chronicled his ex-wife's accusations of abuse in a special issue on domestic violence.

Parish has denied the charges in court papers, but didn't respond to the magazine, *Sports Illustrated,* which basically accepted Nancy Saad's version even though there were no witnesses, evidence, or charges filed against Parish.

The 1985–86 year was an enjoyable one for Parish because, for the only time in his years in Boston, he had a Hall of Famer playing behind him. It was fun being a Celtic that year.

"We had that arrogance, that cockiness, that comes with knowing you're going to win," he said. "We won consistently and we were tough, very tough, to beat down the stretch."

Unlike several of his 1985–86 teammates, Parish has never shown any desire to stay in basketball after retirement. He said the only job he might consider would be as an assistant coach; he wants nothing more.

K.C. Jones continued to coach the Boston Celtics for two more seasons, but the team got old around him and he rode the veterans until they had nothing left. Finally, during the 1988 playoffs, the Celtics announced Jones would move to the front office and Jimmy Rodgers would take over.

Many felt, and still feel, that Jones was kicked upstairs. He was given a title, but little responsibility.

"It was," Jones said years later, "my choice. In fact, I had gone to Red [Auerbach] earlier that year when Jimmy did not get the New York job and told him I would go one more year."

(Rodgers had been offered the Knicks job, but the Celtics would not let him out of his contract. New York hired Rick Pitino instead and Rodgers was furious. He did get the Boston head job in 1988, but lasted only two years.)

"What was there left for me to do in Boston? I had done it all," Jones said.

But the front office did not satisfy him. He was treated as a glorified scout as Rodgers and Volk ran the basketball operation. After one year, Jones left to be an assistant coach in Seattle with his old friend Bernie Bickerstaff.

After one year as a Seattle assistant, Bickerstaff moved to the front office and Jones replaced him as head coach. Although he had young, emerging talent there, he didn't have the success the team anticipated. This was a time when Jones had to coach, and his detractors pointed out that he really didn't have to do a lot of that in Boston.

The Sonics went 41-41 in Jones's first year there. They were 18-18 in his second year when he was fired, replaced eventually by George Karl. He returned to the NBA in 1994 as an assistant to Don Chaney in Detroit, but was not rehired when the Pistons brought in Doug Collins to run the basketball operation.

When the Celtics' head coaching job opened up in 1995, Jones, then sixty-three, expressed an interest. His former sixth man, M.L. Carr, was in charge then but never seriously considered Jones. Carr eventually took the job himself.

It's highly unlikely Jones will ever be a head coach again at any level. He was interested in the University of New Hampshire opening in 1996, but he turned sixty-four that year and was never really a serious candidate for the job.

Then, in a surprising turn of events, he rejoined the Celtics in 1996 as an assistant coach. His place in basketball history is assured. He is in the Hall of Fame. He has been a part of twelve NBA champions. His 67.4 career winning percentage as a head coach ranks him fourth all-time, just ahead of his boss and mentor, Red Auerbach. That is not a bad place to be.

The Celtics themselves had two more good years before everything unraveled.

A couple of weeks after defeating the Rockets, the Celtics selected Maryland forward Len Bias with the second pick in the draft. Two days later, Bias was dead from cocaine intoxication, setting in motion a chain of events that haunts the franchise to this day. Six years after Bias died, another talented player, Reggie Lewis, collapsed and died of cardiac arrest at the age of twenty-seven. Lewis had already appeared in an All-Star

Game and was seen as one of the Celtics' leading players for the 1990s.

The 1986–87 team made it back to the Finals, but by then McHale was playing on his broken foot, Wedman and Walton were unusable, and Bird was dragging. The following season, the Pistons eliminated the Celtics in a rough, six-game series in the Eastern Conference Finals. The Celtics have been unable to string together successive playoff series wins since, earning only first-round wins over the Indiana Pacers in 1991 and 1992 before being eliminated in the second round.

Then Bird retired and McHale followed a year later and, by 1995–96, the Celtics had posted three consecutive losing seasons for the first time since Auerbach arrived in 1950. In Auerbach's first thirty-six years with the Celtics, the team had never gone longer than five years between championships. Now they are working on ten with no relief in sight. The Celtics were barely able to match the total number of wins of the 1985–86 Celtics in M.L. Carr's first two years as the basketball chief.

Carr was determined to bring back the Celtics to their accustomed position of greatness, but, in a twenty-nine-team league with shrewd executives, moneymaking franchises, and a salary cap, he found the slope quite slippery. He also found that the new breed of player did not care for any of the supposed enticements the Celtics could offer: tradition, loyalty, a history of success. The sixteen championship banners meant little to them; they were a generation removed from the days when the Celtics repeated as NBA champions year after year in the 1960s. The values the Celtics espoused and practiced in those days were meaningless in the 1990s, all but assuring that the sixteenth flag, the last banner, might be longing for fresh company well into the next century.

AFTERWORD
SIMPLY THE BEST

The day after their victory over the Rockets, the Celtics were treated to the usual downtown parade and celebration. Hundreds of thousands cheered as the team weaved through downtown for a ceremony at City Hall. Walton sat on a flatbed truck and gleefully sipped a can of beer, much to the consternation of general manager Jan Volk, who thought the least Big Bill could do was pour it into a cup. Walton didn't care. It was a time for celebration and recognition.

Red Auerbach said the 1985–86 Celtics were the best team he had ever been associated with, and that included fifteen previous championship teams. K.C. Jones, an assistant on the great 1971–72 Lakers team, said the 1985–86 Celtics were even better than that one. This was, without a doubt, a great team.

But were they the best ever? Who knows? They were certainly the best team that year. But what made this team so special, more than their sheer greatness, was the fact that they were together for only one year. The 1985–86 Celtics were unique in their greatness. When people talk about this team, they call it the "Walton Team" to differentiate it from the other two title teams in the Larry Bird era.

"That team was the best team I ever coached against," said Bill Fitch, who entered the NBA in 1971. "Of all the teams that have won it over the years, that is the one team I would have most hated to [have to] beat four out of seven."

The game has changed in the ten years since the Celtics won their last title, giving way to a different style of basketball, with bigger, faster players who are long on athleticism and short on fundamentals. That doesn't necessarily mean that the Celtics of 1985–86 couldn't compete with the Chicago Bulls, Orlando Magic, or Houston Rockets of today. Chances are, those teams would have found it much harder in the mid-1980s than the 1985–86 Celtics would have found the game today.

Larry Bird said that the 1985–86 team was the best team he played on, but Bird is reluctant to put any individual or any team in a special place. He has always felt that the stars of the 1950s and 1960s aren't sufficiently appreciated today. He does feel, however, that the "Walton Team" would stack up against any he's seen, and he's right.

"You can't compare any team with that team. It was by far the best," he said. "If you just took our second team with a healthy Bill Walton and Scotty Wedman, today it would win 55 games."

In the fall of 1995, Dennis Johnson was talking with Jo Jo White about great Celtics teams. White said he thought the 1976 Boston title team could beat the 1986 Celtics team. Johnson was incredulous.

"I'd never say we could or couldn't," Dennis Johnson said, "but I would put my money on that team and take my chances. Look at Houston. They won the championship [in 1994]. Take ten years off Robert [Parish] and he'd play against Hakeem. No one could guard Kevin. Robert Horry against Larry? No way. Kenny Smith against Danny? No way. And we had a much, much better bench. It's fun to compare teams. It's like boxing. I still say Muhammad Ali is the best there was. But could he beat Mike Tyson?"

And now, because of expansion, the talent in the NBA is so

diluted that teams that would otherwise be considered ordinary are winning championships. Are the 1994/1995 champion Houston Rockets even better than the 1986 Rockets? One thing is certain: neither of those Houston title teams confronted a team as good as the 1985–86 Lakers in the playoffs. Or, needless to say, the 1985–86 Celtics.

"The league is so watered down now," Bird said. "And wait until they expand again. Then, you'll be able to get to the Finals with one great player and four mediocre ones."

That already seems to be the case. Who, besides Olajuwon on the 1994 champion Rockets was a certifiably great player? In the 1980s, you needed three, maybe four Hall of Famers to even think about winning a championship. The Sixers had Julius Erving and two others who belong there: Moses Malone and Maurice Cheeks. The Lakers had Abdul-Jabbar, Magic Johnson, and two others who will warrant consideration: James Worthy and Michael Cooper.

The 1985–86 Celtics had four, possibly five. Walton made it, but he did so on the basis of his play at UCLA. He was, however, exactly what the Celtics needed in 1985–86. Bird, McHale, and Parish will all be inducted; so might Dennis Johnson.

Even the mediocre teams in the mid-1980s were tough. The Bullets and Nets had rosters full of quality players. They just didn't have enough great ones.

"You needed to have three or four Hall of Famers back then," Cedric Maxwell said. "How many Hall of Famers do you need today? How many does Houston have? One. How many does Chicago have? One. Okay, maybe two. Back then, one Hall of Famer might not have gotten you into the playoffs."

Of all the Celtics on the 1985–86 team, the only one who played on legitimately good teams after leaving Boston was Danny Ainge. He was a member of the 1991–92 Portland Trail Blazers and the 1992–93 Phoenix Suns, two teams that went to the NBA Finals but lost to the Chicago Bulls. Ainge, an erudite student of the game, feels he has seen no team in the last eleven years that could compete with the 1985–86 Celtics.

"In my opinion," he said, "that was the best team ever. I've played on some good teams since, teams that went to the Finals, and they couldn't come close to that team. You had three players in the front line who are going to be Hall of Famers, who were perennial All-Stars, and who were all in the primes of their careers. DJ is going to be a Hall-of-Famer, too. What I think made that team so special was that if there was an incentive to win, we'd win. That's why I think it's the best team I've seen. There was no way anyone could beat us if we really wanted to win."

The Celtics and the Lakers were the two dominant teams of the 1980s, accounting for eight of the ten championships in the decade. The Lakers' best team was, in all likelihood, the 1986–87 squad that acquired Mychal Thompson in midseason and went 65-17. The team defeated an injured Celtics team 4–2 in the NBA Finals.

The real shame was that the two best teams of the decade, the 1985–86 Celtics and the 1986–87 Lakers, did not meet. If they had, McHale feels the Celtics would have prevailed.

"The Lakers teams were good, quality teams, but we were just too strong up front overall for them to beat us," McHale said. "I think with that particular team, we were better and deeper."

Phil Johnson, now an assistant with Utah, was the head coach of the Sacramento Kings in 1985–86. A decade later, when the Chicago Bulls were dominating and bringing back memories of the 1971–72 Lakers team that won 69 games, Johnson advised everyone who inquired that if you want to talk good teams, you were in the wrong decade.

"I'm not sure that Celtics team wasn't better than any of them," he said. "It was so well balanced. It was a very good defensive team and a punishing offensive team. Their perimeter players were excellent. How do you find a better team than that? You can talk all you want about the Bulls now or the Lakers back then, but I like that Celtics team."

Before the Chicago Bulls' 1995–96 season (where they won a record total of 87 games), the only team other than the 1986 Celtics to win 82 games was the 1991–92 Bulls. But that Chicago team lost seven playoff games, including three at home. The

1988–89 Detroit team won 63 games and then steamrolled through the playoffs, losing only twice.

"The Detroit team? We didn't have much trouble with them when we were all healthy," McHale said. "And Chicago? Are you serious? Will Perdue, Stacey King, Horace Grant, and Bill Cartwright were going to stop our front line? I don't think so. Yeah, they had Michael, but he gave everyone problems. When you look at our team versus their team, I don't think there's any way. We just had so much depth. I think the only team that might have given us trouble was that '83 Philly team."

The 1982–83 Philadelphia 76ers, with newcomer Moses Malone anchoring the middle, won 65 games and then went 12-1 in the postseason. The Celtics that season were in a state of chaos—they were eventually swept by the Bucks—but were still able to beat that Philly team not once, not twice, but all three times in Boston Garden. That team's front line of Malone, Erving, and Bobby Jones would have had matchup problems with the Parish-Bird-McHale-Walton quartet. The Sixers backcourt of Maurice Cheeks, Andrew Toney, and Clint Richardson was as good as any in any era, but a healthy Toney never had to deal with a healthy Dennis Johnson. That would have made an excellent matchup.

Statistically, the 1985–86 Celtics had at the time the fourth best winning percentage in NBA history. The 1971–72 Lakers (69-13), the 1966–67 76ers (68-13), and the 1972–73 Celtics (68-14) all had better records. (The 1995–96 Bulls, at 72-10, have since leaped past all these teams.) No team played better at home: the Celtics were 40-1 in the regular season, an NBA record even the Bulls couldn't match, and 10-0 in the playoffs. That's 50-1. Until that season, no team had ever won as many as 37 home games in a regular season.

No team had a better one-two combination in the middle than Parish and Walton, and Bird was, in his prime, as good as any player who ever played. They may have been the best pure passing team that ever played. The one great play in the Finals that typified that Celtics team was when Bird, double-teamed, slipped the ball to Walton for a layup. On his way up, Walton was quickly covered, so he underhanded the ball to a wide-open McHale, who promptly laid it in. That play crystallized the whole season and now, in the new FleetCenter, that play is shown in a video before each game.

The 1985–86 Celtics and the 1995–96 Bulls are the only teams ever to have two winning streaks of 13 or more games in one season. In addition, the 1985–86 Celtics also put together streaks of nine, eight, and eight. In the playoffs, they started every single series by winning the first two games at home en route to a 15-3 playoff total.

The 1994 Dream Team II at the world championships in Toronto was coached by Don Nelson. After one practice session, Nelson was asked for his thoughts on the 1985–86 Celtics. He had, during the 1985–86 season, called that team the best in Celtics history. But when asked in 1994, he seemed to hedge a bit.

"I don't know how good that team could have been. They didn't seem to be any better than the other Boston teams that beat us in the playoffs," he said.

Nelson was told that unlike the 1984 and 1987 teams, this Celtics team not only swept Milwaukee, but won the four games by an average of 15 points a game.

"That is not true," he said. "No team of mine was ever swept by the Celtics."

Nelson was informed again that the Celtics had in fact swept the Bucks that season. He demanded evidence. An NBA guide was produced to reveal that, yes, in fact, the Celtics had swept the series.

"Hmm," he said, finally convinced. "That must have been one pretty good team, then."

Here is a wholly subjective list of the five best teams in NBA history. You'll notice that no team from the last nine years is included. Cedric Maxwell was right: you needed better players to win back then.

This list does not include the 1995–96 Bulls, a team that will probably always be discussed as one of the all-time great teams for two reasons: their 72-10 season and the presence of Michael Jordan. But the feeling here—one seconded by many people, including Charles Barkley and Jordan himself—is that this team wasn't even as strong as, say, the 1992 NBA champion Bulls, who had Horace Grant, Bill Cartwright, John Paxson, and B.J. Armstrong. As for its supposed defensive prowess, it was not as strong a defensive team as either of the Detroit champions in 1989 and 1990.

And let's remember the NBA in 1995–96: the product is so diluted and adulterated that it's laughable to compare the quality of play to that of the mid-1980s. There are 25 percent more teams now than in 1985–86, and the players coming into the game now are, for the most part, all flash and dazzle. Look at the composition of the 1996 U.S. Olympic team: nine of the 12 players were drafted in the 1980s, and four were drafted by 1985.

The Bulls were a great team for their time, which means they had a couple of All-Stars, some useful subordinates, and a so-so bench. In an age of instant gratification, however, they became more known for their celebrity. Dennis Rodman became a bestselling author based solely on the fact that he was on that team. They could play the game well and they came out snarling virtually every night; this same team, however, would not have come close to 72 wins had it played a decade earlier.

If you look at NBA history as a bell curve, the very top would be in the mid- to late 1980s. That's when there were twenty-three teams, not twenty-nine, and when the talent level and the quality of play were both at their peak. That's why the 1985–86 Celtics deserve to be recognized for what they did; they played at a time when the competition was never better and the game was not yet contaminated by the ravages of expansion.

5. The 1970–71 Milwaukee Bucks: This team ranks as one of the greatest, most unappreciated, oft-overlooked juggernauts in

NBA history. It was the first team to shoot 50 percent (50.9) from the field in a season. It finished the regular season 66-16 and then went 12-2 through the playoffs. No team in NBA history has been as dominant in both the regular season (12.2 point differential) and the playoffs (13.2 point differential) as this one. Like the Lakers of the following year, they may not have had a drop-dead starting five, but they had Kareem Abdul-Jabbar, then in his second NBA season. He averaged 31.7 points and almost 16 rebounds a game. They had Oscar Robertson, then 32, in the first of his four seasons with Milwaukee. And they had excellent role players such as Bobby Dandridge, John Mc-Glocklin, Greg Smith, and McCoy McLemore (who, by virtue of a midseason trade, played in 86 regular season games that year). This team had to open its first-round series on the road due to arena availability problems, and they played their games in that round in Madison, Wisconsin. They swept the Bullets in the Finals. Their overall record, however, is slightly less impressive when one takes into account that dreaded NBA phenomenon known as expansion. Seven of their wins were against first-year Portland and Cleveland, and another five against Seattle, a team that had been in the league for only three years.

4. The 1966–67 Philadelphia 76ers: This team at one point was thought to be the best ever and, at one time, it probably was. It went 68-13 in the regular season but only 11-4 in the playoffs. It did, however, have Wilt Chamberlain, five years younger than in his Lakers title days and averaging 24.1 points, 24.2 rebounds, 7.8 assists, and shooting 68 percent from the field. They also had a tremendous supporting cast! Up front the Sixers could throw Chet Walker, Luke Jackson (the 1960s answer to Maurice Lucas), and Billy Cunningham, the aptly named Kangaroo Kid. The backcourt was equally brilliant with Hal Greer and Wali Jones. The Sixers, who won their games by an average of 9.4 points, blew away a very good Celtics team in the regular season and ended Boston's nine-year title run by knocking them out of the playoffs in five games. They did, however, need six games to put away the San Francisco Warriors, who won only 44

games all year. They also dropped two home playoff games in the process.

3. The 1971–72 Lakers: They won 33 straight and finished 69-13, now the second-best record in NBA history. They won games by an average of 12.3 points a game during the regular season, but were less than dominating in the playoffs. Although they were 12-3 in the postseason, they lost twice at home and twice trailed in a playoff series. Their average winning margin was just 3.9 points in the playoffs. This was a consummate team, fueled by an awesome backcourt of Gail Goodrich and Jerry West that averaged 52 points a game. Their forwards—Happy Hairston and Jim McMillian—were standard-sized for the times, but undersized today. And Wilt Chamberlain focused on other aspects of the game besides scoring, and it paid off. But this team also enjoyed the benefits of expansion. Portland and Cleveland were in their second year, and the Lakers were 9-1 against the two teams.

2. The 1986–87 Lakers: This had to be Pat Riley's best bunch. He never had Magic Johnson and Kareem Abdul-Jabbar both playing at their best, but this was pretty close. Johnson won the MVP title for the first time and Abdul-Jabbar got midseason relief help from Mychal Thompson. They also had A.C. Green and James Worthy up front. Michael Cooper played tough defense and Byron Scott got better and better as the season progressed. They blew people away in the playoffs by an average of 14.3 points a game and, had the 2-2-1-1-1 format been in effect in the NBA Finals, would have needed only five games instead of six to dethrone the Celtics. This team went through the regular season at 65-17, winning games by an average of 9.3 points, and shooting 51.6 percent from the field. They then went 15-3 in the playoffs. Their 20 overall defeats is two more than the 1985–86 Celtics, but you still wouldn't mind going to war with this group.

By now, of course, you know who No. 1 is. The 1985–86 Celtics could beat a team inside. It could beat a team outside. It could beat a team with defense. It had the greatest front line in NBA history, the greatest backup center in NBA history, and most importantly, had an almost perfect record at Boston Garden.

Glenn Rivers, who played for Atlanta that season, remembered that Celtics team with equal parts admiration and fright. "You couldn't do anything about it. They had you at their whim," Rivers said. "They were so strong. They had to be one of the best ever, if not the best. All I know is that that year, no one touched them. Or really even bothered them."

INDEX